D1783535

A Guide to
World Fairs
and
Festivals

A Guide to World Fairs and Festivals

FRANCES SHEMANSKI

GREENWOOD PRESS
WESTPORT, CONNECTICUT • LONDON, ENGLAND

Library of Congress Cataloging in Publication Data

Shemanski, Frances.
  A guide to world fairs and festivals.

  Bibliography: p.
  1. Festivals—Directories. 2. Fairs—Directories.
I. Title.
GT3930.S43   1985   394.2'69   84-12810
ISBN 0-313-20786-0 (lib. bdg.)

Copyright © 1985 by Frances Shemanski

All rights reserved. No portion of this book may be reproduced, by any process or technique, without the express written consent of the publisher.

Library of Congress Catalog Card Number: 84-12810
ISBN: 0-313-20786-0

First published in 1985

Greenwood Press
A division of Congressional Information Service, Inc.
88 Post Road West
Westport, Connecticut 06881

Printed in the United States of America

10 9 8 7 6 5 4 3 2 1

CONTENTS

Preface	vii
Fairs and Festivals	3
Calendar of Fairs and Festivals	189
Appendix: Types of Festivals	247
Index	301

PREFACE

Festivals and celebrations have been a way of life almost since the time of Adam and Eve. The changing of the seasons, planting time, harvest time, successful hunts, birthdays, weddings and religious rites have all been reasons for a festival. They still are. Additionally anniversaries are occasions for rejoicing. Most events occur annually, attracting people from all parts of the world. These visitors stay, spend money and help the local economy. Festivals also mean jobs. This is especially true when the festival is keyed to the visual and performing arts, as many are. Such events also give an area a cultural heritage that it previously did not have. Many festivals are well organized, handled by non-profit associations or helped by government subsidy. Other festivals, though held annually, are not so well organized although they do seem to fall into place once begun. Preparation is usually done with volunteer help.

This book is a guide to fairs and festivals throughout the world. It covers 75 countries, encompassing Canada (all of its provinces and territories), Central and South America, Europe (Eastern and Western), Africa, the Middle East, Asia, the Pacific and the Far East. The United States is covered in a separate book, *A Guide to Fairs and Festivals in the United States*, also published by Greenwood Press. All festivals and events in this book are listed alphabetically by country, city and town. In the case of Canada, the province and territory is listed and Mexico by state, city and/or town. All names, with some exceptions, are in English. Dates are by month and time of year rather than specific ones which change constantly. Each event includes information on its origin, history, purpose, special features, successes and future plans, plus a description of each festival or event, consisting of one or more paragraphs.

As in the preparation for *A Guide to Fairs and Festivals in the United States*, special questionnaires were mailed to thousands of festival organizers, government and city tourist bureaus all over the world. As a newspaper editor and compiler of calendars of events for many top newspapers and magazines, I had direct contact with many festivals. I have also attended many events, described in this book and in the United States guide. The questionnaire attempted to obtain more information in addition to what I had collected over the years: when an event began and why; its length; awards and/or recognition; founders and special features; how it evolved; when held and where; how it helped its area; how it is financed and what age group it attracts. I also asked for any available literature about the event. Most complied. Therefore, information came from the questionnaires, brochures, histories, collected materials, newspaper clippings and souvenir programs. The Canadian questionnaires were followed up by telephone interviews. Government tourist offices represented in the United States were also called for clarifications and additional information.

The festivals and events in this book include cultural programs, sports, religious events, humor, agriculture, flowers, New Year's celebrations, historic events and patriotic observances. Obviously, it was not practical to include all festivals and events in this one volume. Those that do appear were selected for various reasons: the age of the festival; the number of people attending; the impact of the event on its area; famous founders. Not only major events and festivals are covered but also smaller ones, especially if research showed that they have a strong impact on their location.

The appendix lists fairs and festivals according to type of event for the benefit of those interested in one special kind of event. Some are listed more than once because they include several activities and features. The volume also includes a general events calendar which lists both the events in the book and some not included. All events are indexed by their English titles. The reader should find this a useful guide to the many fairs and festivals throughout the world.

Frances Shemanski

A Guide to
World Fairs
and
Festivals_____

ANTIGUA

St. John's

POLICE WEEK FESTIVAL

Held annually, August/September
Sports, culture, community, goodwill, competition

Police Week Festival is designed to create good will between local citizens and Antigua's police force through a program of sports events and social and cultural activities. These include football games, shooting competitions, talent and fashion shows, dances and exhibitions. There is also a marathon cycle race, band tattoos in various villages plus performances by the Police Choir. The special event was started in September 1969, adopted from the Guyana Police Force. It is now well received throughout the island, attracting some 6,000 persons to the shows and competitions, adding up to a grand total of more than 100,000 over the years. Police Week is held either the last week in August or the first in September. It is financed by the police force and by donations from private industry. All events, except the dances, are free to the public. Events in St. John's are held at the Police Compound and at the Community Recreation Park.

ARGENTINA

Mendoza

NATIONAL FESTIVAL OF THE GRAPE HARVEST

Held annually, March
Folkloric, harvest, agricultural

The National Festival of the Grape Harvest is always held the first week of March to coincide with the ripening of the grapes and their harvesting in this area. Local people have been celebrating the harvest since 1936. The festival includes the blessing of the grapes, the parade of carts through the city streets and the election and coronation of the queen, Cecilia I. The festival ends with a sound and light performance, involving 2,000 persons and a fireworks display near the Frank Romero Day Amphitheater. There are tours to local wineries, wine-tasting sessions and folk song and dance performances. There is also an exhibit of wines. Thousands of tourists and local people attend the festivities, a help to the local economy.

ARUBA (NETHERLANDS ANTILLES)

Oranjestad

CARNIVAL

Held annually, three days before Ash Wednesday, movable dates.
Religious, Mardi Gras

Carnival is celebrated throughout the island of Aruba and is a pre-Lenten festivity that is a social, religious and cultural event. It ends midnight Tuesday, the day before Ash Wednesday. Actually steel band contests, tumba contests and the elections of Carnival queens from most towns and villages begin two months before. Carnival celebrations were officially organized in 1944 by the Aruba Tivoli Club, the island's oldest social club, which started the event as a club activity. The first islandwide celebration got underway in 1955, handled by the Aruba Carnival Committee, founded by the late Eric Arends, an ex-lieutenant governor of Aruba. The committee still handles preparations for the big parade and various competitions. Work on the Carnival is a serious, year-long project involving hundreds of volunteers. The Carnival Main Parade in Oranjestad takes eight hours and winds through the city streets. It includes brightly decorated floats and people in bizarre colorful costumes who move on foot, usually dancing the jump-up, a half-dance performed to a half-march rhythm. The parade ends at sundown. The Carnival unofficially begins months before, when plans for floats and costumes are made. Various island social clubs try to decide on a theme. Usually by the end of January there's a Calypsonian Competition, followed the next week by the Panorama Steel Band Contest. This is followed by the Tumba Contest, in which local musicians compete playing original compositions, hoping one will become the Carnival's official song. Tumba is the native music of the Netherlands Antilles. A Children's Carnival Parade is also part of the Carnival celebrations in Oranjestad. A few days later the Carnival Queen is selected at a competition in Wilhelmina Stadium. There is usually a music concert by several leading island groups. The Tuesday before Ash Wednesday marks the end of the Carnival with the Old Mask Parade, followed by the traditional burning of "King Momo." The event annually attracts more than 10,000. Almost half a million have attended since the event became an islandwide celebration. Work on the carnival is by volunteers and members of various social clubs, who deal with it year-round. It is financed through private donations and admission charges. The parade, however, is free.

AUSTRALIA

New South Wales

Sydney

FESTIVAL OF SYDNEY

Held annually, December/January
Cultural, circus, sports

The Festival of Sydney is a relatively new cultural event, with the first one held December 31, 1977, continuing through January 1978. It was initiated by the city's lord mayor and local businessmen to replace the October Waratah Festival that ended in 1973. The new festival was needed to fill a cultural void for local residents and tourists. It is held during Australia's summer season and school holidays. The festival has about 1,500 different events, which include art exhibits, jazz, opera, concert music and circus performances. It opens with a New Year's Eve Opera House Gala, special dance week, Hyde Park Festival for children with games, street theater and food booths. There is a vintage car rally, a Grand Festival Parade, rock music concerts, folkloric performances, Australian film festival and sports, including yachting races and golf tournaments. Events are citywide and in the city's old market area, the Haymarket, renovated to include two theaters, a concert hall, arts and crafts exhibition space and audio-visual displays. The festival plays to an audience of more than half a million every year. It features celebrities like Stephen Sondheim and Hal Prince. Work on the festival is done by a paid staff who work year-round on details. The festival is financed by the City Council, State Government and donations from private industry. Most events are free, but there are some admission charges.

New South Wales

Sydney

ROYAL EASTER SHOW

Held annually to coincide with Easter holidays
Economic, agricultural, fair

The Royal Easter Show is like an American state fair. It has livestock exhibitions and judgings for large cash prizes. It has sports competitions, fashion and flower shows, famous celebrities performing and a carnival midway. It is sponsored annually by the Royal Agricultural Society of New South Wales, founded in 1822, for the purpose of focusing on the country's agricultural industry and helping folks sell their products. It is always held during the Easter holidays, when school is closed for vacation and more people can attend. The show attracts more than a million people annually. Only once, in 1977, did the attendance fall below the million mark. The show is described as an "expression of our national character." The Society, through the show and other sponsored events, attempts to "promote, foster and encourage the development of the agricultural, mining and industrial resources of the State of New South Wales." The only times that the show wasn't held was during the 1919 influenza epidemic and during World War II, when the army occupied the showground from 1942 to 1946. Otherwise the Royal Easter Show has been held at the Moore Park Showground continuously since 1882. The total value of the buildings and exhibits of the show has been estimated in excess of $32 million, and industrial displays at more than $12 million. More than 600 exhibitors participate, making it one of the world's largest shows. The Royal Agricultural Society of New South Wales has a yearly budget of more than $1 million. The show always has a theme with all events keyed to it. Over the years, it has taken on an international look, with European countries, like West Germany, exhibitions and performers from the United States participating. The show is financed through ticket sales, exhibit fees, booth rentals and memberships in the sponsoring society. There are also contributions from various businesses.

Queensland

Toowoomba

CARNIVAL OF FLOWERS

Held annually, September/October
Floral, cultural

The Carnival of Flowers is an annual spring event that pays tribute to the local horticulture with a variety of cultural, sports and entertainment events. It was started by the local chamber of commerce, which felt that the city needed a special event for residents and to attract visitors. At first it was to be a street carnival, but at a town hall meeting in 1949 it was decided to focus on the area's lovely spring flowers. A special Carnival Committee was elected, and with the help of a part-time organizing secretary it put together the first Toowoomba Carnival of Flowers in 1950. The group was given a budget by the city with the proviso that any profits realized were to be used for the next carnival and an equal share was to go to the Queensland Bush Children's Health Scheme, Toowoomba Branch. The first carnival was an instant success not only with local people but also with visitors. The event received a lot of publicity and began to grow. It is responsible for the city being known as Australia's Garden City. More than 200,000 attended the eight-day event, which was first held in October but later changed to the end of September into early October. The annual event includes home garden competitions sponsored by the city's daily newspaper, *Toowoomba Chronicle*, with cash prizes. Tours of the home and city gardens are also featured. The highlight is the first Saturday's Floral Parade, with thousands of flowers, beautiful girls, floral costumes and floats. The parade is always held, rain or shine. There is a carnival queen competition and junior queen contest. All city shops display floral exhibits, and the Toowoomba Orchid Society displays exotic and native orchids. There are rides, amusements and special entertainment for children throughout the city. There are golf competitions, a major cycling meet, a special speedway, trotting and racing programs. A top carnival feature is the "Joy of Living," a performing and visual arts program that offers theater, music, children's plays, jazz, films, arts and crafts. The event is supervised by the Toowoomba Carnival of Flowers Association, Inc., a nonprofit group that handles all details for the carnival, working year-round. The carnival is financed through admission charges for certain events, and contributions from businesses and from the city chamber of commerce. It is also supported partially by the Toowoomba City Council, the Queensland Government, Tourist Bureau, Australian Council for the Arts, Community Arts Fund and Queensland State Government. Any profits are donated to a worthy charity or community project.

South Australia

Adelaide

FESTIVAL OF THE ARTS

Held biennially, even-numbered years, February/March; next: 1986, 1988.
Cultural

The Festival of the Arts dates back to 1960, when a group of businessmen decided that Adelaide, the capital of South Australia, needed something worthwhile to attract tourists and entertain residents during the autumn season of February and March. The city, devoid of any cultural event or institution and certainly geographically isolated, needed a special event, like a festival of the arts. The festival, held only during even-numbered years, has put the city on the world's cultural map. Today, it is one of the top performing arts centers around, attracting international performers and orchestras. In 1973, the Adelaide Festival Centre opened a special performance hall, the Festival Theatre, with four other theaters, including the Playhouse, home of the South Australian Theatre Company, the Space, a versatile box-shaped auditorium, the Stone Amphitheatre for free outdoor plays and concerts and the Plaza, where different programs are given. The Adelaide Festival Centre has 4,000 seats, not enough for festival goers, who total more than 100,000. Festival events are held citywide in smaller theaters, town halls, clubs, city parks and streets. The festival usually offers more than 300 events. In 1980, 10 countries participated together with the best of the all-Australian talent also featured. For example, there was the Warsaw National Philharmonic Orchestra and the Freeman Jazz Quartet from Chicago, both performing on the same day. There is chamber music, experimental plays, classical ballet, symphony concerts, mime groups, marionettes, acid rock and modern jazz. During the first two weeks, poets, dramatists, writers, journalists and screenwriters from all over the world meet in conferences and workshops to discuss literary ideas, directions and styles. Another feature, introduced only a few years ago, is the "Food and Wine Frolic," usually held in a city park. It features international foods and wines. There is also an "Old Fashioned Family Picnic," an all-day event held on the banks of the river, overlooked by the Adelaide Festival Centre. The festival has parades with floats, fashion shows and fireworks. It is financed through ticket sales and help from the South Australia government, the Australia Council, the Adelaide Festival Centre Trust and by industry and individual patrons of the arts.

South Australia

Barossa Valley, Tanunda

BAROSSA VALLEY VINTAGE FESTIVAL

Held biennially, April, odd-numbered years; next: 1985, 1987.
Harvest, agricultural, fair

The Barossa Valley Vintage Festival goes back to 1947, when local vintners in Tanunda and neighboring towns in Barossa Valley held a vintage ball to celebrate the grape harvest. It proved so popular that it was repeated every year. More events were added, and festivities were held for seven days and seven nights, starting Easter Monday. Work on the festival took almost a year so it was decided to hold it every two years, during odd-numbered years. The festival's German flavor comes from the early German Lutheran settlers in 1842. The area's soil was right for grapes, and so the grape and wine industry evolved. Today there are more than 30 vineyards and wineries in the valley, which is only 18 miles long and 5–7 miles wide. It is near Adelaide. The festival called attention to the valley and greatly helped the area's economy. Some 200,000 attend every festival. Events in Tanunda include grape-picking contests, the selection of a festival queen, wine tastings, winery tours, art exhibits, and a parade of floats, humorous, floral and traditional. The parade goes from Tanunda to Nuriootpa. There is also a vintage fair with exhibits, competitions, German folk songs and dances and even Maypole dancing. Work on the festival is done by a special committee and it takes them 14 months to prepare for the biennial event, which is financed through admission fees and contributions from local wineries and the local tourist office.

Victoria

Melbourne

MOOMBA FESTIVAL

Held annually, March
Cultural, economic

The Moomba Festival was introduced in March 1955 by the city of Melbourne to provide free popular and cultural entertainment for local residents and visitors. It was the idea of Sir Maurice Nathan, lord mayor of Melbourne from 1961 to 1963, and the late Cr. W. Comedow. The idea can be traced even further back to 1912 as planned by the then City Council, but World War I put an end to it. A second try was made in 1939, but World War II stopped it. It wasn't until 1954 that a third attempt was made, and in 1955 the Moomba Festival was born. "Moomba" is an aboriginal word that means "let's get together and have fun." The annual event does just that with 200 different programs, including a carnival, music, sports, drama, art, literature and a huge street parade of 150 floats, bands and novelty units. More than 600,000 persons enjoy the annual event, which is covered live by four of the city's television stations. It is always held in March, which is autumn in Australia, and the weather is perfect most of the time. Famous performers, many from the United States, like singer Neil Diamond, the Beach Boys and Oscar Peterson, are featured. The 1978 festival also included the international water ski champions from Venezuela, Miami Beach, Florida, and England, all competing in the second largest Masters International Water Ski Championships. Each festival has a King and Moomba Queen, fireworks and plenty of activity in the city gardens, and most of it is free. Other events are held citywide in parks, streets, museums, art galleries and theaters. To date the Moomba Festival has hosted more than 4 million people. It is both culturally and economically successful. The festival is financed through some admission fees, donations from private industry (60 percent) and from the state government and the city of Melbourne (40 percent).

Western Australia

Perth

FESTIVAL OF PERTH

Held annually, February/March
Cultural

The Festival of Perth began in February 1953 as a six-week program of cultural entertainment for students attending evening and summer session classes at the University of Western Australia. It was launched and subsidized by the university because there were no cultural programs in Perth at the time. The idea is attributed to Professor Fred Alexander and John Birman of the university. Local groups presented some music and drama, which attracted other students and outsiders. It began to expand, and so did the costs of handling it. It eventually was funded by the state of Western Australia with additional help from the Australia Council, the City of Perth and donations from businesses and nearby communities and cities. Today, it is a major arts festival, offering drama, music, opera, dance, film festivals, art exhibits, children's programs and even sports competitions, all held throughout the city. The festival also features folk music and dance groups, parades, improvisations and other events. While the festival showcases mainly Australian performing artists, it is also a venue for many famous international performers from Europe, Canada and the United States. The festival is now held for one month and plays to an audience of more than half a million people, including tourists. Work is done by both a paid staff and many volunteers. Many events and programs are free because they are sponsored by private industry, but some events do charge admission.

AUSTRIA

Bregenz (Vorarlberg)

BREGENZ FESTIVAL

Held annually, July/August
Cultural

The Bregenz Festival continues to be famous for performances of opera, operettas, drama, ballet and symphonic concerts, many still presented on the floating stage, outdoors on Lake Constance. The festival also features East European dance companies available through special cultural exchange agreements. The festival was started in 1946 to give local people some cultural enjoyment after the end of World War II. The moving forces behind the festival were ballet dancer Kurt Kaiser, conductor Othmar Suitner, Eugen Leissing in charge of cultural affairs in Bregenz, Dr. Julius Wachter, then mayor of Bregenz, and Adolf Salzmann, a city alderman. In addition to the floating stage, other performances are given at the Theater am Kornmarkt and in nearby towns. In 1979, a new indoor Festival House, located on the banks of Lake Constance, was opened for year-round concerts and events. The festival attracts as many as 100,000 each year. The festival is a member of the European Association of Music Festivals. In 1982, *The Gypsy Baron* by Strauss was presented on the floating stage. Donizetti's opera, *Lucia di Lammermoor* with Jose Carreras was given in the Festspielhaus (Festival House). Goethe's *Egmont* was performed in the Vienna Burghteater and orchestral concerts with the Vienna Symphony Orchestra and the Dresden Philharmonic. Soloists have included Piero Cappuccilli, Walter Klein and Heinrich Schiff. Work on the festival is done by a small staff of 14 paid workers and hundreds of volunteers. The event is financed through ticket sales and grants from the Federal, Vorarlberg region and city of Bregenz governments.

Graz (Styria)

STYRIAN AUTUMN OR STEIRISCHER HERBST

Held annually, October/November
Cultural

The Steirischer Herbst, or Styrian Autumn, is a festival that dates back to September 23, 1968, and is devoted completely to contemporary art, literature, theater and music. Styrian Autumn is often described as the cultural center of avant-garde art in Austria. Festival events include Triog, a three-country biennial exhibition of advanced art, and Music Protokoll, a contemporary world music biennial radio program, broadcast internationally. There is the Styrian Academy, a scientific symposium with special themes. Open House is a free program for youth and first performances of contemporary operas and dramas. More than 80,000 attend each year with a grand total to date of almost a million persons. The 1982 festival was highlighted by the World Music Festival of the International Society of New Music and Music Protokoll, a music and literary symposium, exhibitions, jazz concerts, songs and small theatre. The festival, a member of the European Association of Music Festivals, offers many free programs. Where tickets are sold, the prices are purposely low. The entire event is financed by the federal, provincial and city governments. Performances are citywide.

Hallein, Oberndorf, Wagrain, all of Salzburg

"SILENT NIGHT, HOLY NIGHT" CELEBRATION

Held annually, Christmas Eve
Religious, Christmas, music

"Silent Night, Holy Night" Celebrations are held on Christmas Eve to commemorate the composing and writing of the now famous Christmas carol in this area in 1818. The carol was performed December 24, 1818, in St. Nickola Church in Oberndorf. It was written and composed by Franz Xaver Gruber and Father Josef Mohr. The melody as heard today is different from the original but basically is the same composition. Every year, hundreds come to Oberndorf and the other towns to participate in the candlelight processions to the local churches. All sing the famous song en route to church and again inside the church. It is usually sung in various languages to honor all nations and the birth of the Christ child.

AUSTRIA

Ossiach, Villach

CARINTHIAN SUMMER FESTIVAL

Held annually, June/August
Cultural

The Carinthian Summer Festival is a two-month event of music, opera and choir performances, starring world famous performers and orchestras. Performances are given in both villages of Ossiach and Villach. Part of the festival includes two-week courses in vocal studies under the direction of a leading performer. In the past, such notables as Christa Ludwig, opera and concert star, have taught. The event draws thousands of people. In 1982, the festival honored its founder, Helmut Wobisch, with a special memorial concert. The festival is often the venue for world premieres of operas. The first festival was held in 1969, and the festival has been continuing with much success. It is supported by government grants, donations from art patrons and ticket sales.

Salzburg

SALZBURG FESTIVAL

Held annually, July/August
Cultural

The Salzburg Festival dates back to 1920, when it was launched to educate the world about Austrian culture. It is today one of the major music festivals in Europe, attracting the world's most celebrated conductors, beginning with Richard Strauss, one of the festival founders. That first festival began with the presentation of *Jedermann*, played on the steps of St. Rupert's Cathedral. The festival still offers *Jedermann* but also operas, recitals, instrumental concerts with world famous and top Austrian performers. The festival has survived economic depression and World War II because of the strong cultural interests of the Austrians, led by Max Reinhardt and Hugo von Hofmannsthal.

The 1982 season offered Herbert von Karajan, James Levine, Gerd Albrecht, Lorin Maazel, Wolfgang Sawallisch, Claudio Abbado, Neville Marrimer, Seiji Ozawa and Riccardo Muti as guest conductors. Operas included Beethoven's *Fidelio*, Mozart's *Cosi Fan Tutte* and *The Magic Flute*, Offenbach's *Tales of Hoffman*, Verdi's *Falstaff* and Richard Strauss's *Aradne auf Naxos*. Recitalists were Tom Krause, Hermann Prey, Peter Schreier, Dietrich Fischer-Dieskau and Christa Ludwig. Instrumentalists were violinist Gidon Kremer; pianists Bruno Leonardro Gelber, Rudolf Buchbinder, Claudio Arrau, Maurizio Pollino and Alfred Brendel and cellists Heinrich Schiff, Lynn Harrell and Yo Yo Ma. The festival highlight was Stravinsky's *Oedipus Rex* performed by the Vienna Philharmonic, conducted by James Levine and narrated by Maximilian Schell.

This highly popular festival attracts several hundred thousand people with a grand total of several million since 1920. Performances are given in four theaters, concert halls and churches citywide. Most tickets are purchased a year in advance of the festival. The cost of 1982 festival tickets ranged from $12.50 to $140 per person. The festival, a member of the European Association of Music Festivals, is financed by box-office receipts (74 percent) and by grants from the province, city and local tourism offices (26 percent).

Vienna

VIENNA FESTIVAL

Held annually, May/June
Cultural

The Vienna Festival is a six-week event that offers more than 1,000 performances of concerts, opera, ballet and drama by both Austrian and foreign companies, all famous. The festival plays to an audience of more than a million people annually. Performances are citywide. Music programs are usually handled by the Wiener Konserthausgesellschaft and Gesellschaft der Musikfreunde, two famous concert halls and associations of Vienna. Other performances are handled by the Theater an der Wien, usually for foreign drama and dance groups. There are also independent groups offering programs, so-called fringe events. Among international groups that have participated in the Vienna Festival, founded in 1951, are the Royal Shakespeare Company, Theatron Technis of Athens, Teatr Stary of Cracow, Merce Cunningham and Dance Company, Martha Graham Dance Company and the Malegot Ballet of Leningrad.

During the 1982 festival, Austria's own Leonie Rysanek appeared in two of her famous roles, as the empress in Richard Strauss's *Die Frau ohne Schatten* and as Kundry in Wagner's *Parsifal*. At the State Opera House there was a revival of Verdi's *Otello*, with James Levine conducting. Placido Domingo played the title role, Mirella Freni was Desdemona and Renato Bruson was Iago. After the performance, Placido Domingo went to the podium to conduct *Die Fledermaus* by Johann Strauss. The opera program included other familiar works like *Don Giovanni, La Boheme* and *Carmen*, as well as rare works like Pfitzner's *Palestrina*. At the Volksoper, Cole Porter's *Kiss Me Kate* and Leonard Bernstein's *West Side Story* were performed together with the works of Offenbach, Johann Strauss and Franz Lehar. Haydn's 250th birthday was commemorated with a performance of *Orlando Paladino* at the Theater an der Wien. Other Haydn works were given in the City Hall courtyard, Schonbrunn Palace and St. Stephen's Cathedral, where Haydn was a choir boy. Herbert von Karajan conducted a performance of *The Creation* with the Vienna Philharmonic. Haydn was also honored with a dance program by choreographer Ivan Marko, entitled *Haydn in Dance*, and by a performance of a marionette opera by Haydn, *Die Feuersbrusnt*. Festival participants included the Piccolo Theater of Milan, the Munich Kammerspiele, the Noh Theater of Japan, the Broadway cast of *Ain't Misbehavin'*, the Netherlands Chamber Orchestra, the Pittsburgh Symphony and the Leningrad Philharmonic. Among guest conductors were Herbert von Karajan, Bernard Haitnik, Eugen Jochum, Andre Previn, Claudio Abbado and Leif Segerstrom. The festival is a member of the European Association of Music Festivals. It attracts several hundred thousand persons, which includes tourists. The event is financed through box-office receipts and by a subsidy from the Austrian Confederation, the city of Vienna and the Touristic Confederation of Austria.

THE BAHAMAS

Freeport, Nassau

BAHAMAS GOOMBAY HOLIDAY

Held annually, July/August
Economic, cultural

The Bahamas Goombay Holiday is a two-month celebration of cultural events offered in both Freeport (Grand Bahama Island) and Nassau (New Providence Island), designed to attract tourists in the summer off-season and to entertain local residents. It is also a get-acquainted time for local citizens and visitors. Started in 1971 by the local tourist board, it originally began in May and ended in August with only an every Friday event from 9 a.m. to midnight. Over the years, it expanded to more days in the week and to Freeport as well as Nassau. The tourist business improved in May and June so that the Goombay Holiday is now held July through August. There are performances by the Royal Bahamas Police Band in both cities, moonlight cruises in waters out of Nassau and a water ballet in Freeport, with Goombay parades in both locations. Sundays are usually devoted to taking a visitor to church to hear gospel groups and choirs and to participate in the people-to-people friendship campaign. There are Sunday afternoon concerts at the Nassau Botanic Gardens at 5 p.m., and Mondays and Wednesdays a 9 p.m. moonlight boat cruise from the Prince George Wharf. Goombay bands entertain aboard and refreshments are served. Tuesdays and Thursdays offer a variety of sporting events at the many resort hotels. Folkloric shows by the Bahamas School of the Theatre are given at a local resort hotel. There is a special food and craft market on Parliament Street, which is closed to vehicular traffic from 3 to 7 p.m. The promotion attracts thousands of visitors who also spend money at the local hotels, restaurants and shops. Work on the event is by volunteer groups, directed by the tourist board. The entire event is financed by grants from the government but is almost self-supporting. Most events are free, but a few do charge an admission fee.

Nassau

FOX HILL DAY

Held annually, second Tuesday in August
Historic, commemorative

Fox Hill Day is a Bahamian event celebrated for more than 100 years to mark the abolition of slavery. The one-day event takes place in an area called Fox Hill, a small, quiet township about five miles from Nassau. Most activities take place at the Fox Hill Parade Ground. It becomes a free-for-all carnival with Bahamian foods, songs and dances, starting in the late afternoon. On a more serious note, however, there is an 11 a.m. Thanksgiving Service in the local Baptist church. It's open to the public. Visitors are always given a royal welcome and are ushered to the front. Gospel and Bahamian religious song concerts are part of the service.

Freeport, Nassau, Family Out Islands

JUNKANOO PARADE AND FESTIVAL

Held annually, December 26, January 1
Cultural, legendary, ethnic, parade, New Year

The Junkanoo Parade and Festival is held on Boxing Day, December 26, and January 1, beginning at 4 a.m. starting "over the hill" in Nassau's native quarter. Junkanoo parades are along Bay Street in Nassau as well as in Freeport and the Family of Out Islands. Masqueraded marchers wear elaborate costumes which take months to make and are done in complete secrecy. The dancers bob and weave along in a shuffling step to the beat of an Afro-Bahamian rhythm called Goombay. Musical instruments include cowbells, goat skin drums and trumpets backed by the clicking and clacking of lignum vitae sticks (hardwood), the staccato rattle of pebble-filled "shak-shaks" and the sound of steel drums. The music is infectious, and spectators are soon caught up in it all. Dancing and music are continuous until sunrise, and then comes the judging. The group selected as the best dressed wins cash prizes with other prizes to individually dressed adults and children. Legend claims that this festival was started by a West African tribal chief, John Canoe. Another says that Junkanoo comes from the French "*gens inconnus*," or unknown people, because of the masks worn by the dancers to hide their identities. One of the bonuses of each parade is that often the colorful headpieces worn by the dancers and paraders are given to tourists at the end of the festivity. Junkanoo is described as a combination Mardi Gras, mummer's parade and ancient African tribal ritual.

BARBADOS

Bridgetown, islandwide

JUNE CROP-OVER FESTIVAL

Held annually, June, sometimes in July
Harvest, folkloric, cultural

The June Crop-Over Festival celebrates the harvesting of the sugar cane crop with special events that actually mirror what did happen at harvest time in the 1600s. Today's festival, however, dates back to 1973. It officially begins with a decorated cart parade to recall the last day of reaping, when workers, wearing bright flowers and ribbons, drove in decorated carts to the mills and molasses terminals. They sang happy songs and clapped in rhythm to mark the end of the sugar cane crop and harvesting season. Crop-over parties once held by plantation owners for the workers are now held at resort hotels and villages. The same foods are still featured, including roasted pig, corn pone, sweet bread and pudding 'n souse plus drinks like lemonade, mauby and cane juice and "kill devil" rum. Years ago the slave workers danced to the beat of a tuk band, which included a base drum, kettle drum, flute and improvised instruments. The same music is still played, with calypso and steel band competitions added to the musical offerings. Folk dancing, singing, arts and crafts demonstrations, the crowning of a Queen and King of the Crop with various Crop-Over Festival Queen competitions are also featured. There's a donkey derby, goat racing and contests like climbing a greased pole or trying to catch a greased pig. Country-style fairs are held every weekend in each Bajan parish. The month-long June or July festival officially closes the last night with the ceremony of the "Burning of Mr. Harding." An effigy symbolizing the historic ruthless gang-driver Mr. Harding is carried to its fatal end by a parade of decorated floats, singers, dancers and fireworks. When the parade ends, Mr. Harding burns.

BELGIUM

Antwerp, Bruges, Brussels, Ghent,
Kortrijk, Leuven, Mechelen

FLANDERS FESTIVAL

Held annually, April/October
Cultural

The Flanders Festival, one of Europe's most diverse events, is held in seven different cities. Its purpose is to make international classical music available to Flemish audiences. Centuries ago, Flanders held a prominent position in the arts. This festival traces its beginnings back to 1958, when a Flanders music event and program were held at the World Exhibition–World's Fair in Brussels. A year later, Jan Briers of the Ghent Festival persuaded festival founders in Antwerp and Tongeren to unite and hold one Flanders Festival. Over the years, other cities joined the festival, now held annually April through October. The world's most famous performers, opera companies and ensembles perform. The festival is divided into seven sections spread out over five Flemish provinces. Each section is responsible for its own budget and program. Each is helped with a subsidy from the Belgian Ministry of Culture and Belgian Radio and Television and by donations from private groups. There is financing from ticket sales also. The festival schedule differs from year to year, but all events attract large audiences, ranging from 5,000 to 50,000, totaling more than 150,000 each year. Performances in the different cities are held in churches, museums, stadiums, concert halls and even abbeys. The festival is a member of the European Association of Music Festivals.

In 1982, the Flanders Festival marked two anniversaries. Haydn's 250th birthday was celebrated with a variety of his works, including *The Creation* in Bruges and other cities. Stradella's 300th birthday was observed with a performance of *San Giovanni Battista* in Bruges. Other operas presented in the different cities included Massenet's *Cendrillon*, conducted by John Nelson with Frederica von Stade, Joselyne Taillon and Ann Murray. There was Mozart's *La Clemenza di Tito* conducted by Sylvain Gambreling with Stuart Burrows and Christiane Eda-Pierre; Mozart's *Idomeneo*, conducted by John Pritchard with Mr. Burrows, Miss Eda-Pierre and Robert Tear; Verdi's *Simon Boccanegra*, conducted by Mr. Gambreling with Jose van Dam in the title role. Performing ensembles included the Polish Chamber Orchestra, the Chamber Orchestra of the Royal Academy of Music of London, Der Junge Choir of Aachen, the Bamberg Symphony Orchestra, the Antwerp Philharmonic, Philharmonia Hungarica, the Christ Church Cathedral Choir of Oxford, the Choir of Westminster Abbey, London; the Philadelphia Orchestra, the Warsaw Quartet, the Cleveland Quartet, the London

Symphony Orchestra, the Amsterdam Baroque Orchestra and the Stuttgart Chamber Orchestra. The festival also featured soloists. Among some of them were sopranos Judith Blegen and Mariette Kemmer, pianist Murray Perahia and violinist Arthur Grumiaux and conductors Claudio Abbado, Ton Koopman and Riccardo Muti.

Beselare

PROCESSION OF THE WITCHES

Held annually, last Sunday in July
Folkloric, legendary, parade

The annual Procession of the Witches recalls through pageantry the history of witchcraft in this area. The town's nickname is "Parish of the Sorceress." The procession or parade begins at 3:30 p.m. led by a brass band, majorettes, the town's coat of arms and the marquis and marquess of Beselare. The six-hour parade consists of three segments. One is folkloric with the famous flying goat, the haunted farm, the enchanted mills, the tree of ghosts and witches of Beselare represented in appropriate costumes and floats. The second segment represents local witch sayings, the circle of witches and a cart or float carrying today's local witches. The final phase of the parade is the trial of the witches and the witch scales. If a witch is lighter in weight than the jury estimates, she is a spirit doomed to die. If the jury is correct about her weight, the witch goes free. This is followed by burning at the stakes and the funeral of "Sefa Bubbels." Sefa Bubbels was a witch during the Middle Ages. Her real name was Josepha Bubbels. She was said to be a dreadful shrew, ugly and so tall that she was called the Giant Witch. She became the witch of the witches. Although the annual procession has been held for centuries, it wasn't actually organized until 1958 to give the town an annual event of touristic attraction. The event, based on a folkloric legend, is financed through donations from local residents, who also work on preparations months in advance. The parade does attract thousands of foreign visitors.

Bruges

HOLY BLOOD PROCESSION

Held annually, May on Ascension Day, movable date
Religious, historic, procession

The Holy Blood Procession is always held on Ascension Day, the Thursday 50 days after Easter. Today's procession is the continuance of an eight-century-old tradition, based on history and religious custom. In 1146, the threat of a Turkish invasion of Jerusalem made Baudoin III, king of Jerusalem, ask for help, and a second new crusade. Help came from Thierry of Alsace, who was cited for bravery although the expedition failed. He was given the relic of the Holy Blood, which he brought to the magistrate of Bruges. The entire city celebrated Thierry's return with the relic, April 7, A.D. 1150. The Chapel of the Holy Blood was built on the site of the old one to hold the Holy Blood of Christ relic. There was a procession. This procession and veneration of the Holy Blood relic weren't organized on a regular basis until 1820, when it was legally established. Today, the procession is held at 3 p.m. on Ascension Day and includes (patterned after the Spanish tradition) a parade of the penitents and floats depicting Biblical scenes, ranging from the fall of Adam and Eve to Christ's crucifixion. A dozen or so people reenact the return of Count Thierry to his town. They carry town banners, and some dress like the Flemish Crusaders, the Knights of the Court and the Burghers of Bruges. The procession starts from the town Burg and returns there for the bishop's blessing of the crowd with the relic of the Holy Blood. Actually the day is a Holy Day of Obligation, requiring Roman Catholics to attend mass, so the day begins with an 11 a.m. pontifical high mass in the cathedral. The parade lasts for one and a half hours.

Brussels

BRUSSELS INTERNATIONAL FAIR

Held annually, April/May
Economic, fair

The Brussels International Fair dates back to 1927, when it was started to be a showcase not only for Belgian industry and products but also for the interchange of products, ideas and industries with other countries. The fair has displays, exhibits and various programs. The trade fair aspect of the annual event demonstrates where Belgium stands in the European international commercial scene. Each year, the fair has a theme. For example, in 1977 it was "Deck Brussels with Flowers," and exhibits carried out the theme. The fair includes folkloric performances, special evening dinners and a Forum of the Nations, started in 1977, the fiftieth anniversary of the fair, in which 33 foreign countries participated. It continues to be a program of meetings and exchange sessions between Belgium and guest countries. The fair attracts thousands of visitors, many foreigners. The event is financed through admission charges, rental fees and government help. The annual exposition features laboratory equipment exhibits, hotel and restaurant equipment, educational displays and even a horse show. It also deals with environmental protection and public works equipment.

Lochristi

BEGONIA FESTIVAL

Held annually, August
Floral, economic, horticultural

The Begonia Festival coincides with the full blooming of the begonias, which come in many colors and varieties. The day before the three-day festival begins, the whole town gathers the flowers and sets up exhibits and also carpets the streets with the flowers arranged in exquisite designs, which are floodlit at night. First-day festivities are from 5 to 11 p.m. More than 50,000 people view the floral art works, listen to band concerts and enjoy local foods. From 9 to 11 a.m. the next two days, there's the Floral Parade of Floats with very elaborate begonia-decorated displays, statues and pictures. More than a million begonia blossoms in eight different colors and three sizes are used for the decorations. The festival, held for more than a 100 years, continues to be more organized these days, with local citizens taking a very active part. The monks of Saint Bavo from the Abbey of Ghent are credited for planting the first begonias in this and surrounding areas. The begonia, originally a South American plant, was grown for its leaves and light-colored flowers by Sire Begon, a former administrator of Santo Domingo. After much cross-breeding, begonias became very popular for flower beds because of their color and shape. Begonias can be white, yellow, scarlet, blue, mauve and even pale pink. During the festival, tours are conducted to the begonia fields for viewing. Lochristi is northeast of Ghent.

Ypres

CAT FESTIVAL AND PARADE

Held annually, second Sunday in May
Folkloric, legendary, parade

The Cat Festival and Parade is based on a legend dating back to the year A.D. 962, when Baudoin III, the Count of Flanders, ordered the people of Ypres to throw two or three live cats from the tower of his castle. In those days, cats were sacrificed just as witches were burned. Pagan belief had made the cat into a divinity, more often of fertility, so that popular Christian belief then saw the cat as evil. By throwing live cats from the castle tower, citizens of Ypres would be renouncing pagan superstitions. Although the Cat Festival has been observed for centuries, there were a few times when it was banned. It was stopped in the eighteenth century by order of Joseph II and again after the French occupation. By 1817, however, it was again observed by selecting one citizen, attired in a red jacket and white cap, decorated with multicolored ribbons, to go to the castle tower and throw down a live cat. Luckily the cat often survived the drop to run away. During World War I, it was observed only by a concert of the bells on the second Wednesday in May ("Kattewoensdag") at 3 p.m. In 1938, the local people reinstated the festival the second Sunday in May. Live cats were replaced by toy stuffed ones. The Cat Parade was added in 1955. It continues to include floats and costumes based on the entire feline mythology through the ages. For example, there is the divine cat "Bastet," worshipped by the Egyptians in the sanctuary of Bubastis, two giant cats pulling the chariot of Freya, the Germanic goddess, Puss in Boots and more. After the parade, crowds gather in front of the town belfry. A jester is at the top, and he throws down some toy stuffed cats. There is always a big scramble for the fake cats.

BERMUDA

Hamilton

BERMUDA FESTIVAL

Held annually, January/February
Cultural, economic

The Bermuda Festival was started to give local citizens an opportunity to enjoy the performing arts and to attract visitors during the island's off-season. The first event was held in Hamilton in 1976. More than 40 performers appeared. The festival attracted 90 percent capacity audiences and actually finished in the black with a profit of $3,000. Within a short time, the festival has featured world famous performers, ranging from Dave Brubeck to the Alvin Ailey Dancers and British stars Emlyn Williams and Michael Redgrave. The festival offers concerts in classical music, opera and jazz. There are instrumental and vocal performances, too, plus mime, theater and magic shows. It is an international event in every sense of the word. The festival is financed through ticket sales and grants from the Bermuda Department of Tourism and the Bermuda Chamber of Commerce.

Hamilton, St. George's

BERMUDA COLLEGE WEEKS

Held annually, March/April
Economic

Bermuda College Weeks cover four to five weeks of activities, many free, for college students from all over the United States and Canada who came here for fun and respite from their studies. More than 15,000 come to enjoy the sun and island and special events, offered by the Bermuda government, which annually appropriates about $100,000 toward the programs. These include get-acquainted dances, free luncheons, a Hamilton Harbour boat cruise and steel band concerts. There are also beach parties and volleyball matches. Specially issued identification cards admit the bearer to all events. Over the years the Elbow Beach Surf Club on the island's South Shore has become the unofficial base of operations for Bermuda College Weeks. College Weeks goes back to 1936, when Ivy League rugby teams spent their spring vacations during March and April in Bermuda, competing against Bermudian and British teams. The girls soon discovered where the boys were and followed them there. Eventually serious rugby competition disappeared, but the students continued to come to Bermuda. In 1948, the Bermuda government made College Weeks an official part of the island's annual celebrations. More events are added each year, and some are changed by the students themselves. The Bermuda government keeps a close watch for any illegal drugs used. Students pay their own airfares and for their hotels (which do offer them large discounts). Since 1948, close to a million students have enjoyed College Weeks.

BONAIRE (NETHERLANDS ANTILLES)

Kralendijk

INTERNATIONAL REGATTA

Held annually, October
Sports, competition, boats

The International Regatta is a four-day competition held the third week of October with hundreds of entries from neighboring islands, Venezuela and Puerto Rico. It was originally sponsored by the Lions Club of Bonaire in 1968 to increase tourism to the island and to give the island an official sports event. It consists of races over various water courses for different types of sailboats, including working and fishing boats. The idea for the regatta was based on periodic races that local fishermen and sailors of the Netherlands Antilles ran for their own pleasure. The event attracts not only hundreds of contestants but also thousands of visitors who follow regattas. It has proved to be economically beneficial for the island's hotels. The event is handled by local residents and businessmen who donate money to the project and their time to work out details. Work begins a few months prior to the regatta itself. There are entry fees. The races take place in waters off the island.

BRAZIL

Rio de Janeiro

CARNIVAL

Held annually, four days prior to Ash Wednesday, movable dates
Folkloric, economic

Carnival has become synonymous with Rio de Janeiro and has been celebrated in this city for hundreds of years. Most Carnival events start the Saturday before Ash Wednesday and continue at a frenzied pace right up to the start of Lent. Unofficially, celebrations start long before on New Year's Eve with thousands of local followers of voodoo. Decorated with fresh flowers and carrying lighted candles, they parade hypnotically into the ocean in a pagan tribute to Iemanja, the goddess of the sea. At midnight the city beaches glow with candles and resound with pealing bells and screeching sirens to usher in the New Year. The main Carnival celebrations always come either in February or March, depending upon Ash Wednesday and Easter dates, both movable. Since seasons are reversed in Brazil, Carnival is a summertime event. Carnival is a blend of African and European cultures. In Europe, Carnival was originally celebrated to mark the end of a cold dark winter and was brought to Brazil by the early Portuguese settlers. They wore masks during Carnival time and sprayed each other with flour and liquid to create a wild exotic look. The coming of Black slaves added hypnotic African rhythms and drum beats. Eventually the Blacks painted themselves with whitewash to mark freedom during the Carnival. In 1846, Clara Delamastro, a French actress and wife of a well-known Rio hotel owner, hired an orchestra, decorated the hotel and invited friends to a costume ball, thus giving birth to one of Rio's traditional balls. Today, Carnival festivities get underway, weather permitting, on Saturday afternoon with thousands of spectators lined up along the city's eight-mile beachfront waiting for the parades and dancers to appear. There's street dancing to the beat of drums and *cuicas* (gourds). The disjointed uninhibited dancing goes through the main streets. Local residents mix freely with the dancers, who are doing the samba to the music of all kinds of bands. Various costume balls are held each Carnival night with the famous Artists' Ball at the Gloria Hotel the Saturday before Carnival week. The city's many social clubs hold their own balls, too, and tickets are very expensive and hard to get. The balls start at 11 p.m. and go through daybreak or later the next day. Some guests wear costumes. Some wear black ties, and others only bathing suits. Every year there's always an international celebrity at the Carnival, and the crowd goes wild. In the past such stars as Liza Minnelli, Margaux Hemingway and Racquel Welch have attended. Sunday is the day for the Escola de Samba, or Parade of the Samba Schools, beginning at 7 p.m. and continuing through noon the next day. The Samba Schools, only a little more than 40 years old, are not real schools but neighborhood social clubs whose members are devoted to celebrating Carnival. Each school selects a narrative line or theme, usually from Brazilian history and folklore for dramatic appeal. For example, in 1980, the Beija-Flor School of Nilopolis, a poor workers' suburb in Rio, acted out a series of fairy tales during their 80-minute appearance on the street. Each school selects a samba from the new works of its own member composers. Often the songs are recorded and sold months before the big show so that spectators have time to learn the words to accompany the dancers as they gyrate on Carnival night. The parade features the top 10 samba schools, each with about 3,000 performers or up to as many as 30,000, all dressed in very original costumes, some scanty. About 80,000 viewers are in the bleachers. Both eventually are tired out, but bursts of rhythms from each group's percussion section of kettle drums, tambourines, whistles, rattles, graters and cowbells seem to give all a second wind, and the parade goes on. Each samba school presentation follows an established pattern and is a competition, with judging based on nine categories, from overall impression to the artistry of the floats and costumes to the performances of individuals and how they portray their set roles in the pageant. More than a million people watch the parade that winds thoughout the city. Many of the samba schools have been in the Carnival for over a century. Each has its own customs and history, and members come from all walks of life. It is considered an honor to be among the best schools. As soon as one Carnival ends, the very next day, each samba school is hard at work preparing for the next year's event. Various groups, some poor, sell key chains and headbands with their school's emblem, hold raffles and even feature Saturday night samba parties year-round to raise money to buy materials for costumes and to build floats and props, all done in complete secrecy. The same costume is never used again, nor is the material put into another outfit. Each is made from scratch every year.

BRITISH VIRGIN ISLANDS

Tortola

TORTOLA FESTIVAL

Held annually, August
Historic, commemorative

The Tortola Festival celebrates the freeing of the slaves in the British Virgin Islands in 1834 (three decades before the United States) with special commemorative programs and events. It has been continually observed in one form or another ever since. Festivities begin the first week in August with an 11 a.m.

"August Monday" festival parade. Presiding is the newly selected Miss British Virgin Islands. Special events include horse races, water sports, folkloric programs and fireworks.

BULGARIA

Gabrovo

NATIONAL HUMOR AND SATIRE FESTIVAL

Held annually, May
Cultural, humor

The National Humor and Satire Festival claims to be the only festival in the world devoted to humor. It is held annually in late May, sometimes into early June. The town of Gabrovo, founded in the fourteenth century by a blacksmith, Racho, has the reputation of being stingy, and lots of jokes are told about the town. For example, when Gabrovians go to sleep, they stop their clocks to save wear on the gears. They entertain in the dark, since there's no need to pay for light just to talk. No one knows how these jokes got started. Local people work hard for a living, but they still have a good sense of humor. In 1967, the first festival was held to attract tourism to the area. The ten-day event begins with a carnival procession through town. It has floats, and marchers are dressed like their favorite comic figure. The floats very often are satiric and exceptionally original. After the parade, serious competitions for the best laughs are held at the House of Humor, a modern four-story building that contains more than 12,000 exhibits about humorists and artists from all over the world. More than 1,000 entries from 50 countries participate in the annual festival, which includes cartoonists, filmmakers, sculptors, artists and performers dealing in humor and satire. At the 1979 festival, the United States was represented by the works of Art Buchwald, Woody Allen and Kurt Vonnegut, Jr. Special international awards are given to foreign contestants as well as national ones to Bulgarians in the humor competition. More than 10,000 attend each year's festival. It is financed through grants from the government and from contest entry fees and some ticket sales.

Kazanluk

ROSE FESTIVAL

Held annually, May/June
Floral, economic, harvest, horticultural

The Rose Festival is an annual ten-day event always held in late May into early June, the blooming season for the roses, which are raised for perfume attar and medicine and exported to all parts of the world. Kazanluk is a small town in the Valley of the Roses, where millions of rose bushes are cultivated. Thousands of visitors attend this event, which begins before dawn when farmers and young people dressed in native costumes and carrying baskets and hampers ride in gaily decorated carts for the ritual picking of the rose petals in the acres of red and white roses. All visitors are given rose wreaths and bouquets of roses as a festival souvenir. There is a Queen Pageant, but the queen is not selected for beauty but for her ability as a rose picker. She is dressed in white, wears a white veil and carries a bouquet of white roses. After she is crowned, she leads a long chain dance into Kazanluk, where the official festival flag is flown. This is the signal for the Parade of Roses to begin. Parade floats are rose-decorated. There are marching bands, costumed paraders and folk dancing. The parade takes a couple of hours as it goes through all the nearby towns in the valley. After the parade, there are picnics featuring Bulgarian food and drink. Folk dance and song programs follow. Legend claims that a Persian trader brought rose bush cuttings to the Balkans hundreds of years ago to provide attar for his lady's perfumes. Today, Bulgaria supplies 90 percent of the world's rose attar. Festival goers can also tour the Rose Museum in Kazanluk. It traces the history and production of rose oil through photographs. The Kazanluk Scentific Institute is also open to visitors who get to see the actual process of rose oil extraction. It takes 3,300 pounds of rose petals to make two pounds of rose attar, which is used for medicinal, aromatic and food purposes. One quart of rose oil costs $3,325. The festival is financed through government grants. There are some admission charges, but most events are free.

Slunchev Bryag

GOLDEN ORPHEUS

Held annually, June
Cultural, competition

The Golden Orpheus is held in a resort town on the Black Sea and is an international popular music competition. Some 60 countries, including the United

States and Canada, send more than 500 contestants to compete in every contemporary music medium, ranging from synthesizer to soul, big band to bop. Participants sing Bulgarian and their own national songs. More than 50,000 persons attend the ten-day festival. It is named for the god of song and poetry, Orpheus, who, according to legend, lived in the Rhodope and Balkan mountains. The festival includes a prize competition for the best pop song by a Bulgarian composer, an international prize competition for singers and concerts by top Bulgarian and foreign singers and instrumentalists. After preliminary auditions, the public hears the best Bulgarian and foreign compositions, performed by all contestants. There are also recitals by world famous singers. The festival's jury panel consists of well-known conductors, directors and musicologists. The festival was started 25 years ago to bring a cultural experience to the resort area and attract tourists. A paid staff works year-round in preparing for the annual event. It is financed by government grants.

CANADA

Alberta Province

Banff

BANFF FESTIVAL OF THE ARTS

Held annually, May/August
Cultural

The Banff Festival of the Arts is a two-and-a-half month program with the majestic Canadian Rocky Mountains serving as a setting for music, drama, opera, dance, art and workshops. Performances are given in the 1,000-seat Eric Harvie Theatre and the 250-seat Margaret Greenham Theatre. In addition to professional performances, featuring famous artists, there are also many free concerts given by students and faculty of the Banff School of Fine Arts Division at the Banff Centre and locations throughout the town. Actual festival performances, however, are usually in August to spotlight achievements of students with the extra bonus of famous performers and productions. The festival grew out of the school, which was started in 1933 to help talented students advance in the arts. Originally only for Canadians, it is now international in scope. A limited number of scholarships are available. The school is financed through tuition charges, government contributions and private donations. The festival is supported through ticket sales and contributions from various cultural and civic groups. The festival is a showcase for the school's talent and a source of top entertainment for local residents and vacationers. It offers opera recitals, chamber music, orchestral concerts, readings, ballet, modern dance, visual arts exhibits (with photography) and jazz.

Alberta Province

Calgary

CALGARY EXHIBITION AND STAMPEDE

Held annually, July
Economic, sports, rodeo, competition, fair

The Calgary Exhibition and Stampede is Canada's largest rodeo event and ranks right up there with the famous Cheyenne (Wyoming, U.S.A.) Frontier Days Rodeo. In fact, it was Guy Weadick from Cheyenne who founded this event. A showman and rodeo man, he visited Calgary in 1912 and found the area suitable for a rodeo, cowboys and Indians. He obtained local financial backing. The event was interrupted by World War I, but by 1923 it was on its way to success. It originally was called the Calgary Stampede, but over the years it expanded and the name was changed. The highlight is the daily afternoon rodeo, played to an audience of 25,000 in the grandstand at Stampede Park. Other rodeo events include the chuckwagon race, the Grandstand Show with world famous entertainers and special firework displays. More than a million people attend each year's event, and since its start close to a billion have attended. Each year has a special theme. In 1982, its seventieth anniversary it was "Salute to the Cowboy." In past years, it has honored the Indians and pioneers of the area. The stampede is a world-class rodeo competition in saddle bronc and bareback riding, steer wrestling, calf roping and bull riding. In 1982, there was a purse of $500,000, an all-time high for any rodeo. The chuck wagon races had its own purse of $175,000 in 1982. Rodeo events are held in the 130-acre Stampede Park in downtown Calgary. There's also a midway with more than 40 rides and attractions, including Weadickville, (named for the stampede's founder), a Wild West town with bad guys plus a Frontier Casino with 100 blackjack tables and 10 roulette wheels. There are agricultural and livestock exhibits and a 1,000-population Indian Village with teepees, representative of five Indian tribes from the nearby Plains. They actively participate in the rodeo and share in the profits. Among celebrities who've entertained are comedian Arte Johnson, Bob Hope and singers Helen Reddy and Bobby Vinton. Work on the Stampede is a year-round job with 175 salaried workers and 700 volunteers during the event. The annual event is financed through contributions from civic and business groups, gate admissions and shows.

Alberta Province

Edmonton

KLONDIKE DAYS EXPOSITION

Held annually, July
Historic, pageantry

Klondike Days Exposition commemorates the Gold Rush of 1898 and how it changed the small agricultural village of Edmonton into a boom town overnight. Edmonton was the starting point for the overland trip to the Yukon. This annual event transforms citizens into men and women of the Gold Rush era complete with costumes. Women turn into Klondike Kates and wear long gowns, stockings and high-laced boots. Festivities begin with a two-hour Klondike Days parade through the city's downtown area, followed the next day by a Band Extravaganza at Clarke Stadium featuring Canadian and local marching bands and drum and bugle corps in competition for trophies. There is a Sourdough Raft Race, covering a ten-mile part of the North Saskatchewan River with viewing from the river banks. A highlight of Klondike Days is the Sunday Promenade, when the central part of the city is closed to traffic so that everyone in Klondike costumes can stroll along the streets to enjoy free entertainment, both professional and amateur, performed on eleven stages. Other festival events include Klondike Garden parties on the grounds of the Legislative Building and noontime free entertainment on two downtown stages with one in front of City Hall. Local theater groups perform typical melodramas of the Klondike era, and Klondike-style casinos are in full operation along with citywide Klondike breakfasts and luncheons. Many city hotels offer Klondike Nights entertainment. There is also an Alberta Gold Panning Championship at the Chilkoot Gold Mine daily, with finalists eligible to enter the World Gold Panning Championships. Foods sold at the event reflect the era and various ethnic groups like the Chinese, Italians and Ukrainians. Klondike Days began in 1962, when the Edmonton Exhibition Association incorporated a Klondike theme as a tribute to past history. Today, the event attracts more than half a million folks, and over the years, several million. It is financed through contributions from civic and business groups and through the sale of souvenirs and souvenir booklets.

British Columbia Province

Abbotsford

INTERNATIONAL AIR SHOW

Held annually, August
Economic, aviation

The International Air Show is an annual three-day event held at the local airport and attracting as many as 200,000 people. Since the first one-day show in 1962, a couple of million people have been part of the show, which is usually preceded by a general conference on aviation. Each year the conference and show are keyed to a theme, for example, air cargo and human needs. Operated since 1969 by the nonprofit Abbotsford International Airshow Society, it is officially recognized as Canada's national air show. It has received worldwide recognition, too. It is also Canada's only established aviation/aerospace industry show for the latest civilian aircraft. In 1975, it was the largest fly-in for private aircraft (926) in the Pacific Northwest. The annual show is a big boost for the local economy, with hotels, motels, restaurants and bars all doing well. The air show, of course, features aerobatic performances by the Canadian Armed Forces, Snowbirds Jet Team, the U.S. Air Force's Thunderbirds, members of the Royal Air Force and private performers. There are also displays and exhibits of air equipment and a big banquet with famous air folks presiding. Work on the show is almost year-round with two full-time staff members and hundreds of local volunteers. It is financed through gate receipts (charge per carload, per person and per busload), as well as entry fees for private citizens who fly to the event, program sales, booth rentals and sales displays.

British Columbia Province

Penticton

PEACH FESTIVAL

Held annually, August
Harvest, economic

The Peach Festival is a harvest event in August designed to bring tourists to the area. There are tours of the peach orchards and a chance to help with the harvest, with some peaches going to the picker. There's a Peach Queen Coronation, a peach parade, square dancing, a rodeo, peach exhibits, entertainment and both land and water sports. The Queen Coronation ceremony has expanded to include Peach Royalty from other Canadian provinces and from ten United States regions. The first festival lasted three days in August 1948 and included an air show and agricultural fair. In 1957, a Square Dance Jamboree was added. It now is an eight-day festival with all the added features still offered. Festival events are held in the Peach Bowl and at King's Park. Work on the festival is by volunteers. It is financed through gate fees, trading dollars and corporation grants. More than 25,000 attend each year's festival, with a grand total of more than a million to date.

British Columbia Province

Prince George

SNOWGOLF CHAMPIONSHIP

Held annually, February
Sports, economic, competition

The Snowgolf Championship is an annual three-day winter event designed to get local residents out of the winter doldrums. It also attracts tourists. It's a zany winter sport dating back to 1970, when some members of the Prince George Golf Club tried golfing in the snow for fun. They saw potential in this game and formed a board of directors. Three years later they established a World Championship of Snowgolf. In 1978, it was part of the Prince George's annual Mardi Gras of winter festivities. Every year, a few thousand put on all kinds of fun winter costumes and showed up at the Prince George Golf Course. In 1973, there was the original three-hole course with as many strokes as a person wanted. It grew to a nine-hole course and more normal pars. Plastic six-inch tees were introduced, and billiard ball–size golf balls of bright purple were used. By 1975 proceeds from the Snowgolf Tournament were going to the Aurora Centre for the Physically and Mentally Handicapped. Today, prizes and souvenirs worth more than $10,000 are awarded to almost every golfer for being the most promotion-conscious, snowgolf booster of the year, the best costume and unusual footwear, plus "booby" prizes for such categories as coldest celebrity foursome. The event begins with a "Snow Loa" for visitors and celebrities and a handshake from Snowbera, the tournament mascot. At 8 p.m. there's the "World's Worst Parade" followed by a Celebrity Dinner and Dance. Celebrities include those from the sports and entertainment worlds. Round One of the tournament gets underway the next morning at 9 a.m., continuing to 4 p.m. with a dinner dance from 8 p.m. to 2 a.m. There are three nine-hole courses for the several hundred snowgolfers per course, with foursome tee-offs at five-minute intervals. Round

Two usually on a Sunday is again from 9 a.m. to 4 p.m., with an awards dinner at 6 p.m. This fun event does help the local economy and tourism. Several airlines even operate package trips for the event. Work is done by local volunteers. It is financed through green fees (sorry, white fees), entry fees and grants from local industry. It is a nonprofit event, with any realized profits going to a local charity.

Manitoba Province

Dauphin

CANADA'S NATIONAL UKRAINIAN FESTIVAL

Held annually, July/August
Ethnic

Canada's National Ukrainian Festival is an ethnic event that centers entirely on the culture and art of the Ukrainian people. It has been staged annually since 1966 by descendants of Ukrainian pioneers to preserve their ethnic heritage. Not only are those of Ukrainian descent in Manitoba involved but also those of the same background from all over Canada and the United States. Festival events include demonstrations of the artistic Easter egg decorating that's so famous, traditional foods, ritual breads and cross-stitch embroidery. There are competitions, stage shows, song fests, bandura playing and Cossack dancing, making a very full four days. There are arts and crafts exhibits and demonstrations and a parade with decorated floats, moving orchestras and paraders in authentic costumes. It is financed through private donations and sales of foods and souvenirs.

Manitoba Province

Gimli

ICELANDIC FESTIVAL

Held annually, August
Ethnic

The Icelandic Festival or Islendingadagurinn is an ethnic event that pays tribute to the original Icelandic groups who emigrated to Canada in 1875, soon after volcanic eruptions destroyed their homes in Iceland. Eventually they settled on the shores of Lake Winnipeg and called home New Iceland, later changing it to Gimli, which is Icelandic for "paradise." The three-day festival, one of the oldest ethnic ones in Manitoba and possibly Canada, dates back to 1890, when those early settlers wanted to preserve their customs. Their descendants still do. Events include choir singing and a folk festival with participants dressed in Icelandic costumes. There are theater programs, fine arts, a regatta and air show (modern event), song writing and poetry contests. Icelandic food specialities include *vineterta* (five- to seven-layer torte with prune filling), smoked *rulla pilsa* (lamb) and *skyr* (like yogurt). There's a festival queen, selected for her "outstanding merit," who can be young or old, married or single. With the honor goes the title Maid of the Mountain, or Fjalikona. Thousands come to the festival, which is always held either the last week of July or the first in August. The festival is self-supporting.

Manitoba Province

St. Boniface

FESTIVAL DU VOYAGEUR

Held annually, February
Ethnic, historic

Festival du Voyageur is held in February to honor the *voyageurs* who paddled the fur-trading canoes that opened up Canada's interior in the 1700s and 1800s. It is estimated that about 5,000 of these men traveled from Montreal to the Rockies and from Hudson Bay down to the Gulf of Mexico, opening up the fur trade to the entire nation. These men, whose legendary feats continually grew via stories, are honored every year in this French-speaking city, now a district of Winnipeg. The main festival site is Voyageur Park, as Whittier Park on St. Joseph and Hebert streets is renamed during the nine-day festival. There is always an official *voyageur* (a different person selected each year) dressed in the typical costume of bright shirt, traditional sash, colored garters over leather leggings and either a fur hat or a red toque. He greets all visitors each year, whose number is more than 400,000 (many are tourists from the rest of Canada and from the United States). Since the first festival in 1970, several million have enjoyed the event. Social aspects of the festival include French-Canadian cuisine, such as pea soup, tourtiere and beans with maple syrup. There's a Governor's Ball, attended by guests in costume. Sports events include hockey, ringette (ladies' hockey), snowshoe racing, basketball and a cross-country ski participation race. Snow sculptures line the five blocks of Provencher Boulevard, and there's a demonstration of snow sculpture by a group of Manitoba snow sculptors, winners of an international competition. Both children and adults are encouraged to watch and try to do it. The festival has a beard-growing contest, casinos, fiddling and jigging contest, museum exhibits, handicraft displays and dog sled races. There are souvenir and information booths on the main streets and a midway, five cabins with living exhibits, such as a working blacksmith, plus a heated marquee tent where hot meals and snacks are sold. There are noontime shows in the tent for schoolchildren and live stage shows from 8 to 11 p.m. "Voyageur Park" also has live buffalos, a tally-ho with a mule-drawn sleigh, dog sled rides and a snow slide to keep visitors busy and happy. The festival boasts more than 54 different events. The special school programs of the festival attract as many as 100,000 children of all ages. The festival was originally started in 1970 to generate winter tourism and business. At the same time it is historic in scope because it honors the early fur traders. The event is officially recognized as Manitoba's and Winnipeg's winter festival and is said to be the largest such event in Western Canada. In 1977, the festival brought in $3.2 million to the community. Work on the event is handled by 50 paid workers. During the peak period 1,500 volunteers help out. Monies to operate the festival come from the provincial government (about one-quarter) and from various businesses and civic groups (three-quarters). There are some admission fees, but most events are free. Souvenir journals and buttons also bring in some money.

Manitoba Province

The Pas

NORTHERN MANITOBA TRAPPERS' FESTIVAL

Held annually, February
Economic, sports, heritage, competition

The Northern Manitoba Trappers' Festival is an almost week-long event that pays tribute to the historic contribution and development of the Canadian northland by pioneer trappers who used sled dogs for transportation. Festival events include the World Championship Sled Dog Race, originally a 200-mile nonstop race now consisting of three daily laps of 50 miles each. There are several outdoor trappers' contests, including a 20-mile snowshoe race, tea boiling on the ice and snow, trap setting, muskrat skinning, flour packing, moose, goose and frog calling as well as fish eating. There's beard-growing contest, ice fishing through three to four feet of ice on the Saskatchewan River and a competition for the most fish caught within one hour. Other outdoor events include pulp wood cutting, wood sawing and splitting, tree felling, North Pole climbing all done in outdoor temperatures, ranging from a warm zero to twenty degrees below zero. Indoor events vary from a raw fur competition to native handicrafts (tanned moose and deer hide leather with bead or silk work) made into jackets, vests, gloves, parkas, mukluks, necklaces and handbags. There's also an international art contest and a Fur Queen competition, rendezvous dances, beer fests and stage shows with local talent. The various races and competitions offer cash money prizes, which vary from year to year. The annual winter festival attracts about 15,000 folks, many tourists, who do help the local economy. The current festival goes back to 1948 and the third week in January and is descended from the 1916 World Championship nonstop Sled Dog Race for a $1,000 prize. It was called the Pas Dog Derby and operated intermittently to 1931. It was discontinued during the Depression and not revived until 1948, becoming the Trappers' Festival. It was changed from January to mid-February because the weather was better then. Work on the festival is on a voluntary basis with only one typist who's paid a small honorarium. The event is financed through contributions from local industry and civic groups and through the sale of souvenir booklets. There is an admission charge for some indoor programs. The events are held throughout the town. The festival is administered by the nonprofit Northern Manitoba Trappers Festival Committee, Inc., consisting of more than 700 business people, both men and women.

Manitoba Province

Winnipeg

WINNIPEG FOLK FESTIVAL

Held annually, July
Folkloric, cultural

The Winnipeg Folk Festival is really a music festival, featuring bluegrass, gospel, jazz and old-time music with performers from all over Canada, the United States and Europe. Performances are outdoors at Birds Hill Park, about 14 miles north of Winnipeg, with city bus service available to and from the site. The three-day programs feature regional, national and international folk musicians and dancers. In 1981 there were 150 musicians appearing in more than 90 acts. Well-known performers appear, such as Valdy, Steve Goodman, Odetta and Amos Garrett. The festival, however, does include less famous performers, too. The 1981 festival had a record attendance of 34,000, which was topped in 1982 by 10,000 more. The festival started in 1974, directed by Mitch Podolak, a veteran in the folk music field, who is still artistic director. The event is handled by a paid staff of 4, assisted by 400 volunteers who work at the emporium (an open-air store in the park), the kitchen and at the ticket gate. They also direct traffic to a parking lot on the site. The 1981 festival operated for the first time without a deficit. It costs about $300,000 to operate the Friday to Sunday festival, which is financed through ticket sales, donations, sponsors and city and provincial grants, which make up 85 percent of the total revenue.

Manitoba Province

Winnipeg

FOLKLORAMA

Held annually, August
Ethnic, economic, cultural, folkloric

Folklorama is a one-week multi-ethnic festival of food, music, dance, arts and crafts that seems to appeal to more than half a million people every year. It is always held in mid-August. There are now 40 national pavilions as compared to the original 15. They are located throughout the city in community centers, school auditoriums, churches, tents, theaters and even university halls. Food continues to be the top attraction. Recently the Swedish Pavilion used 1,000 pounds of minced beef for cabbage rolls, and the Greek Pavilion marinated, skewered and froze more than 14,000 shish kebabs. Folk dancers and musicians are popular too, and both professional and amateur dance ensembles, choirs, musicians and artists perform. The dancing has included limbo dancers from Jamaica and Trinidad, Chinese musicians from New York and harpists and dancers from Ireland. Handicraft displays and sales include glassware, wooden shoes, wood carvings, jewelry and even dresses. Work on the event and during it is done by more than 14,000 volunteers, who put in hundreds of hours cooking, serving, manning the booths, selling and even performing. It is entirely operated by seven paid workers (three are only summer help). Tickets are sold in the form of a passport at different cost, but one passport is entry to all pavilions. The event is financed through admission charges, sales and contributions from local industry.

New Brunswick Province

Caraquet

ACADIAN FESTIVAL

Held annually, August
Ethnic, heritage, culture, folkloric

The Acadian Festival's goal is still to promote Acadian culture in all its aspects. It is always held for ten days culminating on August 15, the National Feast of the Acadians and the Assumption of the Blessed Virgin Mary. Events are cultural, social and, more recently, athletic. There are Acadian art exhibits and music with emphasis on the violin, accordion and guitar. There are dances performed to the strains of both French Acadian and modern rock music. There are theater offerings for both children and adults. There are French Acadian foods available, films and choir performances. Sports cover regattas, mini-golf and bicycle races. About 4 million have attended since the first festival in 1962. Between 20,000 and 30,000 come every August. The most popular event continues to be "L'Acadic en Fete," a huge happening with Acadian musicians, singers, artists, actors and actresses. Work on the next festival begins right after one festival ends. Most volunteers are young people interested in preserving their heritage. The event is financed through some admission fees, the sale of food and souvenirs and donations from civic, religious and business groups. Events are held throughout the city.

New Brunswick Province

Newcastle

MIRAMICHI FOLK SONG FESTIVAL

Held annually, June
Cultural, folkloric

The Miramichi Folk Song Festival is a three-day, late June event devoted entirely to songs and ballads, both old and new traditional in the miramichi "come all ye's" style taken from the old-time lumber camps. Local contemporary songs are made up by the participating singers. There are also Acadian French folk songs. Old songs are performed without accompaniment but are followed by old-time fiddling tunes, mouth organs, accordions, guitar and piano playing, plus step and tap dancing. The festival features not only local folk singers and musicans but also groups from all over Canada and the United States. It gives everyone the opportunity to hear authentic regional folk singing in the style of more than 100 years ago. The festival is sponsored by the Miramichi Historical Society, Radio Station CFAN Newcastle and the Newcastle Tourism Bureau. Since the festival is held late in June, in some years it can overlap with the celebration of Canada's Dominion Day, July 1. The very first festival was held August 14, 1957, and was the direct result of Lord Beaverbrook asking Dr. Louise Manny to research and collect folk songs, miramichi ballads and "come all ye's" narrative songs that told true stories of adventure, romance and tragedy. She did, and with the help of Dr. Helen Creighton of Dartmouth, Nova Scotia, and Dr. Edward (Sandy) Ives of the University of Maine, USA, and Dr. Jan

LaRue of New York University developed a one-day festival. It succeeded so well that it evolved into a three-day event that is culturally rich and helpful to the local economy. The first year, only 1,000 attended. Today, it's more than 20,000 and growing. The total to date is close to a million. Work on the festival is done by local volunteers, usually starting six months in advance of the event. It is financed through provincial government grants and sponsorships. There is an admission charge to each night's and day's programs. The festival is administered by a Miramichi Folk Song Festival Committee with a president, vice-president, director, treasurer and a secretary.

New Brunswick Province

Shediac

LOBSTER FESTIVAL

Held annually, July
Economic, food, fish

The Lobster Festival was first held in July 1952 to raise money to build an extension on the Shediac Legion Building. It proved so popular that it was continued the next year, gaining more visitors for the area. It was decided to continue it as a way of calling attention to the local lobster fishing industry. Today it is a six-day event that centers around the lobster, which is in abundance in this area. Festival programs include lobster-eating contests for all, daily public and private boiled lobster meals, a cabaret and a lobster trap expedition. There are family stage shows, artifact displays, a casino and a midway. Festivities begin with an opening day parade and a Grand Ball that same evening. Specialities include a children's costume parade, a 50-mile bicycle race and fireworks. The idea for the festival came from Joseph E. LeBlanc, a member of the provincial parliament for 25 years. By 1975, the festival had really come into its own, putting more than $500,000 back into the community, with motels, restaurants and stores doing a booming business. It is estimated that from 40,000 to 50,000 attend each year, and since 1952, several million. Of course, there's a Lobster Queen, rock music concerts, dances, other entertainment and plenty of lobster to eat. Festival work is done by a paid staff who work year-round preparing for the big event. It is financed through admission fees, the sale of lobster meals, souvenirs and rides. It has become self-supporting. All events are held on the festival grounds.

New Brunswick Province

Tracadie

BITOWA OUTDOOR FESTIVAL

Held annually, June
Conservation, ecology, economic, fish, sports

The Bitowa Outdoor Festival is keyed to the protection, conservation and recreation of renewable natural resources. The first festival was June 16-17, 1974, sponsored by the Association Chasse et Peche Bitowa. The association wanted folks to know more about the outdoors and its conservation. Events continue to center around camping, canoe racing and workshops in orienteering, canoeing, archery and fly fishing. There are competitions in wood cutting, horse hauling, four-wheel drive and a rally. It is always held the third full weekend in June, covering four days of activity and involving more sponsoring organizations. The festival attracts about 5,000 to the outdoors, many from outside the region. It's not all nature, however, since there's a wine cellar, beer tent and beer garden to help defray expenses. It is also financed by admission charges for the day and for camping. Work is by volunteers, who start six months before the event. Camping and events are held at Park Le Royer.

Newfoundland Province

Provincewide

NEWFOUNDLAND DRAMA FESTIVAL

Held annually, Easter vacations, movable date
Cultural

The Newfoundland Drama Festival is held annually to coincide with Easter vacation week, and each year it is held in a different part of the province. Its purpose is cultural and to help develop an interest in drama and talents of major amateur and community theater groups. It was started by several well-known citizens in St. John's. The festival features a full-length play with six evening performances. Originally, back in 1950, it ran for four days. Now it runs for six days. It is culturally successful because the audience represents all age groups. Almost 100,000 have attended performances. Work on the event is by volunteers. It is financed through ticket sales and sponsorships. Performances usually take place in local theaters and high school auditoriums.

Newfoundland Province

St. John's

SUMMER FESTIVAL OF THE ARTS

Held annually, July
Cultural

The Summer Festival of the Arts is a month-long event offering drama, music and the arts at the Arts & Culture Centre. It goes back to July 1967, when it began as a three-week cultural program for local residents. It became so popular that it was expanded to a full month in July. Its purposes is "to make some form of theatrical and concert programming available to the public in a time which would otherwise not have normal theater activity." Involved in setting up the event was Michael Cook, a Canadian playwright, and John C. Perlin, cultural affairs director for the province of Newfoundland. The festival features one main stage production, classic films, pop and country and western music and performers, crafts displays, children's theater and free outdoor noontime concerts. The festival provides employment for performers and technicians and aids the local economy since more than 15,000 people attend. To date, a grand total of 150,000 have attended performances. Both a paid staff and volunteers work on festival details. It is supported by box-office sales and by a government subsidy.

Northwest Territories

Frobisher Bay

TOONIK TYME

Held annually, April/May
Sports, legendary

Toonik Tyme is a combination winter carnival and welcome-to-spring festival held in memory of the legendary Toonik. Toonik belonged to a race of people living in Baffinland before the time of the Inuit. It is a week-long event held in late April into early May. The Tooniks were strong but short on brains, which eventually led to their extinction. The Inuit, however, believe that Mr. Toonik was such a workaholic that he never had time to socialize. So during Toonik Tyme, the Inuit of the Northwest Territories enjoy the fun that Toonik never did. Every year, a Miss Toonik is chosen instead of a carnival queen to reign over the festivities, which begin with the arrival of Mr. Toonik by dog sled. Festival events feature competitions in beard growing, ice sculpture, igloo building, tea brewing, fishing through the ice and even the toughest snowmobile race in the world. During the week, a group of hunters go off to bring back as many seals as possible, and upon their return there is a seal-skinning contest. There's a fireworks display and, on the last day, a barbecue and parade of decorated floats. Since Toonik Tyme is based on a legend, no one knows how long it's been going on. In recent years, more events have been added, including a queen to keep Mr. Toonik happy. It is financed through local contributions and admission and entry fees for some of the events.

Northwest Territories

Inuvik

TOP OF THE WORLD SKI MEET

Held annually at Easter, movable date
Sports

The Top of the World Ski Meet is held to coincide with Easter weekend because then the weather, though cold, is not too stormy. Inuvik is the capital for cross-country skiing in Canada. This event started in 1968 "to focus attention on accomplishments of Northern skiers, of whom most are of Indian and Eskimo origin." The event has been sanctioned by the Canadian Ski Association. One of the original organizers was Bjorger Pettersen, a former coach for the Canadian National Ski Team. The event features the top skiers of the world. Ski meet events include the regular cross-country ski races, demonstration biathlon, tour day and entertainment for visiting skiers. Some 200 skiers participated the first year. Now it is well over 1,000. Work on the meet is performed by local volunteers. It is financed through local government grants and self-funding. There are also entry fees for the races. All events are held at the Inuvik Ski Club Cross Country Trails.

Northwest Territories

Inuvik and local area

NORTHERN GAMES

Held annually, July
Sports, heritage

The Northern Games are a showcase for the traditional Inuit and Indian sports, dances, drumming competitions, displays, crafts and the now highly popular

Good Woman Contest, enabling Northern women to show their skills at animal skinning, bannock baking, sewing and other "bush skills." The four-day mid-July games are now competitions for the Inuit and Indians of Alaska, the Yukon, Labrador and the Northwest Territories. Each year, the games are held in another area of the Northwest Territories. The Inuit have always held the games as part of their culture, but they did not go public until 1970. And they went public to show other cultures "the beautiful aspects of the Inuit culture" and to preserve it. The Northern Games Association was formed for this purpose and to "maintain respect and knowledge of the Inuit traditions." It is held in summer because the weather is best then. The games are run and directed by the natives themselves, so that they remain authentic. About 400 participated, but over the years it has increased to thousands. Work is done by the association with a paid staff and lots of volunteer help, and details are worked out months before the games. The games are supported by government and oil company fundings. There is no admission charge to any of the events, which are held in local schools and halls.

Northwest Territories

Yellowknife

CARIBOU CARNIVAL AND CHAMPIONSHIP DOG DERBY

Held annually, March
Sports, economic, competition

The Caribou Carnival and Championship Dog Derby has grown from a three-day weekend in late March to a week-long program of sports and fun to chase away the winter blues and the long dark nights in this part of Canada. There's a solid week of entertainment and contests like igloo building, log sawing, Indian wrestling, tea boiling, snowshoeing, speed-skating derby and skiing. The Carnival Capers show stars local talent and a skit revue and features Northern celebrities. The highlight is the Canadian Championship Dog Derby race, which attracts competitors from all over North America. It is a three-day, 150-mile race on Great Slave Lake. It offers more than $20,000 in prize money for speedy mushers. The carnival, dating back to 1967, was started to lift local morale and to add to the local economy. It even lures thousands of tourists, who brave the cold to join in the fun. There's also a Miss Yellowknife Tournament, a Pee Week Hockey Tournament, special dinners, a cabaret and a casino. The event is self-supporting, and all work is done by local volunteers.

Nova Scotia Province

Annapolis Valley Region

ANNAPOLIS VALLEY APPLE BLOSSOM FESTIVAL

Held annually May/June
Economic, cultural, floral

Annapolis Valley Apple Blossom Festival events are held in small towns and cities throughout the Annapolis Valley, which is famed for its apple crops and orchards that flower in late May or early June, weather permitting. The very first festival was held in 1933 and was started for three reasons: to let all of North America and Europe know about the valley's apple industry; to call attention to the area's scenic beauty and historic background as the Land of Evangeline, and to develop local talent via special competitions for vocal soloists, quartets, orchestras, choirs and bands. The first festival was localized to Kentville, whose citizens organized the event and were successful in obtaining a grant from the provincial government to finance it. Festivities included the coronation of a queen, selected from entries from nearby towns, and concerts and parades. Two years later the festival was incorporated under the laws of Nova Scotia. It began to expand in scope and length until World War II, when it added historic and patriotic pageants. After the war, the festival was reactivated to cover four days, and the "Royal Tour" of other valley towns was introduced. This led to the festival events being held throughout the valley. Today there's an Apple Blossom Queen and Princesses, a children's parade, sports, tours to view the blossoms, apple pie baking and eating contests and an apple recipe cooking competition. Today the Apple Blossom Queen is known as Queen Annapolisa, and she is chosen from 18 local princesses. About 60,000 visitors and residents attend festival events. Since that first one in 1933, and despite World War II curtailment in travel, more than a million have attended. Work on the five-day festival is done by volunteers in each valley village and town, and it's almost a year-round project. The festival is supported by civic and business group contributions and sponsorships, some admission fees and exhibit space charges. Events take place throughout the entire Annapolis Valley, covering about 60 towns and villages.

Nova Scotia Province

Antigonish

EASTERN NOVA SCOTIA EXHIBITION

Held annually, September
Economic, fair, agricultural

The Eastern Nova Scotia Exhibition is the equivalent of a state fair. Its purpose continues to be to exhibit superior livestock, seed grains and vegetable crops. It is held the first week in September. It is also held to help farmers improve the quality of their produce and to have a place to learn and exchange ideas. This event dates back to 1900, when it was known as the Antigonish Fall Fair. Its name was changed to the present one in 1965. This local fair has grown into a regional one, thus the need for a name change. Exhibition events include a light horse show, a draft horse show, a horse pull, a tug-of-war and a talent program. There are cattle, beef and dairy displays. Prize money is more than $10,000 and increases each year. The exhibition after wages and expenses are paid realizes a profit every year. Several thousand attend the event, handled by a paid manager and staff members. It is financed through entry fees, exhibit space fees and both provincial and federal grants. It is held at the exhibition grounds.

Nova Scotia Province

Dartmouth

MARITIME OLD TIME FIDDLING CONTEST

Held annually, July
Cultural, economic, competition

The Maritime Old Time Fiddling Contest was first held in May 1952 as a one-day fund-raising event to help build the St. Thomas More Church. Not only was enough money raised and the church built and paid for but also it led to a highly successful competition, now held for two days and nights in July. It has become a vehicle for promoting the area's heritage and culture of old-time fiddle music. Monies realized from each year's competition are given to worthwhile charities. The contest continues to be sponsored and handled by the St. Thomas More Council of Catholic Men. The competition has four classes: open, Scottish, 60 and over and 16 and under. Small cash prizes are presented to the winner of each class, judged by prominent performers and fiddling experts. Some prizes include trips to compete in other contests, and there are trophies for second- and third-place winners. Contest rules stipulate that contestants may enter one class only. Open-class competitors are required to play a waltz, jig and hoedown, in that order. Scottish-class contestants must play a march, strathspey and reel, in that order. Time limit for each is three minutes maximum. The 16 and under and 60 and over entrants may play either a waltz, jig or hoedown or a march, strathspey and reel, in the correct order. All tunes played must be of accepted old-time variety, and a contestant may be accompanied on one instrument only. The accompanist may chord or play melody. All contestants have to compete in the Friday night preliminary. Finalists in open-class (top ten), Scottish-class (top five), 16 and under (top five) and 60 and over (top five) then compete Saturday night. All finalists can play any waltz, jig and hoedown or march, strathspey and reel of his or her choice. Judging is based on contest rules, accuracy, technique, tempo, tone and overall style. In addition to the competition, there is also a public dance and entertainment by well-known local performers. About 5,000 attend each year's contest. The first year, 3,000 participated. To date more than 100,000 have participated and listened. Work on the contest is by volunteers from the parish of St. Thomas More Church. It is financed through gate receipts and other charges. Contest events are held at the Prince Andrew High School on Woodlawn Road. Advance registration is required.

Nova Scotia Province

St. Ann's

GAELIC MOD

Held annually, August
Cultural heritage, ethnic, sports, competition

The Gaelic Mod, patterned after the National Mod in Scotland, is the way this Canadian province preserves its Scottish heritage. A mod is a competition of athletic skill, bagpipe playing, dancing and singing. This one marks the end of a five-week summer school for 150 teenagers at the Gaelic College of Celtic Folk Arts and Highland Home Crafts. The mod is held the first full week in August. Special events include visits by Scottish clan chiefs in full regalia plus competitions and displays in highland dancing, band demonstrations, Gaelic singing and bagpiping. The annual event is both economically and culturally successful, attracting as many as 100,000 persons for the entire week. Celebrities, such as famed Scots and clan chieftains, are always in attendance. Several million have participated and attended since the first Gaelic Mod. That first mod was held in 1939, when the college was incorporated by a special act of the Nova Scotia Legislature. Students teach, produce and perform all over Canada and in several foreign countries. Work on the mod is done by the college, which also finances the event. There are admission fees to some demonstrations and contests. All events are held on the Gaelic College campus.

Ontario Province

Bancroft

GEMBOREE

Held annually, July/August
Economic, rockhound

The Gemboree was developed to attract tourists to the area, and it has succeeded. The first event in 1964 attracted about 25,000 people. It is designed to be a rock collector's paradise, but over the years a handcrafters show, country music and a midway have been added. The idea for the event was developed by local residents, including Carl Bosiak, Rockhounds Club president and operator of mines in the area. He also was the Tourist Association president. To date, almost a million people have attended the Gemboree. Events also include rock-swapping sessions, mineral displays, field trips, a children's day and entertainment. The event is financed through admission fees and sale of souvenirs and food. Work is done by 20 volunteers, each contributing ten days of work each month year-round. Most events take place at a 16-acre park, under six large tents with approximate space under cover of 16,000 square feet. Field trips are within the vicinity of Bancroft. It is held in late July into August, usually a full weekend of four days.

Ontario Province

Guelph

GUELPH SPRING FESTIVAL

Held annually, April/May
Cultural

The Guelph Spring Festival grew out of a national vocal competition held in Guelph during Canada's Centennial Year in 1967. Guelph was the hometown of the famous Canadian tenor and general manager of the Metropolitan Opera, Edward Johnson. The great interest in that competition led to the festival, founded by Nicholas Goldschmidt, who was director of the Performing Arts Centennial and is still the festival's artistic director, and Dr. Murdo MacKinnon, dean of arts at the University of Guelph and president of the Edward Johnson Music Foundation. The first festival was held May 1968 and went on to become known for offering top international and Canadian performers in concerts of orchestral, instrumental and vocal music. The festival also became known for its unusual opera productions. Each year's three-week festival program now offers theater, dance, film and art exhibits as well. It has also commissioned operas, musical compositions and held world premieres of dramatic works. It is held late April to mid-May. The festival attracts about 120,000 people, many visitors. The event has contributed greatly to Canadian culture. World famous performers who have appeared include violinist Yehudi Menuhin, tenor Jan Pierce, opera singer Marilyn Horne and violinist Isaac Stern. The festival is truly international in scope. It is sponsored by the Edward Johnson Music Foundation and is also financed through ticket sales and grants from the Canada Council, the Ontario Arts Council and the Ministry of Culture and Recreation. It is also helped by the city of Guelph, University of Guelph, corporations and individual patrons of the arts.

Ontario Province

Kitchener, Waterloo

OKTOBERFEST

Held annually, October
Economic, ethnic, beer

The Oktoberfest is a nine-day beer festival that successfully emulates the famous Munich Oktoberfest but differs a bit. In this Canadian area, events take place in more than 200 beer halls, and there's dancing, folklore songs and more. This area has a large German heritage and four large German Canadian clubs. The event offers oompah bands, ethnic dance groups and beer. It claims to be the second largest Oktoberfest in the world, next to the Munich one. It does attract about 350,000 people every year, and since the first 1969 festival, almost 5 million people. It was developed by local citizens with the help of the Kitchener Chamber of Commerce to help the community economically and to preserve its German heritage. It originally was a five-day event, but a year later it went to nine days. It always begins the Friday before Canada's Thanksgiving Monday in early October. Events now spill over into nearby Waterloo. In 1977, it was estimated that $10 million was put back into the local economy each year, making

Oktoberfest a paying event. The most popular events are the Festhalles (beer halls), foaming beer steins, oompah bands and the general carnival atmosphere. Celebrities who've been to the event include the real Pied Piper of Hamelin, Germany, John Diefenbacker, and comedian Arte Johnson. Work on the Oktoberfest is done by three paid staff members and hundreds of volunteers, who donate two evenings per week year-round. The event is financed by admission fees, sale of beer and souvenirs.

Ontario Province

Niagara-on-the Lake

SHAW FESTIVAL

Held annually, May/October
Cultural

The Shaw Festival is a 22-week summer season of Shavian drama plus plays by contemporary playwrights. It is also a fully year-round professional enterprise with its own performing arts center, concert series and touring company. The festival became a year-round project when the new Festival Theatre opened in 1973. It was designed by architect Ron Thom. Thousands of visitors come for the summer festival season, which begins in May and continues through October. The festival started out in 1962 as a "Salute to Shaw" amateur event, offering Shaw's *Don Juan in Hell* and *Candida* with a company of ten unpaid actors directed by Maynard Burgess. It played to an audience of 200 in a nineteenth-century court house made over into a theater. A local resident and retired lawyer, Brian Doherty, Q.C., helped organize the event and he together with some theater people founded the Shaw Festival. Doherty decided to create a fully professional Shaw Festival and in 1963 established the theater as a nonprofit organization with a board of directors and obtained the services of Andrew Allan as artistic director. Allan's tenure (1963–65) was one of expansion. With money from a pre-Toronto engagement of Mavor Moore's *Spring Thaw*, he increased the company to 14 and the season to three weeks with three Shavian plays. In 1964, he extended the season to four weeks and four plays, adding 2 full-time designers to the staff and increasing the company to 25. In 1965, the festival received a government grant from the Ontario Arts Council, and a full-time company manager and publicity director were hired. Brian Doherty also introduced a seminar series that has continued ever since. It was also the first year that a non-Shavian play was performed, also establishing the practice of offering plays of Shaw's contemporaries. The play was Sean O'Casey's *The Shadow of a Gunman*. In 1966, the Canada Council made its first grant to the festival, and

Andrew Allan was succeeded by Barry Morse, who only served one year. Paxton Whitehead took over in 1967, a year that featured an end-of-season tour, part of a cooperative program with MTC (Manitoba Theatre Centre). Whitehead was artistic director through 1977, and during his term there were several festival changes. In 1968, the English-language world premiere of Feydeau's *La Main Passe*, retitled *The Chemmy Circle*, was featured in the festival's season. The following year there was a post-season tour to Ottawa with the production of *The Guardsman*. There was an hour-long documentary, "The Summer Is for Shaw," produced by Toronto's CFTO-TV and telecast throughout Canada and New York State. By 1970, music had become part of the festival, and the festival continued to grow in popularity. The 1977 festival budget was $1.6 million, with monies realized from ticket sales, private donations and grants from foundations and from federal, provincial and city governments.

Ontario Province

Ottawa

FESTIVAL OF SPRING

Held annually, May
Floral, commemorative, cultural, sports

The Festival of Spring, originally the Canadian Tulip Festival, is a multifaceted event held in Canada's capital city, Ottawa. It is always in May, usually mid-May. Weather conditions determine the blooming of more than 3 million tulips of 200 varieties. The nine-day festival dates back to 1949. It was a thank you to the Dutch royal family for their continued gifts of tulips to Canada. During World War II, the Dutch royal family lived in Ottawa and in appreciation gave 20,000 tulips in 1946 to Canada. Every year more tulips arrived. More than 150,000 tulips bloom in a single bed at Dow's Lake at the south end of the Rideau Canal. They also grow at Parliament Hill and cover miles of roadways, city cycle paths, parks, squares and grounds around all major public buildings. Tours are conducted during the festival to all the areas. Festival events today include a procession of decorated boats on the Rideau Canal, a bathtub race on Dow's Lake, a giant craft market and beer garden in Major's Hill Park and fireworks. Over the years, the festival has added open-air entertainment for all ages, with free live concerts and performances by talented young artists as well as international, national and local stars at Major's Hill Park. There's also singing and dancing every evening at the Festival of Spring Terrace. On the first Sunday of the festival, there is a morning race covering 42 kilometers on roads past Parliament Hill. The National Capital Marathon is considered to be one of the world's largest and top events. About 300,000 attend the annual festival, and it is estimated that several million have enjoyed it since the first 1949 Tulip Festival. Work on the festival is done entirely by volunteers and is financed by civic group contributions, fund raising and admission charges to some programs.

Ontario Province

Ottawa

FESTIVAL OTTAWA OPERA PLUS

Held annually, July
Cultural

Festival Ottawa Opera Plus, originally Festival Canada when it began in July 1971, has grown to be an international event with world famous opera stars, orchestras and musicians performing at the National Arts Centre. The three-week festival was launched with the help of Lester B. Pearson, then prime minister of Canada and Nobel Prize winner, and G. H. Southam, director general of the National Arts Centre, and conductor Mario Bernardi. This fulfilled the 1952 wish of Governor General Vincent Massey for an international arts festival in Canada. Its purpose was to give the country a cultural event of gigantic proportions, and it has succeeded. More than 40,000 persons attend the annual performances, and since its beginning, more than half a million. The festival continues to focus on the presentation of three grand operas, two smaller operas and a series of chamber music and symphony concerts. Additional opera films and videotape screenings are also featured. Work on the festival is by a paid staff working year-round on the details. The festival also uses world famous designers for sets and costumes and famous stage directors. The event is subsidized by the Canadian government, and there are admission charges with season subscriptions available. Performances are in the center's three houses: Opera House, Theatre and Viewing Centre.

Ontario Province

St. Catharines

NIAGARA GRAPE AND WINE FESTIVAL

Held annually, September
Harvest, economic, agricultural

The Niagara Grape and Wine Festival is held in late September for ten days to coincide with the harvest season. The event goes back to 1952, when the local wine industry decided to call attention to Canada's vineyards and to develop tourism in the area. The Canadian Wine Institute, with the help of a local vintner, Bevis Walters, began to offer one-day tours of Niagara's vineyards and historic sites in the St. Catharines–Niagara Peninsula district. It attracted tourists who wanted more than a tour, and so different events were added and the festival became a ten-day event. Besides tours, there are wine-sampling parties, ethnic concerts, street parades, the selection of a Grape King and sports. The Grande Parade continues to be a popular festival event with half a million spectators. It is estimated that more than 10 million people have attended the festival over the last 30 years. Work on festival details is done by volunteers and takes about a half-year before the event itself. The festival is supported by help from the city of St. Catharines, the Ontario Grape Growers, Marketing Boards and the Wine Council of Ontario. There are some admission fees, but most events are free. Events are held on a citywide basis.

Ontario Province

Stratford

STRATFORD FESTIVAL

Held annually, June/October
Cultural

The Stratford Festival started in 1953 as a six-week theater event, based on the idea of local journalist Tom Patterson to hold a Shakespearean drama festival in a town that bore the name of the Bard's birthplace. Originally the plan called for a simple open-air offering, but later it was decided to build a tent theater. This decision was based on the advice of the late Sir Tyrone Guthrie, called in to help with the project. A festival committee went along with Guthrie's recommendation, and they approved a $150,000 budget to build the enclosed tent theater. Negotiations were also conducted for Alec Guinness and Irene Worth to head the festival company. An application was made for a charter to the provincial government, and by October 1952, a nonprofit organization, the Stratford Shakespearean Festival Foundation of Canada, had been established with Harrison A. Showalter as president and A. M. Bell vice-president. Although there were some minor setbacks, the curtain went up on schedule. At first, the festival was handled by a local board of governors and a small summer staff. Today, it has a year-round staff of more than 100 and, during the summer, an additional 650 staffers. The festival's board of governors now includes men and women in the arts and business world from all over Canada. As the festival grew, it added traveling tours to all over the world. In 1974, from February through April, the Stratford Company made its first tour of Australia, playing to audiences in Perth, Melbourne and Sydney. Today's festival performances are given in the Festival Theatre, which replaced the tent in 1957. It is a modern version of the Elizabethan stage. The festival has presented all of Shakespeare's plays and repeated 21 of them. It has also added Sophocles, Ibsen, Moliere, Chekhov, Sheridan, Brecht, Beckett and Canadian playwrights in repertory. It has added concerts, opera, exhibits, seminars and films. Programs are given in rotating repertory in the 2,258-seat Festival Theatre, the 1,102-seat Avon Theatre and the 300-seat Third Stage, a small theater used for seminars and experimental drama. The festival, held June through October, has an audience of more than half a million. It continues to grow.

In 1975, the festival ran 21 weeks and had a total attendance of 437,302, who watched 362 performances, earning a gross income of $2,637,549. Two years later, the festival season was extended to 23 weeks. It had an audience of half a million. There were 342 performances, and the gross box-office receipts totaled $4,237,106. The festival is financed through box-office receipts, private donations and government grants. The festival has been under the artistic direction of Robin Phillips since 1975. Other directors have included Cecil Clarke in 1954, Michael Langham, 1956–67 and Jean Gascon, 1968–74.

Ontario Province

Toronto

CANADIAN NATIONAL EXHIBITION

Held annually, August/September
Economic, fair

The Canadian National Exhibition claims to be the world's oldest and largest annual exhibition or fair with a large midway, many exhibits, an air show and top entertainment at the Grandstand in Exhibition Place. The first one was held in 1879, when the city of Toronto decided to keep the traveling provincial exhibition permanently in Toronto. Although buildings were erected, the fair went to Ottawa the following year, but Toronto didn't give up. The Toronto Industrial Exibition became a reality and was called that until 1921, when the name was changed for broader appeal to the entire country. The size of the fair has changed, and it's been extended from two to three weeks. It has a record 3.5 million visitors annually. The exhibition headlines famous celebrities like Bob Hope and many political figures. The exhibition was a 100 years old in 1978, and it's still going strong. The exhibition is located on the shores of Lake Ontario, about ten minutes from downtown Metro Toronto. It is on 350-acres of land, which hold Victorian-style display buildings, modern pavilions, lawns, flower gardens and trees. There are exhibits of all kinds, an air show, a horse show and food booths. Each year's event includes a Scottish World Festival with concerts, demonatrations and competitions every evening at the grandstand. Work on the exhibition is year-round, performed by both paid staffers and volunteers. The event is self-supporting, and there are admission fees.

Ontario Province

Toronto

CARIBANA

Held annually, July/August
Ethnic, cultural, folkloric

Caribana is a Caribbean folk festival of music, art and dance. It includes a costume parade at Toronto Islands Park. It is based on the Carnival of Trinidad and Tobago in the West Indies. In 1967, when Canada marked its centennial year, the Caribana Festival was Toronto's West Indian community's contribution to the event. It caught on, and it's been held even since, expanding into a full week of gala programs in late July and early August. The annual event has been cited by the mayor of Toronto for its contribution to tourism. Events include ferry cruises the first three nights, a ball on a Friday and the night of the Caribana Queen's Coronation. There is a Saturday masqueraders parade with several bands and revelers from the sidelines joining in the line of march. There are also handicrafts and special foods. The Caribana is always held so that it ends with Toronto's Civic Holiday, the first Monday in August. The festival attracts almost a million people annually. Work on the event is done by volunteer help, usually from the West Indian community. It is financed through ticket sales, grants from the city and donations from private enterprise. Programs are held at the Centre or Olympic Island and Royal York Hotel.

Ontario Province

Windsor

INTERNATIONAL FREEDOM FESTIVAL

Held annually, June/July 4
Patriotic, historic

The International Freedom Festival is a joint friendship celebration between Windsor in Ontario, Canada, and Detroit across the border, in Michigan, U.S.A.

It has grown from a 9- to a 13-day celebration that commemorates Canada Day on July 1 and U.S. Independence Day on July 4 with events on both sides of the border. It attracts up to a million to both cities and countries, with local citizens going back and forth for the festivities. The events include a Freedom Festival Ball at Windsor's Cleary Auditorium, ending with a giant parade down Vernon Avenue in Detroit. In between are motorboat, tug boat, canoe and bicycle races as well as firework displays. There's a celebrity golf tournament, Las Vegas Casino, the beer haus and a drum corps competition, plus family picnics, street dancing, a track and field event and more. The idea for the festival is credited to some journalism students in 1930. However, it wasn't until 1959, with the pending visit of Queen Elizabeth II and Prince Philip to Windsor, that the festival was launched to mark the occasion. Detroit decided to join in the honors, and the festival has continued ever since for different reasons, attracting several million people over the years. The festival also honors a person who has "contributed to peace and international amity" with the presentation of the Freedom Award. Past recipients have been John F. Kennedy, Lester B. Pearson, Martin Luther King, Jr., and the Gordie Howe family.

Prince Edward Island Province

Charlottetown

CHARLOTTETOWN FESTIVAL

Held annually, June/September
Cultural

The Charlottetown Festival is devoted to musicals by Canadians. It includes the first one ever offered in 1965, *Anne of Green Gables*, a story about rural turn-of-the-century life in the island province, based on a local writer's novel. It was adapted for the musical stage by Norman Campbell and Donald Harron. It is a favorite by novelist Lucy Maud Montgomery and is repeated every year with the addition of two other full musicals. There are also plays for children in the Circus Tent Theatre, several short plays and music in the Lunchtime Theatre. Sunday evening pop concerts are in the Confederation Centre. The event is financed through box-office receipts and by a $500,000 grant from the Canada Council and Board of the Confederation Building Trusts plus extra grants from city, provincial and federal governments.

Prince Edward Island Province

O'Leary

POTATO BLOSSOM FESTIVAL

Held annually, July
Economic, floral, agricultural

The Potato Blossom Festival dates back to 1950, when the town of O'Leary was looking for a way to raise money to help finance a community rink. The festival was successful and was continued till 1964, when it became part of a centennial festival, and in 1967 it was part of the Charlottetown Confederation and Dominion centennial observance. It then became a separate event and remained so. It is held the last week of July, when the potato plants are in bloom. Festival events include a celebrity banquet and dance, horse racing, a Potato Blossom Queen competition, talent night, fireworks, midway, parade, display booths, golf tournament and interfaith song service. There are also tours to view the potato blossoms. The Potato Blossom Queen usually attends the Royal Winter Fair in Toronto, where she is in charge of the Prince Edward Island potato booth for publicity purposes. The festival does boost the local economy, since it attracts 4,000 visitors annually, adding up to several hundred thousand over the years. Local volunteers work out festival details. The festival is supported by village and provincial grants and by contributions from civic and business groups. There are admission charges to festival events also.

Quebec Province

Quebec City

CARNAVAL

Held annually, February
Economic, sports, pageantry

The Carnaval is a ten-day winter festival designed to boost winter tourism and the spirits of local citizens. It is usually held the first Thursday in February through the second Sunday. It began in 1955, developed by several local businessmen who wanted to better the economy. Today, the event is world famous. Mascot of the event is Bonhomme Carnaval, a seven-foot walking, talking live snowman, who together with the Carnaval Queen and her duchesses reigns over the festivities. More than 500,000 people converge on Place Carnaval on Dufferin

Street in front of the Parliament Buildings to join in special programs. Most events are citywide. The Ice Palace is at Place Carnaval and the setting for the crowning of the Carnaval Queen, who is paid great respect by local citizens. There is a sugar shack, a slide, an international snow sculpture contest and Bonhomme games, all free. Sports rate high during Carnaval and include the International Pee-Wee Hockey Tournament for those 12 years old and younger. Teams come from all over Quebec, Canada and the United States to compete. There is also the well-known Chateau Frontenac toboggan slide and skiing on the hills of the Plains of Abraham. There's the hazardous ice canoe race across the St. Lawrence River between Quebec City and Levis. Teams of five men per canoe race across the river and back, sometimes rowing, sometimes running across ice packs, pushing and pulling their boats with them. Other sports include motorcycle races on ice with contestants from across Canada and the United States. Snowmobile racing covers the half-mile track at speeds of up to 90 miles per hour. There are street dances, costume balls, speed skating and barrel-jumping contests and two night parades with illuminated floats and firework displays. Carnaval Street is lined with ice and snow sculptures done by local artists competing for prizes. Today, the festival attracts 2 million visitors, a boon to the local economy. Work on the Carnaval is by paid workers, assisted by volunteer help. It is financed through sponsorships, subsidies and contributions from businesses. There are some admission fees, but many events are free. A principal source of income for the Carnaval Association is still the candle sale or "bougie." Buyers of the bougies increase the chances of their representative duchess (they come from all over Quebec) being selected Carnaval Queen and of participating in a giant lottery and win many prizes. During bougie night, the actual night the candles are sold, more than 10,000 participate in the sale and distribution process.

Quebec Province

Quebec City

SUMMER FESTIVAL

Held annually, July
Cultural, economic

The Summer Festival is a showcase for Quebec and Canadian artists, musicians, actors and actresses. It gives them employment and gives local residents and visitors a flavor of Quebec culture. The first festival was held in July 1967, organized by local people interested in enjoying culture during the summer. The ten-day festival offers 150 different programs citywide, featuring classical and popular music, folk songs, art exhibits, a film festival and theater. The festival continues to be a popular summer diversion for as many as 400,000 people, several million since the first event. Street shows have recently been added to the list of festival programs. Work on festival programs is performed by 100 local volunteers and 4 paid staffers. It is supported by money grants from both the Quebec and Canadian governments and by contributions from various businesses and civic groups who match the government funds. There are some admission fees, but many festival events are free.

Quebec Province

Saint-Tite

WESTERN FESTIVAL

Held annually, September
Economic, sports, rodeo, competition

The annual Western Festival, or Festival Western, is a rodeo complete with the traditional competitions. Saint-Tite is a small town located midway between Montreal and Quebec City. The festival was started by local businessmen in 1968 to help the local economy. This is the only French rodeo in the world, and it has become the biggest one in eastern Canada. More than 300,000 folks go Western with a French accent at the Western Festival. Since the first one, several million have enjoyed it. Rodeo events include bronco busting, Brahama bull riding, calf roping, bull doggin' (wrestling a steer to the ground and quickly roping its legs), calf cutting (separating a calf from the herd by tying it up), wild cow milking and horse racing. Contestants come from all over Canada and the United States to compete for cash prizes. All the town's people wear Western outfits and costumes, and a local industry turns out cowboy hats and boots for sale. There's even a Western-style wedding on Saturday morning of the festival. The bride and groom and relatives wear traditional Western clothes for the ceremony. On Sunday, there's a parade through the town streets. All floats are built by local residents with life in the Old West as the theme. No motorized floats are allowed. There is a three-day Texas Western Horse Show with both U.S. and Canadian quarter horse associations participating. Judging is held all three days. TV personalities entertain in the rodeo ring, and there's plenty of food but with French-Canadian cuisine taking precedence over Western grub. There's pork and beans, lamb, meat pies and other Quebec goodies. Work on the annual event is by a group of 75 volunteers who work year-round preparing for the festival. It is financed through donations and entry and admission fees.

Saskatchewan Province

Nipawin

NORTHERN PIKE FESTIVAL

Held annually June/August
Sports, economic, competition

The Northern Pike Festival is a fishing competition that was started in 1969 to create tourism in the area. It was organized by the Nipawin Retail Merchants Association, the Nipawin Chamber of Commerce and the Nipawin Wildlife Society to promote fishing in Tobin Lake, created by the Saskatchewan Power Hydro Development of Squaw Rapids. From 1969 to 1976, record-breaking catches of northern pike, walleye, goldeye and perch were made. In 1975, the Tobin pike was caught, and the lucky angler won $5,000. In 1976, a northern pike weighing more than 30 pounds and a walleye of over 10 pounds were caught. The festival was lengthened June to August because the fishing is better. All fishermen who pay the festival entry fee (which differs every year) are eligible to compete in the more than 50 awards categories and for the big Tobin pike prize. About 22 other tagged pikes are worth $100 each if caught and registered. Besides fishing competitions, the festival also has a family compfire night with a singalong and dancing and a family breakfast sponsored by the Nipawin Fish and Game League, and there are church services on Sunday. Most events are at the Nipawin Regional Park. The festival hosts about 2,000 visitors, most fishermen. Since the first festival, a grand total of 26,000 visitors have attended events. The local economy does well, with outfitters and sporting good stores doing business with the visitors. Local volunteers work on festival details. The event is financed through entry fees, admissions to some events and donations from local businesses. The fishing is at Tobin Lake–Squaw Rapids.

Saskatchewan Province

Regina

BUFFALO DAYS

Held annually, July/August
Economic, sports, rodeo, fair

Buffalo Days is a combination fair, rodeo and entertainment event held for six days. It goes back to 1884, when it was the Provincial Exhibition. Today, the annual event features a parade, livestock judging, a midway, stage shows, casino, outdoor grandstand shows, chuck wagon races, tractor pull, programs in the Agradome Building plus evening events and fireworks. The most popular event is the entertainment, which does have some well-known performers and name bands. Formerly held in October, Buffalo Days was changed to mid-summer because of the weather. About 250,000 people attend every year. Work is performed by both a small paid staff and lots of volunteers. Buffalo Days is financed through entry and admission fees. All events are held at the Exhibition Grounds.

Saskatchewan Province

Saskatoon

PIONEER DAYS

Held annually, July
Heritage, economic, folkloric, sports

Pioneer Days honors the pioneer heritage of Saskatoon and surrounding areas. Although it was first held May 10, 1974, its roots date back to 1905, when the area held its first exhibition. The event's present name comes from two other events, Pion-era and Saskachimo. It was changed to attract more visitors. The day before the official start of Pioneer Days is designated as Louis Riel Day (a famous local pioneer) and a Riel Relay Race is held along the river in the city center. Teams of canoe paddlers, horseback riders, backpackers and foot racers compete along a predetermined route. It is a test of skill and endurance. Once festivities are underway, there's a checkers tournament, pancake breakfast, arm wrestling and street dances. There is a Traveller's Day Parade and professional entertainment at several outdoor stages citywide all week. Hundreds participate in the Pioneer Days Fly-In, and there is the "Great Race" of questionable vehicles in front of City Hall. There's gambling, a midway and a tractor-pulling contest. Work on the annual event is by a paid staff and volunteers, who work a few months before and during the event. It is financed through a lottery, permitted by the provincial government. There are admission fees to most events, which take place at Western Development Museum grounds, the Saskachimo Exhibition Grounds and citywide.

Saskatchewan Province

Saskatoon

VESNA FESTIVAL

Held annually, May
Ethnic

The Vesna Festival pays tribute to the Ukrainians of Western Canada. "Vesna" means "spring," and so the event, which was first held in 1973, is held in May for six days. It is held to keep young Ukrainian-Canadians informed about their heritage and to educate others about the culture of these East European people. Highlights include exhibits of Ukrainian art, embroidery, handicrafts and folk songs and dances. Ukrainian folk groups from other parts of Canada often perform during this festival. In the past the Rushnychak and the Sunystepiw, two Ukrainian Folk Rock Bands from Montreal, have starred. The Vesna Chorus, a Saskatoon Ukrainian Youth Chorus, gives concerts, and there are Ukrainian foods to sample. The festival was started by the Saskatoon Ukrainian Professional and Business Club and is still under its auspices. The festival has grown from three to six days. Since the festival is registered with the Canadian Trades Act, sponsors can also help other cities with Ukrainian groups to set up a festival. The Vesna Festival attracts some 3,000 visitors annually. Work on the event is by a special Vesna Festival Committee. It is financed through a grant system and admission charges. Most festival events are held in the Centennial Auditorium.

CAYMAN ISLANDS

George Town, Grand Cayman

PIRATE WEEK FESTIVAL

Held annually, October
Pageantry, economic

Pirate Week Festival is described as a counterpart to fiestas and Mardi Gras celebrations of other Caribbean islands. It takes inspiration from history and legends about the origin of the Cayman Islands. Famous pirates like Henry Morgan, Edward "Blackbeard" Teach, Neal Walker and Thomas Anstis often visited these islands during their seventeenth- and early eighteenth-century raids. The Caymans were named by Spanish sailors who mistakenly identified large iguanas as alligators, calling the islands "Caiman," the Carib word for alligator.

In 1670, the islands with Jamaica were transferred from Spanish to British rule, but the name remained. The festival begins with costumed pirates landing at Hogsty Bay, jailing the royal governor of the islands and taking over his power for a week, the third week in October. They usually run up a skull n' crossbones flag over the Old Court House. The festival was started to attract more tourists, to serve as a showcase of the islands' sports and entertainment activities and to encourage residents to mix more with visitors, making them welcome. Visitors are greeted at the airport and at dockside by pirates, who give them "honorary admiral" certificates entitling them to a free rum punch drink in the customs area. Visitors are later treated to island tours, beach parties, a "Pirate Feast" at Pedro Castle and an all-day fair or band concert. A film, *The Caymanian Triangle*, is shown in George Town. During the festival, treasure maps showing where hidden treasure prizes are hidden are handed out to everyone. The festival ends with a Pirate's Ball at a local hotel and includes a buffet dinner and dancing. Later the ruling pirates are overthrown, "hanged and buried." At midnight, the pirate flag is burned and the royal governor released from jail to receive a 21-gun salute from a warship in the harbor. Additional events added since the first festival in 1977 include coconut-shucking contests, "District Days," with special events on all three islands, parades, dances, film and photography competitions, costume contests and native foods to sample and pirate's grog to drink. The festival is sponsored by the government and various resort hotels and businesses. Several hundred people come each year, and though a young festival, it is continuing in popularity. There are some admission fees, but most festival events are free.

CHINA, REPUBLIC OF (TAIWAN)

Nationwide

CHINESE NEW YEAR

Held annually, movable dates
Traditional holiday

The Chinese or Lunar New Year is one of the most colorful and important of Chinese festivals. The New Year can be observed as early as January 21 or as late as February 21. Dates of Chinese holidays are based on the lunar calendar, which varies from year to year. The lunar calendar divides the year into 12 months. Each month has 29 or 30 days, beginning with the appearance of the new moon. Every 30 months, there is an extra month to adjust to solar time. For example, in 1966 there were two "third moons." When translated into terms of the Gregorian calendar, dates of the New Year and other Chinese celebrations differ every year. Lunar New Years are named for either domestic, wild or mythical animals, including the rat, ox, tiger, rabbit, dragon, snake, horse, sheep, monkey, chicken, dog and pig. On the sixteenth day of the last month, businessmen close their accounts, thanking the gods for a prosperous year. Even customers celebrate by paying their debts so that everyone can start the New Year with a clean slate. On the twenty-fourth day of the twelfth month, each household honors the Kitchen God. According to legend, the Kitchen God returns to heaven at the end of each year to report on the family, so the custom is to make sure he tells as little as possible or only good things. A special malt candy is smeared on the mouth of the god's image or statue to seal his lips during the heavenly visit or so that only sweet words are spoken. Before he returns on New Year's Eve, the house is cleaned thoroughly, with every family member doing some cleaning job. A new statue is placed in the kitchen, usually above the stove, and a rich feast awaits the returning deity. Children receive new clothes at this time and usually spend New Year's Day playing games and eating forbidden sweets or ones not available the rest of the year.

Nationwide

LANTERN FESTIVAL

Held annually, movable date
Traditional

The Lantern Festival is always celebrated on the fifteenth day of the first moon and marks the end of New Year's celebrations in all Chinese communities. The festival once featured torches, which were used to help people find the heavenly spirits they believed could be seen flying past in the light of the first full moon. Today's festival has become a carnival with puppet shows, operas and dragons dancing in the streets. Dragons are traditional symbols of Chinese royalty. During this festival, the dragon, a mythical animal, is an imaginative creation of papier mache and painted cloth and is manipulated by men hidden under the artificial scales. Dragon dances vary. In some, the dragon chases a fiery pearl held out by another dancer a few feet away. In other dances, the dragon prances and plays with a lion to the noisy clamor of gongs, drums and firecrackers. The dances are usually held in city squares or along city streets. Today's festival also includes competitions for the best and most original lanterns.

COLOMBIA

Barranquilla (Atlántico Department)

CARNIVAL

Held annually, before Ash Wednesday, movable date
Religious, folkloric

Carnival in Barranquilla is officially ushered in on the Friday before Ash Wednesday, ending on Shrove Tuesday. It begins with a huge "Battle of Flowers," with thousands parading in outlandish costumes. This is the time of year when local residents dance to African and Indian rhythms and sing songs like "The Devil's Little Bull," "The Congo," "Corn-Huskers" and "Pothook," to name a few. The city has been observing this pre-Lenten festivity for over a century. The parade has beautiful floats decorated with the area's many exotic flowers. The Carnival also features folklore shows, water festivals, a beauty contest, private and public costume balls and the night before Ash Wednesday, the burial of "Joselito Carnaval," the spirit who ruled over the festivities. While the wealthy in the city hold pageants and balls in their own private clubs, competing for the most original and ornate costumes, some very expensive, the less affluent have their own fun. Each local barrio, or neighborhood, selects its own beauty queen and holds informal parties in homes and public places. The partygoers dance around the clock and drink *ron blanco*, the local rum. Thousands participate and thousands more watch the parades. The expense of the Carnival is borne by the different groups, with the poorer residents selling arts, crafts and souvenirs to finance their annual fun.

Neiva (Huila Department)

FESTIVAL OF BAMBUCO

Held annually, June
Folkloric, cultural

The Festival of Bambuco is a Spanish folkloric dance. It is a pursuit dance in which the man chases the woman, all done to a very rhythmic beat. It is usually performed to the music of guitars and mandolins. It is a typical folk dance of the Huila region. It also includes poetry and love songs and the parade of Queens, on decorated rafts in the Magdalena River.

COLOMBIA 65

Popayan

HOLY WEEK OBSERVANCES AND PROCESSIONS

Held annually, movable date
Religious, procession

Holy Week Observance in Popayan date back to soon after the founding of the city in 1536 by the Spanish conquistador Don Sebastian de Belalcazar. The religious processions are held every evening, with the sons of the city's leading families participating. They wear the hooded robes of medieval penitents and carry on their shoulders heavy platforms, holding priceless antique bejeweled religious statues from the city's many churches. They parade along torchlit streets filled with thousands of pilgrims and visitors from all over the world. Candle-bearing monk choirs sing Gregorian chants, and a beautifully decorated float carrying a chamber music ensemble follows. The ensemble plays solemn religious music in keeping with the solemnity of Holy Week. It is considered a great honor to be a bearer of one of the heavy platforms and is a tradition from father to son. If a bearer tires and has to be substituted, this is a great dishonor, and he's not allowed to take part in the next year's processions.

San Martin (Meta Department)

QUADRILLES OF SAN MARTIN

Held annually, November 11
Folkloric, ethnic, economic, equestrian

The Quadrilles of San Martin is an equestrian show and performance held November 11, the Feast of Saint Martin, patron of the town. No one seems to know when or how the Quadrilles got started, but they have been going on for a couple of centuries. San Martin is an older city than Bogota. It was founded in 1538 by conquistador and German explorer Nicholas de Federman, who was looking for gold. The Quadrilles are often described as "an equestrian ballet" and are a tribute to heroic action, honoring Spaniards and Moors (Arabs), Blacks and Indians, who are all responsible for today's Colombian nationality. The all-male Quadrilles consist of 48 expert riders mounted on Creole horses. They are divided into four groups, each with its own leader. They take their place at the four corners of the town's large square, where the event is held. The Moors are dressed in white, Oriental-looking robes and grand turbans and are armed with scimitars. The Spaniards wear a modern combination of black riding jackets, white breeches, tall boots and cowboy hats, and they wield sabers. The Blacks are dressed in exotic African headgear and the skins of jungle animals and carry long machetes. The Indians wear genuine feather headdresses, elaborate necklaces, breastplates and various decorations of the Guajibos and other Indian tribes from the Orinoco Basin. They are armed with bows and arrows. The performances are carefully staged, but often there is spontaneous improvisation with fast riding and split-second timing absolutely necessary. The Quadrilles perform ten separate acts covering the Middle Ages with battles between the Spanish and Moors to the discovery, conquest and settlement of South America to the wars of independence waged against Spain. The different acts have poetic titles: the Challenge, the Salute, the Great Comb, the Half-Charge, the Cockleshell, the Snake and the Parade. Strategy and tactics in the battle scenes follow strict military and historical rules. The grand finale pays tribute to the present Colombian nation, where Whites, Creoles, Blacks, Indians and many European races live and work. After the performances, local residents and visitors meet in open-air cafes and native restaurants on the main square for a few drinks (*aguardiente*, the local anise-flavored liquor) and to eat *ternera a la llanera*, or barbecued baby beef, and watch the fireworks over the city. Participation in the Quadrilles is an honor handed down from generation to generation among the city's oldest families, who spend a great deal of time and money during the year in preparing their costumes, which change each year, and taking care of the horses. They also have to rehearse.

CYPRUS

Curium/Limassol

CURIUM FESTIVAL

Held annually, June/July
Cultural

The Curium Festival is devoted to performances of ancient Greek and Shakespearean plays at the ancient Roman amphitheater of Curium, about 12 miles west of Limassol. The amphitheater (dated from A.D. 50 to 175) seats 2,400 at a time and overlooks Episkopi Bay. Performances are given by both Cypriot and international drama companies. Festival performances also include moonlight concerts. The festival started in 1961 to give local people a cultural event that would also appeal to tourists. The event is financed through ticket sales and mostly by grants from the Cultural Service of the Ministry of Education in Nicosia.

Limassol

LIMASSOL WINE FESTIVAL

Held annually, September 15–30
Economic, harvest, agricultural, wine

The Limassol Wine Festival is a harvest event, held since 1962, giving local people and visitors a chance to sample the area's top industry, wine and spirits. During the festival, there's free wine at all restaurants, where special festival food is sold. Other foods are sold in special booths set up in the streets to accommodate the thousands who come for this event. The two-week festival includes folk dancing and singing performances and Cypriot theater sketches in the city's Public Gardens.

CZECHOSLOVAKIA

Bratislava (Slovakia)

BRATISLAVA MUSIC FESTIVAL

Held annually, October 1–15
Cultural

The Bratislava Music Festival is a festival of opera, symphonic concerts, chamber music, ballet and recitals. It is concerned with "the development and advancement of young artists who are part of the International Tribune of Young Performers, organized in cooperation with UNESCO." Bratislava is the capital of Slovakia, the southeastern part of Czechoslovakia. Festival performances are held in the city's six concert halls. The first festival was held in 1965. It is international in scope, with all performances open to the public. Both young and famous artists perform. The 1982 festival was highlighted by Mozart's *Cosi Fan Tutti*, performed by the German State Opera of Berlin with tenor Peter Schrier. Other participants included Emil Gilels, pianist, the Moscow Chamber Chorus, the Moscow Philharmonic Orchestra and the Birmingham (England) Symphony Orchestra. The festival is supported by ticket sales and by subsidies from the government. The festival is a member of the European Association of Music Festivals.

Postupice (Bohemia)

MAYPOLE AND BURNING OF THE WITCHES

Held annually, April 30–May 1
Folkloric, legendary

Maypole and Burning of the Witches Festival is an annual two-day spring event in this town, about a three-hour drive from Prague. On the afternoon of April 30, the young men of the village put up the Maypole, decorated with ribbons and colored wreaths, in the center of the town square. The Maypole symbolizes the tree of life for the whole community. The next day, both men and women of all ages, dressed in peasant costumes, weave the ribbons in and out as they dance around the Maypole, celebrating the coming of spring. This is followed by the burning of the witches as a means of warding off the bad forces opposing life. The rites begin the night before, when the villagers protect themselves against the hag witches by burning their broomsticks and the witches in effigy. Local bands play music, and villagers gather around the bonfire to drink brandy or beer and to roast sausages as the witches go up in smoke.

Prague (Bohemia)

PRAGUE SPRING

Held annually, May 12–June 4
Cultural

Prague Spring is an international music festival offering symphonic, choral, instrumental and chamber music as well as opera and ballet performances. The first festival was held in 1946 to celebrate the victory and end of World War II and to mark the fiftieth anniversary of the Czech Philharmonic Orchestra, a major event in the city of music, Prague (Bohemia Conservatory of Europe). Local citizens and musicians decided to continue the event, calling it Prague Spring, a musical welcome to the spring season. The festival is a member of the European Association of Music Festivals.

The 1982 event honored three native sons, Smetana, Dvorak and Janacek. It opened with a tribute to Janacek by the Prague Wind Quintet. The Czech Philharmonic played Smetana's *My Country*, Dvorak's Symphony No. 9 in E-minor *From the New World*. The festival also offered Mozart's *Don Giovanni*, which had its world premiere in Prague. It also featured Smetana's *Dalibor*, Dvorak's *Requiem* and Haydn's *The Creation*. Among participating ensembles were the Netherlands Dance Theater, the Janacek Philharmonic of Ostrava, the Netherlands Chamber Orchestra, the Bolshoi Ballet, the Zagreb Chamber Soloists, the Vienna Symphony and the Dresden Staatskapelle.

The festival is financed through ticket sales and is subsidized by the government. Performances are citywide in concert halls, churches and theaters.

Prague (Bohemia)

SPARTAKIADE

Held once every five years in June; next: 1985, 1990
Sports, competition

Spartakiade is a national exercise competition for the entire country, held once every five years since 1955. Millions of young and adult men and women compete in elimination contests, with more than 70,000 selected to participate in the eight-day national competition. Millions of spectators have come from all over the world to watch this physical fitness event. This type of competition is not new to this country, which has had mass physical culture performances for more than 100 years, although not as well organized as it is today. Ages 3 to 70 compete in the various contests, which can be as many as 14. Gymnastics are performed by boys and men with polystyrene bricks, flying saucers, rods and bells and even tambourines. Girls and women add dance performances. There are army drills. The event is held once every five years to give competitors a chance to train. The purpose behind Spartakiade is to have a physically fit nation.

Straznice (Moravia)

FOLKLORE FESTIVAL OF STRAZNICE

Held annually, June
Cultural, folkloric

The Folklore Festival of Straznice was started soon after World War II ended, encouraged by the Czech government to help preserve and perform traditional folk songs and dances. The three-day festival deals with two types of folklore, original and adapted. The original comes from villages and individual associations and is the basis for the festival, which attracts more than 100,000 people annually. Adapted folklore is represented by professional ensembles of folk song and dance. Performances are in a castle park. Over the years, folkloric groups from other East European countries have participated as well as Czech groups, giving the festival an international air. Groups from the Soviet Union, the German Democratic Republic, Yugoslavia, Hungary and even Cuba have performed. The festival also features contemporary folk singers and dancers and offers lectures on folk customs and art. The festival is subsidized by the Czech government and also financed through ticket sales.

Znojmo (Moravia)

ZNOJMO FEAST

Held annually, June/September
Folkloric, historic, pageantry, food

The Znojmo Feast is a historical pageant commemorating the victory of the Battle of Znojmo in 1404. It was won by the local people against King Sigismund of Hungary and Duke Albrecht of Austria. The pageant begins with a blare of trumpets and a parade of the King and Queen and their Court, all in medieval costumes. They go from the castle through the courtyard to preside from a small stage. After a mock trial and sentencing of King Sigismund and the duke, both are brought in chains and neck braces. This is the signal for the medieval fun and games to begin. There's fencing, jousting, bow and arrow competitions and performances by trained falcons flying back and forth from their master's gloved hands. Pretty maidens are tossed high into the air from rubber mats, held by strong young knights in shining armor. In between the competitions there are mandolin concerts and a quartet of medieval song performances. The audience, sitting at long tables, cheers the performers while they eat barbecued chickens and drink beer. After the performances and competitions are over, the stage is turned over to the crowd for dancing. The pageant is performed every Friday and Saturday. The event is subsidized by the government.

DENMARK

Aalborg, Rebild (North Jutland)

REBILD FESTIVAL OR FOURTH OF JULY CELEBRATION

Held annually, July 4
Goodwill, patriotic

The Rebild Festival or Fourth of July Celebration pays tribute to the United States for all the opportunities given Danes who moved there, and at the same time it honors the old country, Denmark. The celebration started July 4, 1912, the idea of Americans of Danish descent, led by Dr. Max Henius of Chicago. He bought 200 acres of land in Rebild and formally deeded the land to King

Christian X on condition that his fellow Danish-Americans be allowed to celebrate the Fourth of July there every year. The king opened the area to all people by establishing it as a national park. The event is held every year, attracting more than 35,000 people, many not even Danish or American. The one-day event lasts for three hours. At 2 p.m. a replica of the Liberty Bell tolls to officially begin festivities. Both American and Danish flags are raised high above the park to the accompaniment of a long roll of drums. Stars from the Royal Danish Opera sing both countries' national anthems. Both U.S. and Danish military bands perform, choirs sing and renditions of the Declaration of Independence and Lincoln's Gettysburg Address are given in both Danish and English. The day's events are highlighted by famous guest speakers, who in the past have included actors Danny Kaye, Raymond Burr, performer and pianist Victor Borge and TV newscaster Walter Cronkite. The only time the observance wasn't held was during World War I. In 1934, Dr. Henius was in charge of a project that built a replica of the Illinois cabin President Lincoln lived in as a young man. Dr. Henius had one log come from each state of the Union where Danish-Americans settled. The cabin was dedicated with the king and queen of Denmark attending. It is a permanent shrine for Americans of Danish ancestry. Although the festival was temporarily stopped during World War II, a small group of Danes went to the park July 4 to raise both the Danish and American flags during the Nazi occupation of their country. Nazi soldiers ripped the flags down, but determined Danes continued to slip into the park and replace and raise both flags. The celebration is always held at Rebild National Park and is sponsored by the Rebild National Park Society, Inc., founded by Danish-Americans who wanted to honor both countries. Both the city of Aalborg and the hills of Rebild have become the center of Danish-American ethnic events held in conjunction with the Independence Day celebrations. Exhibits, receptions for American guests, concerts and dinners are held a few days before. The day's celebration is financed through an admission fee and through the funds of the Rebild National Park Society. The park is about 20 miles south of the city of Aalborg.

Aarhus

AARHUS FESTIVAL WEEK

Held annually, September
Cultural

The Aarhus Festival Week is festival of opera, concerts, exhibits, drama, dance, opera, vaudeville and even sports. It was started in 1965. The nine-day festival entertains more than 20,000 people, who can choose to enjoy either indoor or outdoor programs that are made available to them. Daily shows are featured for children, and actors from the Aarhus Theater go to hospitals and senior citizens' homes to entertain those who can't attend the festival programs. Both Danish and international artists perform as do international orchestras and choirs.

In 1982, performances of opera, classical and modern music, jazz, rock, ballet and drama were held in the new Aarhus Concert Hall. Highlights of the festival included Nielsen's comic opera *Masquerade*, Vladimir Ashkenazy playing Brahms's Concerto No. 1, Loesser's *How to Succeed in Business Without Really Trying*, and the world championship of Latin American dances. Festival participants included the Amadeus Quartet, the National Ballet of Canada and Buffy Sainte-Marie and her group. Some events are free, while others require tickets. The festival is financed through ticket sales and grants from both the national and city governments. The festival always begins the first Saturday in September and continues for eight more days. It is under the patronage of her majesty the queen of Denmark.

Frederikssund

VIKING FESTIVAL

Held annually June/July
Pageantry, folkloric, cultural

The Viking Festival is a series of open-air Viking pageant plays with a cast of 200 local people and an audience of thousands, many tourists. The plays, based on Viking legend, are sometimes especially written for this festival. For example, in 1978, *Amlet* was a drama about the real Prince Hamlet, made famous in Shakespeare's tragic drama. Performances are always followed by Viking feasts of barbecued meat and drinks of mead. The festival started in 1952, when a group of local residents formed a Council of Initiative and put on a three-day festival, the Viking Festival. Many of today's actors have been in the plays since 1952, starting out in children's roles and growing up to play adult parts. The town of Frederikssund is on the Roskilde Fjord in Zealand, where burial mounds and hundreds of relics prove that the Vikings had a large settlement in the area, which would have given their long ships easy access to the sea. The plays are given on the site of the ancient Viking settlement of Calf Island. Each year new Viking plays are added to the repertory. Authentic costumes are used in the performances and plays, which are based on classical themes from Viking literature. The event is financed through ticket sales, sale of Viking meals and drink and local contributions. The festival has gone from three days to two weeks.

Odense

HANS CHRISTIAN ANDERSEN FESTIVAL

Held annually, July/August
Cultural

The Hans Christian Andersen Festival, or the Hans Christian Andersen Play, is almost a month-long event that brings this famous author's works to life through theater performances featuring 35 children, 4 professional actors and a 12-member orchestra. It dates back to 1965, when theatrical director Klaus Pagh of Copenhagen got the idea of making Andersen's works come to life. It originally began with Danish actor Freddy Albeck dressing up like the author and dramatically reading the stories to children. Not only did the children enjoy the readings but so did the accompanying adults, and in turn it attracted tourists. It evolved into a real theater that it is today. Over the years the following works have been presented: *The Swineherd*, *The Nightingale*, *Simple Simon*, *The Tinder Box*, *The Hill of the Elves*, *The Ugly Duckling*, *Little Ida's Flowers*, *Anderseniana*, a montage of his works, and *Little Claus and Big Claus*. By 1977, the festival, whose performances are only an hour long and given throughout the day, were attracting more than 30,000 visitors, many foreign tourists. All performances are given in the Funen Village in Odense. More and more events, including music concerts, were added to the festival, which to date has entertained more than half a million people. A paid staff handles all festival details, including rehearsals three months in advance of the event. There are admission charges, which help support the festival, which is also aided by private donations and grants from the government. Peformances are in the Open Air Theater, and each performance is played to 3,000 people.

Sonderborg

SONDERBORG TILTING TOURNAMENT

Held annually, July
Sports, folkloric, competition

The Sonderborg Tilting Tournament has been an annual event since 1888. Tilting has been a riding sport in southern Jutland for centuries. Tilting tournaments are held in many small villages, and the big one for riders is in July in Sonderborg. Its popularity has grown over the years from 192 contestants to more than 500 today. The event now attracts foreign visitors, who number in the thousands. To date, since the first tournament, it is estimated that 2.5 million people have either participated or watched the event. Men up to the age of 70 compete, and more recently the event has included women who are as skilled. The rules for the tournament remain basically the same. Each rider while in full gallop must strike his lance through a small metal ring suspended between two upright poles. The one who succeeds in getting the most rings is the winner and is proclaimed tournament king. There is usually a country fair held together with the tournament and refreshments of apple fritters, cakes and drinks are available. The tilting tournaments are all-day competitions, but opening day begins with an impressive mounted procession through the streets. All the riding competitors wear white trousers, dark jackets and white caps and hold raised lances decorated with colored streamers. They usually wear medals won at other tournaments or as a sign of continued interest in the ancient sport. It is considered quite an honor to compete in the annual three-day tournament, and there has been a tendency toward the development of tilting dynasties. It is not unusual to see several families represented by three generations. The tournaments were originally intended for amusement among local townspeople. Work on the tournaments is by local citizens. It is financed through entry fees and admission to the fairgrounds.

ETHIOPIA

Addis Ababa

GENNA

Held annually, January 7
Religious, Christmas

Genna is the Christmas celebration in Addis Ababa and nationwide. "Genna" is derived from the ancient Greek "jevva," meaning birth, nativity. The Julian calendar is still used in Ethiopia, and so Christmas comes January 7. Genna is also the name of a special ballgame played on Christmas. Genna observances begin at 3 a.m. in all churches. In Addis Ababa, the country's capital city, services are held at the Church of the Nativity and at Trinity Cathedral. Services begin with a hymn, "Mahlet," sung by the Coptic priests dressed in ceremonial robes and carrying long prayer sticks and *tsenatsel*, or church rattles. They walk in a special procession accompanied by ceremonial drums, with poets and singers following. The service ends around 9 a.m. This is followed by Christmas meals and celebrations. The ballgame is traditionally played in late afternoon. In Addis Ababa it is played at Janhoy Meda. The game is played by men and older boys only and is similar to hockey, with two teams competing until sunset. The winning team celebrates by visiting one house after another. Each household honors them with refreshments and gifts.

Addis Ababa

MASKAL FESTIVAL

Held annually, September 27
Religious, folkloric

The Maskal Festival celebrates the finding of the True Cross and is one of the most important and interesting of Ethiopian holidays. It is observed September 27 and is both a public and religious holiday. The True Cross of Christ, according to legend, was found in the fourth century by Queen Helena, mother of the Roman emperor, Constantine. *Maskal* is the name of the yellow daisy that blooms at this time of year. It is also a religious way to mark deliverance from heavy seasonal rains. This festival is therefore a combination of Christian and pagan traditions associated with the coming of the spring season. The event recalls now how a fragment of the True Cross came to the remote mountain monastery of Gishen Mariam in Wollo Province. There is a book, the *Tefut*, written during the reign of Zara Yacob, 1434–68, that details how the relic was acquired during the Middle Ages, when Christian kings of Ethiopia protected Coptic minorities from invaders. They were rewarded with a relic of the True Cross a week before Maskal, and to this time the event has been observed at this time of year. In Addis Ababa there is a special procession to Maskal Square from Africa Hall and Jubilee Palace, where large tents are erected to hold guests. As many as 100,000 watch the parade, compete with floats, some carrying a giant electric light cross. Priests carry colorful parasols, followed by marching bands, scout troups, school children and civic groups. At 5 p.m. the marchers, carrying lighted torches, sing and throw the *chibbos*, or flaming torches, onto a pyre, which burns throughout the night. Maskal has been celebrated in Ethiopia for more than 1,600 years.

FINLAND

Helsinki

HELSINKI FESTIVAL

Held annually, August/September
Cultural

The Helsinki Festival is the largest continuous Nordic country cultural event. It offers opera, theater, ballet, classical, pop and jazz music in the 1,750-seat Finlandia Hall built in 1972. Today's festival evolved from the Sibelius Festival in 1951, the idea of conductor Martti Simila, composer Nils-Erik and Seppo Nummi. The Sibelius Festival was held in June and the first Helsinki Festival in May, but as time went on, the founders of each event decided to join forces for one festival, the Helsinki Festival, holding it for two weeks late August into early September. More people attended at the end of summer, with the festival attracting more than 300,000 including tourists. The grand total is well over a million people. The festival features both Finnish and other Scandinavian performers as well as international ones. The festival is a member of the European Association of Music Festivals. Among some of the international performing groups featured have been the Polish National Theater of Warsaw, Dance Theater of Harlem, La Mama E.T.C. of New York, Tientsin Acrobat Company of China, Gorki Theater of Leningrad and Theater Kefka of Cologne. International performing groups are selected on the basis of cultural agreements between Finland and other countries. The 1982 festival scheduled the Finnish Radio Symphony, the Helsinki Philharmonic Orchestra, the London Philharmonia, the Cleveland Quartet plus conductors Gerd Albrecht and Jesus-Lopez Cobos. Also participating were pianist Claudio Arrau, flutist Jean-Pierre Rampal and tenor Jose Carreras. The festival is financed through ticket sales and through a budget of almost $1 million, heavily subsidized by the city of Helsinki.

Jyvaskyla

JYVASKYLA ARTS FESTIVAL

Held annually, June/July
Cultural

The Jyvaskyla Arts Festival is a ten-day chamber music event now featuring international groups and performers. It was started in 1956 to give this middle region of Finland a cultural experience. The festival offers not only concerts but also films, theater, exhibits and seminars based on a different theme each year. In addition, the festival conducts a summer Academy of Chamber Music, which has been awarded the Pro Musica Fund. The festival was started and organized by Professor Timo Makinen, composer Seppo Nummi and the late Professor Paivo Oksala, all well known in the music world. In 1982, the festival saluted the Renaissance. Participants included the London Early Music Group, Prague Madrigal Singers, Bartok Quartet, Hortius Musicus from Tallinn and cellist Heinrich Schiff. The festival plays to an audience of more than 30,000 annually and is financed through ticket sales and funds from the Education Ministry of the city. Performances are held citywide, usually at the University Auditorium Maximum, local churches, museums, theaters and sometimes city parks.

Kaustinen

FOLK MUSIC FESTIVAL KAUSTINEN

Held annually, July
Cultural, folkloric

Folk Music Festival Kaustinen is an international folk music and dance event held in the Finnish countryside. The first festival was held in 1968, started by local residents to preserve Finnish folk music, dance and art. Originally only Finnish amateur groups participated, but the festival began to attract large audiences and many tourists. The festival now offers Finnish and foreign folk ensembles, both amateur and professional. As many as 80,000 come to the performances. Foreign groups have come from Japan, Greenland, Canada and the United States. In addition to the scheduled programs held in town local banquet halls, there are impromptu performances and competitions between musicians and dancers in the open air. Finnish folk songs and dances, however, are still an essential part of the festival. There is also spiritual music and new forms of folk music. Special festival events include the Kaustinen Cavalcade, or performances by local musicians, a review of Finnish amateur musicians and foreign groups. The event ends with a festival grand folk music parade on the last day. The festival is financed through ticket sales and through donations from residents and the city.

Pori

PORI JAZZ

Held annually, July
Cultural

Pori Jazz, started in 1965 to showcase Finnish jazz artists, has grown into an international event and one of Europe's top jazz offerings. Famous jazz artists from all over the world, including the United States, perform in more than 50 concerts. A major program is an outdoor concert in the park at Kirjurinluoto Island. This one concert plays to an audience of more than 10,000 jazz fans. Round-the-clock concerts featuring all styles of jazz are held in nightclubs, in restaurants, in jazz clubs, on the street, in churches, in art galleries, in concert halls and in schools. There are also lectures, films and exhibitions on jazz and its influence. There is free admission to several concerts and jazz clubs, but the rest require admission fees, ranging from $5 to $10 for some performances and jam sessions and from $12.50 to $15 for the main park concerts. The event is financed through ticket sales and aid from the city.

Rovaniemi

OUNASVAARA INTERNATIONAL WINTER GAMES

Held annually, March
Sports, competition

The Ounasvaara International Winter Games date back to 1927, when they were started to give northern Finland winter games, centering around various ski events. It has developed into an international event, with foreign countries very active. About 20,000 attend the annual two-day mid-March event, and over the years, close to a million. The most popular event continues to be jumping. Local people volunteer time to work two months before the event. It is financed through entry fees, admission charges and private contributions.

Savonlinna

SAVONLINNA OPERA FESTIVAL

Held annually, July
Cultural

The Savonlinna Opera Festival is held every July for three weeks with opera performances in the 500-year-old Olavinlinna Castle. Famous opera stars perform in such operas as Mozart's *The Magic Flute*, Verdi's *Don Carlos*, and Wagner's *Flying Dutchman*. Different operas are offered each year, catering to thousands of fans. In addition, the festival offers concerts which vary from year to year. More recently, in 1982 Sibelius's symphonies and violin concerto were performed by the Bournemouth Symphony Orchestra in Mikkeli at the Kerimaki Church (the world's largest wooden church), and at the castle. The festival is financed through ticket sales and private donations. Premiere tickets cost from $22 to $33 per person. Other performances are less.

FRANCE

Besancon (Doubs)

BESANCON INTERNATIONAL MUSIC FESTIVAL

Held annually, September
Cultural, competition

The Besancon International Music Festival offers symphony concerts, chamber music and recitals performed amid Roman ruins and in the Cathedral of St. Jean.

It was started for cultural reasons, with the first one held in September 1948. It has grown to play to an audience of more than 20,000 annually. The 17-day festival is rather interesting since it encompasses two other important cultural events: the International Competition for Young Conductors, and the International Festival of Musical and Choreographic Film. Sometimes a foreign dance company is featured. In the past the Ballet Nacional Festivales de Espana has performed. The festival is a member of both the Association of International Festivals of France and of the European Association of Music Festivals. The festival is financed by ticket sales and private donations plus grants from the state and local governments.

Bordeaux (Gironde)

MAY INTERNATIONAL MUSICAL

Held annually, May
Cultural

The May International Musical is a festival of drama, symphony concerts, chamber music, recitals, ballet and art exhibits. The 17-day festival also features a series of programs, headlining young soloists. It is considered to be one of the best events in Europe. Among some of the past festival participants have been the Murray Louis Dance Company of the United States, the Tokyo Ballet, the Cullberg Ballet of Stockholm and The Dancers of Bali. From time to time, the festival features drama, usually French companies. The art of mime has been performed by Ladislav Fialka and Marcel Marceau. The festival goes back to 1949, introduced to attract visitors and to revive culture programs in the area. Performances are held in public gardens, churches, theaters and castles. Thousands attend annually. It is supported by ticket sales and donations from private industry and local government grants. The festival is a member of the European Association of Music Festivals.

Lourdes (Hautes-Pyrenees)

EASTER FESTIVAL OF SACRED MUSIC

Held annually, coinciding with Easter Sunday, movable date
Religious, cultural

The Easter Festival of Sacred Music is a ten-day event, directed by Kurt Redel. It begins on Good Friday and continues through Easter Sunday, ending a week later. International concert and choral groups perform Bach's *Magnificat* and Masses by Beethoven and Mozart. In the past, top German, Polish and Japanese groups have been featured. Religious music by Telemann, Vivaldi, Bach and

Haydn are often featured, with concerts held in the Rosary Basilica at Lourdes. The festival began in 1968 to call attention to the famous area, consecrated to St. Bernadette Soubirous who saw visions of Our Lady in 1858. It is the site of the world famous Catholic shrine, where countless miracles have been experienced. The festival also includes exhibits of sacred art. Tickets for the concerts vary from $3.30 to $16.50. The festival is financed by ticket sales and by donations.

Lyon (Rhone)

INTERNATIONAL FESTIVAL OF LYON

Held annually, June
Cultural

The International Festival of Lyon or Festival of Lyon dates back to June 29, 1946, when it was a month-long Festival de Lyon-Charbonnieres, under the direction of George Bassinet, who wanted a cultural event established in this city, known in Roman days as Lugdunum. By 1960, the sponsor of the festival, La Societe des Eaux Minerales de Charbonnieres, headed by Andre Bassinet, brother of George, decided to withdraw financial support from the event. At this point the festival had attracted so many people from all over France and from other countries that the then mayor of the city, with the approval of the city council, decided to back the festival financially. The Festival of Lyon was officially born with this decision. Today's festival lasts 16 days and offers concerts, ballet and even opera. The city's Roman ruins provide the setting for many concerts, while other programs are given in the Ravel Auditorium, the Theatre du Huitieme and the Maison de la Danse. Highlights of the 1982 festival included the Lyon Orchestra, the Lyon Opera Ballet and the Leningrad Philharmonic Orchestra. The festival is a member of the Association of International Festivals of France and of the European Association of Music Festivals. It is financed by ticket sales and subsidies from the city of Lyon.

Nuits-St. Georges, Beaune, Meursault (Cote-d'Or)

THREE GLORIOUS DAYS

Held annually, the third Saturday through Monday, November
Economic, folkloric, wine

Les Trois Glorieuses, or Three Glorious Days, is a wine festival held in three Burgundy wine-producing towns. This is celebrated with a winetasters' banquet at Nuits-St. Georges. On Sunday there's a wine auction at Hospices de Beaune.

This charity hospital has served the community for more than 500 years, supported by its vineyards, which produce top grapes and wine. The hospital's wine cellars are opened to the public for a fee to sample the new wines, followed by professional tasters. The Sunday auction is open to merchants from all over the world. The Brotherhood of the Knights of the Winetaster's Cup (Confrerie des Chevaliers du Tastevin) was formed in 1934 to help put the wine industry back on its feet after some disastrous vintage failures. The membership now totals 17,000. A series of banquets is held throughout the year by the group to promote the wines, but the best banquets are now part of the wine festival. They are held in Beaune and Meursault. Folk dancing and merrymaking add to each day's celebration.

Paris

PARIS AIR AND SPACE SHOW

Held once every two years in June; next: 1985, 1987
Economic, fair, aviation

The Paris Air and Space Show is held once every two years in June at Le Bourget Airport, about ten miles north of Paris. It attracts more than 600,000 visitors. Events and exhibits are held in the airport's hangars and on the runways. The show goes back to 1908, when it was held to indicate the role of aviation in the future. Today, more than 700 exhibitors from 23 nations participate. Featured are aircraft, launching and ground equipment, missile propulsion units, control and navigational aids, anti-aircraft detection devices and aeronautic components. Presentation and demonstration flights are held the first nine days of the show from 10 a.m. to 5:45 p.m., followed the tenth day by an official International Flying Display and on the final day a special fly-in show especially for the public. The show is self-supporting and is financed through entry fees, rental charges for exhibitors and admissions to the show. Work on the fair is by a paid staff.

Paris

PARIS MARATHON

Held annually, third Saturday in May
Sports, competition

The annual Paris Marathon, open to both amateur and professional runners, now includes American runners. It officially begins at 1 p.m. and covers 26 miles of Parisian streets and riverbanks, from the Arc de Triomphe to Notre Dame and from Les Bois de Boulogne to Les Bois de Vincennes. It is open to athletes of all ages and countries. Several thousand compete. Runners are electrically timed at designated points. A certificate and medal is awarded to those who reach the finish line by at least 6 p.m. The first marathon was held in 1975, and the event has continued ever since. It is financed through entry fees and industry sponsorship.

Paris

SUMMER FESTIVAL OF PARIS

Held annually, July/September
Cultural, economic

The Festival Estival de Paris, or Summer Festival of Paris, offers more than 100 different musical and theater events that can include Mozart symphonies at the Church of St. Germain des Pres, Spanish medieval music at the Sainte-Chapelle and a music cruise on the Seine. It is one of the country's longest and most popular festivals, attracting thousands of visitors. International performers, instrumentalists and orchestras perform everything from medieval to contemporary music. The festival was first held in 1967 to give Parisians and other French people a summer cultural program. It also helped entertain tourists. Part of the festival since 1976 is "Paristory," an audio-visual program about Paris history. It's shown nightly during July and August. The 90-minute program is presented in the classical courtyard of the Palais Royal at 10 p.m. in July and at 9:30 p.m. in August. There is an admission charge of $6 per person. The show is subtitled in English with commentary by Jean Gabin, Michele Morgan, Arletty and Ludmilla Tchernina. A 100-piece orchestra accompanies the voices of Mireille Mathieu and Daniel Guichard.

The 1982 festival scheduled a series of concerts every night in the churches of St. Merri and St. Juilien le Pauvre, the Musee de Cluny, Hotel Intercontinental, the Auber Metro Station and aboard the *bateaux mouches* on the Seine. Highlights included the performance of *David and Jonathan* by Charpentier and Stravinsky's *Mass* in Notre Dame Cathedral. Participants included the Philharmonic Orchestra of Lille, the Academy of Ancient Music, the Boston Camerata, the North Carolina Symphonic Orchestra, the Freiburger Vokalensemble, the Kammerchor of Stuttgart, the Polish Chamber Orchestra and the English Bach Festival Baroque Orchestra. The festival is financed through ticket sales, contributions from private industry and city and government grants.

Strasbourg (Alsace), (Bas-Rhin)

INTERNATIONAL MUSIC FESTIVAL

Held annually, June
Cultural

The International Music Festival in Strasbourg marked its fiftieth anniversary in 1982 with the performance of Bach's B Minor Mass, performed in the Cathedral of Notre Dame. There were performances by the world's top organists (in the past, the late Albert Schweitzer performed at the festival). The idea for the festival was that of a music professor Pautrier and Roger and Gustave Wolf, who met with a group interested in developing a music festival for the city. The Societe des Amis de la Musique was formed to produce the festival. The first one in 1932 featured the Berlin Philharmonic and a Parisian orchestra, Le Ste. L'amoureux. It was an instant success, attracting hundreds of visitors. Each year after, the festival began to feature concerts and programs by more famous orchestras and conductors. Opera also became a part of the event. The festival in 1939 was the last one because of the outbreak of World War II. It was resumed in 1947 and attracted thousands of visitors. The 16-day festival is self-supporting and financed by ticket sales and private donations. The festival is a member of the European Association of Music Festivals.

GERMAN FEDERAL REPUBLIC

Bayreuth (Bavaria)

BAYREUTH FESTIVAL/RICHARD WAGNER FESTIVAL

Held annually, July/August
Cultural

The 35-day Bayreuth Festival, or Richard Wagner Festival, is one of the oldest and most formal of European music festivals. Almost the entire audience is dressed in formal evening clothes. It is such a popular event that tickets are reserved a year in advance. The Wagnerian operas are performed in the Festspielhaus, which was designed especially for Wagner with the help of King Ludwig II of Bavaria. Concerts and recitals are held in the rococo Margrave's Opera House, the oldest in Germany. It was Wagner himself who launched the festival in 1876 with the performance of his four-opera *Ring of the Nibelungs*. It was revived after World War II by his grandsons, Wieland and Wolfgang

Wagner. The world's top conductors and singers perform. Tickets cost from $7 to $80 and are difficult to obtain. Opera performances are staged by world famous directors, who use the latest equipment to enhance the Wagnerian operas. Performances begin at 4 p.m. Over the years, hundreds of thousands have attended. The event has seen royalty, the very wealthy and the not so wealthy. Seven to eight operas are presented annually. The one-hour intermission is also a social festival event. The festival is self-supporting.

Berlin, West

BERLIN FESTIVAL

Held annually, September/October
Cultural

The Berlin Festival offers opera, concerts, soloists and guest conductors. Performances are in the Berlin Opera House and other city halls and theaters. The main center for programs is the Philharmonic Hall, completed in 1963. It's the home of the Berlin Philharmonic Orchestra, led by Herbert von Karajan. The orchestra marked its one hundredth anniversary in 1982. In the past, the festival was keyed to a theme, but later it got away from that. The month-long festival was launched in 1951 to give the divided city cultural enjoyment. It evolved from a local music festival to an international one.

The highlight of the 1982 festival was a Mahler cycle with all ten symphonies, including the Eighth (*The Symphony of a Thousand*), *Das Lied von der Erde*, *The Ruckert-Lider*, *Das Knaben Wunderhorn*, *Das Klagende Lied* and the *Kindertotenlieder*. Participating orchestras were the Philadelphia Orchestra, the Vienna Philharmonic, the London Symphony Orchestra, the Leningrad Philharmonic Orchestra, the Amsterdam Concertgebouw, the Bavarian Radio Symphony Orchestra and the Polish Chamber Orchestra. Guest conductors were Riccardo Murti, Claudio Abbado, Bernard Haitnik, Rafael Kubelik, Leonard Bernstein and Jesus-Lopez Cobos. Featured soloists were violinists Gidon Kremer and Igo Oistrach, pianists Maurizio Pollini, Dirk Joeres, Anthony and Joseph Paratore and Peter Serkin, sopranos Lucia Popp, Jessye Norman, Julia Varady and Margaret Marshall, mezzo-sopranos Brigitte Fassbaender and Agnes Baltsa, tenor Simon Estes and baritone Dietrich Fischer-Dieskau. The festival is a member of the European Association of Music Festivals. It is financed through ticket sales and by an annual budget from the Berlin Senate and the Federal Republic in excess of 1.6 million Deutsche marks.

Landshut (Bavaria)

LANDSHUT WEDDING 1475

Held once every three years, June/July; next: 1985, 1988
Pageantry, historic

The Landshut Wedding 1475 is a traditional pageant presented once every three years. It recreates the festive celebrations of the royal wedding in 1475 of Prince George, son of the reigning Bavarian duke, to Princess Hedwig, daughter of the king of Poland. More than a 1,000 people actively participate, dressed in the costumes of the period to bring the fifteenth century to life. Festivities continue for three weeks, with wedding dances and pageantry on four successive Sundays. The original wedding had 10,000 guests. Today's pageant has 100,000 visitors. Landshut is an hour's drive northeast of Munich. Every Saturday afternoon there is a play and dance performance at the Town Hall. Sunday events begin at 9:30 a.m. with a pageant at the same Town Hall, followed by a 1475 music concert in the courtyard of the Residenz. The festival pageant is repeated between 10:45 a.m. and 1 p.m. at the Town Hall. Sunday is also for the reenactment of the historical wedding procession of 1,000 beginning at 2:30 p.m. and going through the town streets to 4 p.m. This is followed by jousting tournaments, and at 7 p.m. historical dance performances are held at the Town Hall. Wandering minstrels roam the streets singing songs of the Middle Ages. Jolly jesters parade, and knights in armor ride horseback. The pageant is financed by the city. There are some admission charges, but most events are free. Landshut was chartered as a city in 1204 and once was the capital of Bavaria.

Munich (Bavaria)

MUNICH OPERA FESTIVAL

Held annually July/August
Cultural

The annual Munich Opera Festival, which began back in 1901, continues to feature world famous conductors, singers and ballet companies in its opera productions. The Bavarian State Opera performs works by Richard Strauss, who was born in Munich, and by Mozart, Wagner and others. Performances are in the National Theater and Cuvillies Theater, with concerts at the Residenz, a former royal palace. Chamber music programs are given by the Bavarian State Orchestra. Each year the festival has an audience of 50,000 over the 25-day period. Despite the discontinuance of the festival during the two World Wars, the grand total of attendance adds up to a few million. The festival always uses the most famous singers, conductors, directors and designers. A paid staff handles details. The festival is supported by ticket sales, private donations and grants from the government.

Munich (Bavaria)

OKTOBERFEST

Held annually, September/October
Fair, economic, folkloric, beer

The Oktoberfest continues to be one of the country's most important events and is a combination fair and folk festival with the accent on beer, dancing, folk singing and eating. Despite its name, it always begins in late September, continuing for 16 days. It beings with a parade of antique beer wagons pulled by horses, decorated with colored ribbons and accompanied by brass bands through the city streets. The parade ends at Theresienwiese, the fairgrounds. There's a 12-cannon salute, and the burgomaster (mayor) knocks the plug out of the first keg of beer, which continues to flow from other kegs for the next two weeks. The Munich Oktoberfest has been celebrated since 1810, when the first one was a big party given by Bavarian King Maximilian to celebrate the marriage of his son, Crown Prince Ludwig, to Princess Therese of Saxony-Hildburghausen. The fairgrounds were named for her. Most of the activity takes place in six huge 6,000-seat tents of the major brewers at the fairgrounds. Originally the event was held entirely in October, but early winter snows changed it to late September. There's oompah band music, folk singing and dancing in each tent as well as food and beer for sale. Each year, large amounts of food and beer are consumed. In an off-year (1980), 5 million people ate 43 oxen roasted on the spit, 552,198 barbecued chickens, 287,693 pairs of pork sausages and 42,102 roasted pork knuckles, washed down by 1,015,535 gallons of beer. There are children's events and rides, too. The annual event entertains close to a billion people, many tourists. It is financed by admission fees, food and beer sales and sponsorship of the breweries.

Oberammergau (Bavaria)

OBERAMMERGAU PASSION PLAY

Held once every ten years, May/September; next: 1990
Religious

The Oberammergau Passion Play is held once every ten years in thanksgiving to God by the villagers for being spared from the Black Plague. The first play was held in 1634, and it has continued ever since. The play celebrated its 350th anniversary in 1984 with special performances. It has a cast of 1,700, with most of the town's inhabitants from children to the elderly actively participating. Work in preparation for the event, which attracts hundreds of thousands of visitors, is done two years before the actual play is presented. The original play text has been rewritten many times. An 1860 version by a Bavarian priest, Alois Daisenberger, was used until 1970. The play's director discarded it and returned to the 1750 one written by Father Ferdinand Rosner. It is presented in the style of a medieval mystery play. Performances are given in a large amphitheater built in 1930 and with a seating and standing capacity of 6,500 persons. The cast consists of the townspeople, but by law every actor and actress has to be native born in Oberammergau and have resided there for 20 years. A man has to be married for more than 10 years to a woman of the village. All are selected by a special committee, consisting of the mayor, Town Council and a pastor. The event is financed through ticket sales and private donations.

Rothenburg on the Tauber (Bavaria)

MASTER DRAUGHT PAGEANT

Held annually, July
Folkloric, historic, pageantry

The Master Draught Pageant recalls a historic time when this still well-preserved medieval town was saved from destruction. It was during the Thirty Years' War in 1631, when the town was threatened with destruction by the invading imperial troops commanded by General Count Johannes Tserklaes Tilly. The general made a wager with the town's former mayor, George Nusch. If Nusch could drink a gallon flagon of wine in one swallow, the town would be spared. Nusch did, and ever since the event has been commemorated with a pageant reenacting the story. The play is performed by local citizens in authentic costume at the Market Square several times during July and is preceded by a historical costume parade, followed by a "camp life," in which the entire city's population participates. Performances marked their centennial year in 1981. The pageant and other events are free, attracting thousands of visitors. It is financed through souvenir sales and private donations.

Wiesbaden (Hesse)

INTERNATIONAL MAY FESTIVAL

Held annually, May
Cultural

The International May Festival, or Wiesbaden May Festival, offers opera, drama, ballet, song, chamber and symphonic music performed in the Hessian State

Theater and in the Kurhaus. This is West Germany's second oldest music festival. It began in 1896. It is international in scope and features top performers and groups from all over the world.

Nine countries beside West Germany participated in the 1982 three-week festival. Among the participants were the Soviet Union's Kiev Opera, Austria's Theater am Schwedenplatz of Vienna, Britain's Sheer Madness Street Theater Group, France's Trio Tomasi of Paris, Switzerland's Zurich Opera, East Germany's Deutschesoper of Berlin, Greece's Greek National Ballet, Italy's La Fenice Opera of Venice and Finland's KOM Theater of Helsinki. The Opera Studio of Nuremberg was also featured. The festival highlight was Haydn's *The Seasons* with soprano Reri Grist, tenor Robert Gambill and bass Hans Keimer. The festival is supported by ticket sales and subsidies from the city.

GIBRALTAR

Local waters from City Wharf

INTERNATIONAL SHARK ANGLING COMPETITION

Held annually, April/May
Sports, competition

The International Shark Angling Competition is a one-day event in late April or early May, depending upon the weather. It is held at this time of year because the sharks come closer to shore then. The first competition was held in April 1967 and proved such a success that its been continued ever since, attracting up to 1,000 competitors and an equal number of spectators and tourists. It was introduced on a small scale in 1964 by Bing Hopwood and Mr. Terry Venables, a former correspondent for *The Angling Times* of Great Britain, expanded to attract tourists by J. A. Russo, director of the Queens Hotel. The competition offers prizes for the heaviest shark and aggregate weight. Boats leave at 9 a.m. and return at 6 p.m. for the weighing at the City Wharf, which is decorated with flags of competing countries and where spectators and the minister for tourism wait. Both men and women compete. The local record for the largest shark is still 203 pounds. Work on competition is by volunteers, some members of the Tarik Deep Sea Angling Association. It is financed through entry fees and contributions.

GREAT BRITAIN

England

Aldeburgh (Suffolk)

ALDEBURGH FESTIVAL OF MUSIC AND THE ARTS

Held annually, June
Cultural

The Aldeburgh Festival of Music and the Arts was established by the composer Benjamin Britten and tenor Sir Peter Pears in 1947 as a personal event with performances for friends. Its setting is a small fishing town. The festival has grown in importance. Its thirty-fifth anniversary in 1982 was an expansion of programs of opera, concerts, lectures and exhibits. It included *The Beggar's Opera* performed by the Tent Opera Group, and the English Chamber Orchestra gave concerts. The Sadler's Wells Royal Ballet appeared for the first time, and the Royal Shakespeare Company gave *The Hollow Crown*. The two-week festival aims for excellence in music and performances without attracting a mass audience. Performances are in the 300-seat Jubilee or Festival Hall. Some concerts are performed in local churches. It is financed through ticket sales and sponsorships.

England

Bath (Avon)

BATH FESTIVAL

Held annually, May/June
Cultural

The Bath Festival only dates back to 1959, but is has become one of the most important music festivals in Great Britain and throughout Europe. It owes its beginning and success to American violinist Yehudi Menuhin. He helped train the Bath Festival Orchestra, now recognized as among the best small orchestras of the world. He also helped to organize the festival.

In 1982 the festival featured the music of seven centuries, ranging from the *Messe de Notre Dame* by Guillaume de Machaut (born around 1300) to new works by composers Dominic Muldowney (a piano trio) and Colin Matthews.

The festival also honored Haydn with an all-Haydn program by the Monteverdi Choir and Orchestra, directed by John Elliot Gardiner. One of the highlights was the performance of *King Arthur*, a dramatic opera by Purcell and one rarely performed. This festival has fringe benefits such as tours of the area, exhibits and a festival ball held at one of the area's historic homes. In 1965, for example, it was held at Farleigh Hungerford Castle. The ball commemorated the victory of King Henry V over the French at Agincourt in 1415. About 18,000 persons attend each year's festival, which helps both the arts and local tourism. Work on the event is both by a paid staff and volunteers. It is financed by box-office sales, grants and sponsorships. Concerts and other performances are held at citywide locations.

England

Broadstairs (Kent)

BROADSTAIRS DICKENS FESTIVAL

Held annually, June
Cultural

The Broadstairs Dickens Festival features a play adapted from one of Charles Dickens's novels, with a different one each year. Since the first festival in 1936, all of Dickens's works have gone the full circle more than once. The players are all members of the Broadstairs Dickens Players Society. The adaptation and rehearsals take almost eight months. The eight-day festival is still handled by the Broadstairs branch of the Dickens Fellowship. It was the idea of Gladys Waterer, who still continues as honorary secretary of the Broadstairs branch. Charles Dickens lived in Broadstairs at Bleak House, the home of the original Betsey Trotwood in *David Copperfield*. Ms. Waterer lives in Dickens's house. During part of the festival, there are open house programs at both Dickens's house and at Bleak House, also the setting for a Dickensian or Victorian garden party with prizes for the best costumes. There are Victorian music concerts, exhibits and lectures on Dickens. There is a festival dance, and the whole town dresses Victorian for the occasion. Shop windows go Victorian, and people in the streets become Dickens's characters in costume, too. It is financed through ticket sales and private contributions.

England

Chichester (West Sussex)

CHICHESTER FESTIVAL THEATER SEASON

Held annually, May/September
Cultural

The Chichester Festival Theatre Season features four plays from both classical and contemporary repertoires. The festival, started in 1962, was the idea of one man, a local optometrist, city councilor and former mayor, Leslie Evershed-Martin. The first festival, chaired by Sir Laurence Olivier, was an instant success. Today, it is considered to be one of the top drama events. It plays to a 90 percent capacity audience, even though the hexagonal-shaped theater only seats 1,400, with all seats not more than 60 feet from the stage. The festival has also been directed by John Clements until 1973 and by Keith Mitchell in 1977. Originally only three plays in repertory were offered, April to September, and then the season was changed July to September. It is now May through September. It is financed through ticket sales and sponsorships.

England

Gloucester, Hereford, Worcester

THREE CHOIRS FESTIVAL

Held annually, August
Cultural

The Three Choirs Festival is one of Europe's oldest continuing music festivals, reaching its 255th year in 1982, when it was held in Hereford in the rural countryside of Herefordshire. The cathedral cities of Gloucester and Worcester are festival sites in alternating years. In other words, it will be three years, or 1985, before it returns to Hereford. The 1982 festival was highlighted by Verdi's *Requiem*, Vaughan Williams's Symphony No. 5, Walton's *Belshazzar's Feast*, Britten's *The Spring Symphony*, works by Haydn, Mozart, Kodaly and Stravinsky, a commissioned work by William Mathias and a new work by Geoffrey Burgon. The festival was founded before 1719. It still opens with a service of praise and thanksgiving in the host cathedral. A festival choir of 300 voices accompanied by a symphony orchestra perform. The rest of the week usually features about nine or more concerts in the cathedral, with chamber concerts performed in a local theater and nearby historic homes, which open for the occasion. There are many exhibitions and social events in conjunction with the festival, which are attended by thousands of visitors, who must purchase tickets well in advance. The music program offers many first performances, choral works of the Tudor period and recent British works. Early festival records from the eighteenth century indicate that then, as now, the festival was held in succession at the cathedral of Gloucester, Hereford and Worcester and that the cathedral choirs sang sacred songs in the cathedral while secular music was performed elsewhere. Little has changed over the centuries. The nobility and gentry of the eighteenth century patronized the festival with at least two or more of them acting as stewards, thereby guranteeing the continuance of the event. Today, festival subscribers for the weeks are still called stewards, but in name only. Those eighteenth-century stewards came up with the idea that money given at the doors of the cathedral after the performances would be given to the Charity for the Relief of Widows and Orphans of Clergy in the three dioceses. This charity became associated with the festival in 1724 and still benefits from it.

England

Glyndebourne (East Sussex)

GLYNDEBOURNE FESTIVAL

Held annually May/August
Cultural

The Glyndebourne Festival Opera season is one of Europe's more formal festivals that spans two and a half months, or ten weeks. Five operas are presented every season, usually from the third week in May to the first week of August. Performances begin at 5 p.m., and there is a 75-minute intermission during which either dinner is served in the local restaurants or the audience, attired in evening clothes, brings picnics to eat in the gardens. Performances are in the 300-seat opera house in the gardens of the festival founder's estate at Glyndebourne. The festival was started in 1934 by John Christie, a wealthy physicist whose family has owned the Glyndebourne estate since Elizabethan times. Christie decided to form an opera company at his home, as a gift to his bride, Audrey Mildmay, an opera singer. He hired experts like conductor Fritz Busch and director Carl Ebert to help launch the festival. Christie, a Wagnerian opera fan, wanted to produce the "Ring" cycle, but his wife and the two artistic friends convinced him that it was impractical. So for the first season in 1934 there were six performances each of *The Marriage of Figaro* and *Cosi Fan Tutte*. The two productions were successful, and so the festival continued dealing mostly with Mozart operas. It gradually became accepted as one of the leading music festivals in the world and expanded its repertory, especially after World War II, to all kinds of opera, including new ones. The Glyndebourne Festival grew in popularity within five years from its start. Later the cost of operatic production led Christie in 1946 to transfer the festival's operations to the newly established Edinburgh Festival. There was no opera that year in East Sussex. Four years later, outside help from several British industrial companies and the formation of the Glyndebourne Festival Society helped to reestablish the festival at Glyndebourne and ensured it annual financial support. Mozart continued to be part of the festival, but in the 1950s it included several Rossini comic operas, and in the 1960s it became a leader in the revival of baroque opera. By the 1970s, the festival turned to the more unfamiliar Strauss comedies and in 1979 offered its first Haydn opera, *La Fedelta Premiata* and other Haydn works, now part of the 1980s scene. The Glyndebourne Festival is also credited with the discovery of important singers before they became international stars. In 1939, it was American mezzo-soprano Rise Stevens. In 1951 it was Birgit Nilsson, and in 1956, Joan Sutherland. Italian tenor Luciano Pavarotti performed at the festival in 1964. The Glyndebourne Festival Opera Season is well known throughout the world and is often featured in radio and television programs. The operas are recorded. After the festival season, Glyndebourne productions tour the entire United Kingdom. George Christie, son of the founder, is chairman of the Festival Society, and the administration of the event is handled by Moran Caplat, who succeeded Rudolf Bing in 1949. Literally thousands over the years have attended performances. Tickets are difficult to obtain so that advance reservations are now required. The festival receives no state or public subsidy. About 75 percent of its revenue comes from the sale of tickets, and the remaining 25 percent is raised from individuals, trusts and industry.

England

King's Lynn (Norfolk)

KING'S LYNN FESTIVAL

Held annually, July
Cultural

The King's Lynn Festival got its start in 1951, when the market town was selected as one of the British Festival towns for the Festival of Britain celebrations. It continued on its own as the Festival of Music and the Arts annually at the end of July, attracting thousands from all over Britain. Its purpose is to bring culture to this ancient and historic town. In 1982, the festival opened with a concert by the Halle Orchestra conducted by James Loughran with Dame Janet Baker singing Mahler's *Das Lied von der Erde*. This was followed by the Cambridge Buskers in late night programs with fireworks. The festival's other participants have included the English Chamber Orchestra, Humphry Lyttleton and his band, the Cornell University Glee Club, the Pasadena Roof Orchestra and the Scottish Chamber Orchestra. In 1982 there was also a premiere of a festival commission from John Hopkins, *Cantilever*, an entertainment based on the life of Captain John Smith, *Turks and Tomahawks*, and *The Play of Daniel*. The festival also has children's programs. It is financed through tickets sales and private sponsorships and contributions.

England

London

CRUFT'S DOG SHOW

Held annually, February
Sports, dog show

Cruft's Dog Show is considered to be the largest and most attended dog show in all of Great Britain. It goes back to 1886, organized by Charles Cruft, who was responsible for another dog show at the Paris Exhibition of 1878. The show was held for a few years at the Royal Aquarium, Westminster. It won the patronage of Queen Victoria. More recently it was held at Olympia and now the Earls Court on Warwick Road. More than 10,000 entries are received annually. Hundreds of thousands attend the three-day show. It is financed through entry fees and ticket sales.

England

London

FESTIVAL OF THE CITY OF LONDON

Held biennially, even-numbered years in July; next: 1986, 1988
Cultural

The Festival of the City of London was first held in 1963, originated and directed by Ian Hunter "to show the beautiful and historic buildings of the 'square mile' as a superb setting for the finest performances of music, opera and theatre, presented on a scale specially suited to the buildings." An outdoor production of *The Yeomen of the Guard* was given the first year at the Tower of London, marking its 900th anniversary. It has been repeated even since. Concerts are given in various city locations and by both famous British and international artists, orchestras and chamber music groups. There are prose and poetry readings, art exhibits, ethnic festivals, lunchtime programs and more. Different events and programs are sponsored by various commercial firms and companies. It is promoted by the City Arts Trust Limited together with the Corporation of London and the Arts Council of Great Britain.

England

London

CHELSEA FLOWER SHOW

Held annually, May
Floral, economic, horticultural

The Chelsea Flower Show is the annual Royal Horticultural Society show, held since 1888. Originally it was staged in the Temple Gardens, but by 1913 it was changed to the grounds of the Royal Hospital in Chelsea, where it has remained. The hospital is a building designed by Sir Christopher Wren as a retirement home for old soldiers. The flower show, except for wartime breaks, has been held here ever since. It is always held the last full week in May. Its main feature is a giant marquee spanning 3.5 acres and filled with exhibits of new and rare flowers. Both professional and amateur gardeners exhibit miniature landscape gardening. Leading floral designers also construct rock and formal gardens for display. There are about 500 exhibitors of flowers and plants, garden supplies and the latest in horticultural achievements. The show attracts about 250,000 every year. It is financed through admission fees and exhibit charges.

England

London

SWAN-UPPING SEASON

Held annually, last Monday in July
Traditional

The annual Swan-Upping Season is the ancient tradition of marking newborn swans, observed for the past six centuries by two of London's livery companies (trade guilds), the Company of Dyers and the Company of Vintners. The swan was classified as a royal bird in the Middle Ages, with a license from the Crown necessary for anyone else to own one. However, this was changed to give both the dyers and the vintners the right to keep swans on the Thames between London and Henley. "Swan-upping" means that every member of both trade guilds have to go out on the river and mark newborn swans with their own guild identification. Those not marked belong to the queen. Every year since 1363, both the queen's swan master and the swan wardens of both companies perform their duties. A party of men, representing the companies, go out in six skiffs, each flying a large silk standard. They row up the Thames from Blackfriars in the center of London to claim ownership of new swans or cygnets on the river between London and Henley-on-Thames, a distance of 40 miles to the west. Three teams of markers in six boats, two for the Crown and two for each of the companies, cut marks on the beaks of hundreds of cygnets. Ownership is decided by how the beak of their parents were marked in previous summers. One nick on a swan gives it to the dyers, two to the vintners. No mark means it belongs to the Crown. Should the parents of swans bear different marks, the half of cygnets are given to one guild and the rest to the other. An odd number of newborns means that the last bird follows the father's mark.

England

Olney (Buckinghamshire)

PANCAKE RACE

Held annually, Shrove Tuesday, movable date
Traditional, folkloric, competition

The Pancake Race is traced back to pre-Reformation days when everyone went to the priest to confession for absolution on Shrove Tuesday, the day before Ash Wednesday and the start of Lent. Housewives used any excess butter and eggs to make pancakes, a way of preserving perishable food before the Lenten fast. The beginning and end of Shrove Tuesday was marked by the ringing of a bell, called the pancake bell. It is still rung today to mark the start of the pancake race, a survivor from those ancient Shrove Tuesday events. For a certain time only women who lived in Olney were eligible to enter the race. They had to wear a skirt and apron and either a scarf or hat. Contestants are still required to run from their homes with the pancake hot, tossing it once at the official starting point, and again at the start of the 400-yard course to the church and third time at the church. Surviving pancakes are given to the bell ringer, who in turn kisses the winners. The first to deliver a pancake is declared champion. The race is always run before noon, and thousands come to watch. Contestants take the race seriously, but onlookers think it's funny. Many of the contestants have been competing for years. The origin of the race goes back more than 500 years. At the same time, there is a similar race in Liberal, Kansas, U.S.A. It is patterned after the Olney one and is run simultaneously. There is much rivalry between the two cities.

England

Stratford-upon-Avon (Warwickshire)

ROYAL SHAKESPEARE COMPANY/ SHAKESPEARE FESTIVAL

Held annually, April/December
Cultural, drama

The Royal Shakespeare Company or Shakespeare Festival is said to be the longest festival in the world. It offers a selection of Shakespeare's plays in repertory performed by the finest actors in Great Britain. Over the years, all of Shakespeare's works, including *Pericles*, which is not in the First Folio, have been performed. An early ancestor of the festival was one set up by actor-manager David Garrick. It died with Garrick in 1616. But this led Charles Flower to establish another festival in 1864, the basis for today's event. The first Shakespeare Memorial Theatre opened in 1879. It burned down in 1926. The name of the rebuilt theater became Royal Shakespeare Theatre in 1961. It became the first state-subsidized theater in England and the first permanent company in Stratford. Prior to this, famous stars and directors were in the festival. Today, the theater offers in repertory five or more Shakespearean plays and even a non-Shakespearean one. The Royal Shakespeare Company also performs at London's Aldwych Theatre, July through March, in a varied drama program.

England

York (Yorkshire)

YORK FESTIVAL AND MYSTERY PLAYS

Held once every three years, June/July; next: 1987, 1990
Cultural, religious

The York Festival and Mystery Plays began in 1350, produced by the medieval craft guilds on Corpus Christi Day until 1570. Today, the event, revived in 1951 as part of the Festival of Britain, is a triennial event, always held from mid-June through early July. York, a medieval city whose center is surrounded by ancient walls, provides a setting for the plays in the garden of the Abbey of St. Mary. The plays are reenactments of dramas that recount the story of mankind from the Creation to the Last Judgment. Today's plays have been adapted by Canon S. J. Purvis, without losing their effect. Performances are nightly, except Mondays. There is one play that is not featured in the garden but given in medieval style on a wagon in the city streets, daily, except Sundays and Mondays. The festival always opens on a Friday with a special ceremony and performance of sacred music by the minister choir. In addition to the mystery plays, there is also a festival of music and the arts. The music phase ranges from classical to modern, with well-known orchestras performing.

There are evening piano and violin recitals and chamber concerts in the guild hall with other concerts in historic homes. There are art exhibits and sometimes opera performances.

Isle of Wight

Cowes

REGATTA WEEK

Held annually, July/August
Sports, competition

Regatta Week is a yachting race sponsored and organized by the Royal Yacht Club, the only one to fly the White Ensign. This particular regatta goes back to 1812 with the founding of the Royal Yacht Squadron, known for the first eight years as the Cowes Yacht Club. It was given royal patronage in 1820, and since then a member of the royal family either gives out trophies to winners or actually races. The first monarch to present a trophy was William IV in 1834, and King George V was an active yachtsman. More recently, the Duke of Edinburgh has kept up the royal tradition of sailing in the yachting races.

Jersey, Channel Islands

St. Helier

BATTLE OF FLOWERS

Held annually, second Thursday in August
Floral, pageantry, historic

The Battle of Flowers is an annual one-day event centering around flowers, millions of blossoms. All the flowers are grown without charge for this battle.

It begins with a parade of floral floats and coaches, many decorated with flowers. The floats have a flower-covered working windmill and even floral peacocks. All are quite imaginative in their use of flowers. One float is for Miss Jersey, who often rises from a sea of blooms, while other floats recall the island's history, including the 1871 Battle of Jersey. After the parade, there is actually a battle of flowers, with participants belting each other with blossoms. More than 100,000 come for the event. It was formerly held the last Thursday in July but changed to the second Thursday in August. The Battle of Flowers dates back to when it was first staged as part of the coronation celebrations for King Edward VII and Queen Alexandra in 1902.

Scotland

Edinburgh (Lothian)

EDINBURGH FESTIVAL

Held annually, August/September
Cultural

Edinburgh Festival has become one of the most important musical and dramatic events in Scotland and in Great Britain within a short time. The first one, held in 1947, was designed to bring the "pleasure of listening to and seeing great works performed by great artists" to the local citizens, according to John Falconer, then lord provost of Scotland. The idea for the international festival came from the directors of the Glyndebourne Festival Opera, Rudolf Bing and Harvey Wood of the British Council, with the hope of staging a festival of arts in Britain to promote international good will. With the cooperation of John Falconer, the festival began. It was financed through contributions from many people, firms and the Edinburgh Corporation. Basically the festival programs include opera, drama, orchestral concerts, chamber concerts, recitals and art exhibits. Performances are citywide at concert halls and theaters. The Scottish National Orchestra officially opened the 1965 festival and continues to do. Today, it is considered to be one of Europe's most varied festivals. In 1982, the accent was Italian. The festival began with Verdi's *Requiem* with the London Symphony Orchestra conducted by Claudio Abbado. The 1982 festival theme was "Exploring the Influences of Italy and Italians on European Culture." The festival includes 150 performances given under the sponsorship of the Festival Society. It has proven to be economically successful, too. It is estimated that to date more than 6 million people have attended. The festival also has a military Tattoo, an evening performance on the esplanade of Edinburgh Castle. In 1965, the tattoo was performed by soldiers from the Pacific island of Fiji. The dance, song and regimental band music was impressive. The tattoo is also performed by Scottish regiments, who march across the area to the wail of bagpipes. There is highland dancing by men of the Highland Brigade and the Lowland Brigade. Added later to the festival was the International Film Festival, with entries from 40 countries offering more than 200 films. An outgrowth of the Edinburgh Festival but not sanctioned by the official Festival Society is the "Fringe Festival," which goes all out for all kinds of drama, especially experimental. Performances are given in smaller theaters, schools and halls. Some productions make it to the London stage. The official Edinburgh Festival operates with a budget in excess of $1 million. It is financed by the city of Edinburgh, the Scottish Arts Council and private donations. Half of the festival's income is derived from box-office receipts.

Wales

North and South Wales

ROYAL NATIONAL EISTEDDFOD

Held annually, August
Cultural, competition

The Royal National Eisteddfod is a week-long festival of choir singing, harp playing, trumpet playing and poetry reading that alternates in site between North and South Wales. It has been held annually since 1176, when one of the Welsh princes, Lord Rhys ap Gruffydd (Reece, son of Griffith) launched it in Cardigan, South Wales. At this festival, musicians and men of letters competed against each other for valuable prizes. The festival is basically the same today. About 200,000 attend each year. Main events include the Tuesday crowning of the Bard ceremony and the Chairing of the Bard, usually on a Thursday, a formal welcome on Friday to Welshmen who've returned from overseas for this event, and Saturday is for choral music. The Eisteddfod is devoted to Welsh culture with competitions in drama, poetry, music, arts and crafts. Welsh dramas are performed to try to win a special medal. "Eisteddfod" once meant a meeting of the bards to discuss their art and the rules of their society. Over the centuries, its meaning changed from consultation to competition. The chair poem must still be written according to the same metrical rules, an unbroken five-century tradition. The first Eisteddfod that took on a modern look was held in 1451 at Carmarthen, when Queen Elizabeth I made a royal proclamation to regulate the "conventions" of bards, musicians and singers. By the end of the eighteenth century, the Eisteddfod changed to what it still is today. This is entirely a Welsh event, and there is no attempt to seek out the participation of other countries. The festival is also a homecoming for Welshmen who live in other parts of the world. They do return for this annual event. During the modern Eisteddfod, the

Druids are in the limelight, with the Arch Druid in a flowing gown and supported by the elders of the orders, who take the lead part in the festival ceremonies. The site for the festival is selected two years in advance by the Royal Eisteddfod Committee.

Wales

Llangollen (Denbighshire)

INTERNATIONAL MUSICAL EISTEDDFOD

Held annually, July
Cultural, competition

The International Musical Eisteddfod was started in 1946 to unite the world through music and dancing. The festival's motto is "Happy is a world that sings, gentle are its songs." The international competition attracts about 10,000 entries who compete before audiences of more than 180,000. Once the contestants arrive in Great Britain, the festival organizers accommodate them free of charge. Contestants perform in their national costumes. Opening day is marked by performances of a well-known group or professional opera company. The second day's sessions are usually for folk singers and dancers from as many as 30 different countries. The rest of the event features choral and instrumental competitions with evening concerts by visiting choirs. The last concert on a Sunday is a choral and orchestral program. Season tickets are available and entitle the buyer to the same seat for all performances. If only certain concert tickets are wanted, they have to be reserved in advance. The festival's official program is always printed in June so that festival fans will know the events ahead of time.

GREECE

Athens

ATHENS FESTIVAL

Held annually, June/September
Cultural

The Athens Festival was established in 1955 by the Greek government and handled by the Greek National Tourist Organization to promote ancient Greek drama and make Athens an international center of the arts. Originally, the festival was held July through September, but because of its popularity it was changed to June through September. World famous performers appear at the 5,000-seat open-air Herod Atticus Amphitheater, built in A.D. 161, at the foot of the Acropolis. Featured are programs of orchestral and chamber music, classical and popular theater, grand opera and modern dance. In 1982 there were performances by the Paris Symphony Orchestra, Ballet of the Opera of Paris, English Bach Festival, Hungary State Orchestra, Royal Winnipeg Ballet of Canada, Bolshoi Opera and twentieth-century ballet of Maurice Besar. Ancient Greek drama is presented by the National Theater and Opera, the State Theater of Northern Greece and the State Orchestra was well as by various independent companies like the Theater of Piraeus and the Art Theater of Athens. The festival is financed through government grants and admission fees. Tickets are a definite must for this event, which has already played to an audience of several million over the years.

Epidaurus

EPIDAURUS FESTIVAL

Held annually June/August
Cultural

The Epidaurus Festival offers weekend theater productions of ancient Greek tragedy and comedy, with summaries of the plays in English. They are produced annually by the National Theater of Greece, the Northern Greece State Theater and Art Theater. Performances are in the 14,000-seat third century B.C. Theater of Epidaurus, located in the northern part of the Peloponnese. In 1982, the National Theatre of England opened the festival with Aeschylus' trilogy, *Oresteia*. The festival goes back to ancient days, when productions were given once every four years. People went there to be healed by Asclepius, the god of healing, Epidaurus was the ancient sanctuary of this god, born of Apollo and a Boetian princess. The festival was held to honor the god with games, musical competitions and theatrical performances. Modern productions started in 1954, and a year later the festival was on its way. Now it is an annual event, always held in summer to attract tourists. About 90,000 come every year, and more than a million since the first modern event in 1955. Famous Greek performers and the ancient Greek plays are still a vital part of the festival, which is handled by a paid staff. It is financed by grants from the Greek government and by ticket sales.

Rethymon (Crete)

WINE FESTIVAL

Held annually, July
Economic, folkloric, wine

The Wine Festival goes back to antiquity, when it was a religious tribute to Dionysus, god of wine. Today's two-week celebration features free wine, visiting dance groups and *bouzouki* music. For a small entrance fee (which changes yearly), visitors can stroll around the wine exhibit grounds to sample local wines and ouzo, a strong licorice-flavored liqueur made from the distilled residue of grapes left over after the wine is made. About 3,000 tourists came for the event, and over the years, the number could be staggering. It is economically beneficial to the area. Work on the festival is by a paid staff of local merchants and members of the Greek National Tourist Organization. It is financed through local sponsorships and government grants.

Thessaloniki

FESTIVAL OF DEMETRIA

Held annually, October
Cultural

The Festival of Demetria is one of Byzantine music and dance honoring St. Demetrius, the city's patron saint. Originally it was part of the International Trade Fair and a revival of the Demetria fair held in the twelfth century. It changed and in 1966 became the Festival of Demetria, following the International Trade Fair. It offers opera, ballet, concerts and performances of ancient Greek tragedies with both Greek and foreign drama companies. About 5,000 attend annually. Work on the festival is done by paid actors and some church volunteers. It is supported by government subsidies and ticket sales. Performances are in the Theater of the Society of Macedonian Studies on the waterfront.

Thessaloniki

INTERNATIONAL TRADE FAIR, FILM AND SONG FESTIVAL

Held annually, September/October
Economic, cultural, fair

The International Trade Fair, Film and Song Festival dates back to 1935, when it began for both economic and cultural reasons. The fair helped to promote international trade, especially with the underdeveloped Balkan countries. The international film festival runs concurrently with the fair and is a competition. The song festival, which also includes drama, was made part of the fair to revive the city's Byzantine religious and artistic traditions, with both Greek and foreign performers. The fair features all kinds of international, industrial, commercial and agricultural exhibits and displays. The Festival of Greek Light Song is held at the Palais des Sports, and the film competition in the Theater of the Association of Macedonian Studies. All are well attended. Over the years, the number of film entries and theater productions has increased in direct response to visitor demands. It is estimated that more than 40 million have attended since the fair's beginning. It is financed by government grants and donations from private industry and individuals. There are also admission fees.

GUADELOUPE (FRENCH WEST INDIES)

Pointe-a-Pitre

COOKS' FESTIVAL

Held annually, Saturday nearest August 10
Folkloric, food

Fete des Cuisinieres, or Cooks' Festival, is a one-day event that centers around the cooking and cooks of Guadeloupe. It is always held the Saturday nearest August 10, the Feast of St. Laurent, patron saint of cooks. Festivities start on a solemn note with attendance at a 10 a.m. high mass in the Cathedral des Sts. Pierre et Paul and the blessing of the food that will be part of the free five-hour banquet to follow later in the day. A very animated parade follows through the streets of downtown Pointe-a-Pitre. The ladies are dressed in Creole costumes with headdresses decorated with miniature cooking utensils. They march to the beat of the *beguine*, a music born in the French West Indies. They laugh, talk, gossip, and sing, often toppling the statue of St. Laurent that accompanies them. After the parade, the ladies (about 100, and many owners of small island restaurants) begin to prepare a marathon meal behind the doors of the local Palais de la Mutualite. When the doors open later in the afternoon, all residents and visitors are greeted with rum drinks and invited to enjoy the five-hour gourmet meal. St. Laurent sits at the main table decorated with tons of flowers, platters of seafood, spicy sausages, grilled clams, rabbits marinated in wine, loaves of fish, (fish fashioned in loaves of bread) and a large selection of marvelous desserts. The hall only holds 500 people, and it's always full. The meal is served to a continuous stream of people coming in and out for the five hours, which means that about 2,500 people sample the feast. The entire event is financed by the ladies, who donate the food and their cooking talents.

HONG KONG

HONG KONG ARTS FESTIVAL

Held annually, January/February
Cultural

The Hong Kong Arts Festival was founded in 1973 by its continuing sponsors, the Hong Kong Arts Festival Society, Ltd., the Urban Council and the government of Hong Kong. Its purpose continues to be to inspire and aid locally talented artists and to be a showcase for local and international performing arts. The festival is highly successful, culturally and economically, since it attracts thousands of visitors. It is a top performing arts event in Asia.

In 1982, the festival marked its tenth anniversary with performances by the Cleveland Orchestra from the United States, Verdi's *Macbeth* with singers Peter Glossop and Margaret Kingsley. Shakespeare was the inspiration behind several festival events, including *The Taming of the Shrew*, which ran for six days. Judi Dench and Michael Williams recited Shakespearean verse. Other anniversary highlights included the London Festival Ballet, the Gabrieli String Quartet, the Cambridge Theatre Company and the Philippe Gentry Puppet Company, who all made their first appearance in Hong Kong. A special appearance was made by Maxim Shostakovich as conductor and Dmitri Shostakovich as soloists with the Hong Kong Philharmonic Orchestra. Another first in 1982 was the addition of a children's festival within the framework of the festival with a variety of programs. The festival always offers music, opera, film, theater, dance, art exhibitions and performances by Chiuchow and Cantonese operas and Chinese puppets, and storytelling sessions. Performances are in the Hong Kong City Hall, the Hong Kong Arts Centre, the Tsuen Wan Town Hall and the Yuen Long Town Hall. During the month-long event there are fringe events organized by the Urban Council to include many free outdoor programs at the Hong Kong Central Statue Square, parks and playgrounds. The festival is financed through some ticket sales in addition to subsidies from the Urban Council and Hong Kong government.

CHEUNG CHAU FESTIVAL

Held annually, May
Religious, folkloric

The Cheung Chau Festival or Festival of the Bun Hills is a four-day religious event celebrated for centuries and always in May to appease some angry spirits doing damage to the island of Cheung Chau because their graves were disturbed. Legend says that an old Taoist priest told the island people to prepare buns to satisfy the spirits. Apparently it worked, and local citizens have been holding a Bun Festival every year. Today, the event is marked by religious rites and processions plus Chinese opera programs and parades. Three large statues of gods are the festival theme, but the climax is the third day parade of residents, dressed either like a historical or legendary figure, walking on stilts or riding on a parade float. There's a children's tableau with each child suspended from wires attached to a harness hidden under their clothing. The children seem to float in the air. The festival takes its name from the giant cone-shaped bun hills, each more than 60 feet high and decorated with steaming buns. The gigantic bun hills are constructed on a playground near the Pak Tin Temple. The festival ends the fourth day at midnight with the scrambling by hundreds of people to the top of the bun hills to collect from the top as many buns as possible. The more collected, the more luck for that person for the rest of the year. The event attracts thousands of tourists, who also join in the scramble for the good luck buns. The actual festival dates are not officially announced until three weeks before.

DRAGON BOAT FESTIVAL

Held annually, May or June, movable date
Folkloric, sports, competition

The Dragon Boat Festival (Tuen'ng) is a major event that marks the death of a national hero, Chu Yuan, who drowned himself in protest against a corrupt government in power, 403-221 B.C. The date, based on the lunar calendar, varies from late May to June, usually coming between May 28 and June 28. According to the lunar calendar, the event falls on the fifth day of the fifth moon. When Chu Yuan threw himself into the Milo River in Hunan Province, the local people tried to save him. Many took out their dragon boats, racing to the spot, but all in vain. Peasants threw cooked rice into the water to keep the fish from eating his body and to comfort his spirit. They wrapped the rice in bamboo leaves, and this started a custom. Today, the event is commemorated with dragon boat races and the eating of rice dumplings, wrapped in bamboo leaves. In Hong Kong, International Dragon Boat Races are held during the festival, with participants from Hong Kong, Malaysia, Singapore, Macao and Japan. The competition was started in 1976, and the first international one in 1978. More than 300 rowers competed, and thousands came to watch. The first event was held along the East Tsimshatsui waterfront. Now it is held at the Wanchai waterfront across the harbor. In 1981, 80 teams and more than 2,000 rowers participated in 21 races and 9 separate championship races. Three "Row for Charity" races raised $100,000. The rest of the year, the dragon boats are not used. The Dragon God is ceremoniously sent back to heaven at the end of the festival. In the twelfth moon, the boats are brought out for repairs. Before racing practice can begin, a ceremony is performed at the temple of Tin Hau, Goddess of Fishermen. The eyes of the dragon are dotted to symbolize rebirth. The International Dragon Boat Races were organized by the Hong Kong Tourist Association and the Urban Council to attract more tourists to the area and to place more emphasis on the holiday with other Asian countries. The races are financed through entry fees and subsidies from the Urban Council and Hong Kong government. Any profits realized are donated to charity.

FESTIVAL OF ASIAN ARTS

Held annually, October
Cultural

The Festival of Asian Arts is a fairly new visual and performing arts event. The first one was held in November 1976, and the following year it was held the last two weeks in October. The festival is still held the last two weeks in October and is a festival concerned solely with Asian theater, music, dance, folk music, arts and crafts. In 1981, there were traditional performers from 16 Asian countries, which included for the first time Pakistan and Papua New Guinea. A record crowd of 274,000 attended. The 1981 festival programs featured a folk drama from Papua New Guinea, a historic saga from Sri Lanka (Ceylon), a traditional Pansori play from Korea and a sword-play epic by the Hong Kong Repertory Company. As to dance events, there was a pop ballet based on the Ramayana from the Philippines and a new interpretation of the Life of Buddha presented by India's Kalakshetra. There was a Japanese Kabuki dance performance, dancers from Nepal and Bangladesh, the traditional dance-dramas from Thailand, Malaysia and Indonesia and contemporary ballet from Turkey, Australia and Hong Kong. Traditional Chinese instruments, like the *erhu* and the *pipa*, were used by a chamber ensemble from the Hong Kong Chinese Orchestra. Chinese opera with the Guangdong Opera Academy offered some famous Cantonese operas. Additionally there were lectures on traditional folk arts and crafts from Malaysia and other countries. Each year the festival adds to the number of performances and events to accommodate its growing popularity. Performances are held at City Hall, the Arts Centre, the Space Museum lecture hall and the new Queen Elizabeth Stadium (opened in 1981) and in five outdoor parks and playgrounds. Art exhibitions are held in the galleries of City Hall and the Museum of History. In 1981 there were four special exhibits of contemporary paintings, sculpture, calligraphy and prints by Hong Kong artists with modern works from Bangladesh. The festival is financed through some ticket sales (some events are free), donations from the participating countries and subsidies from the Urban Council and Hong Kong government.

HUNGARY

Debrecen

NATIONAL FLORAL CARNIVAL

Held annually, August 20
Folkloric, economic, fair

The National Floral Carnival, although based on traditional fruit and harvest festivals, only goes back to 1968. Its revival was to perpetuate old folkloric customs and to promote the sale of flowers. It features an exhibition of all European cultivated flowers, a parade with floral floats and a flower arrangement competition. There are various displays of fruits as well as flowers. Over the years, more and more exhibits have been added to the one-day event, always held August 20, St. Stephen's Day, a Hungarian saint and king. It is also Constitution Day and a traditional harvest festival day, celebrated by baking the first bread from the newly harvested wheat. The carnival attracts more than 10,000 people, many foreign visitors. To date a grand total of 140,000 have attended. The most popular events include folk dance performances and the parade of floral floats. Work on the carnival is by professional and amateur gardeners. The flowers are donated by the growers. The event is financed by funds from the regional council. There is no admission charge to the carnival.

ICELAND

Reykjavik

REYKJAVIK ARTS FESTIVAL

Held biennially, even-numbered years, June; next: 1986, 1988
Cultural

The Reykjavik Arts Festival, first held in June 1970, was called the North Atlantic Festival. Two men were responsible for the event, which has grown into a top arts festival, attracting more than 16,000 every other year. The famous pianist Vladimir Ashkenazy (still active in the festival) and Ivar Eskeland, former director of the Nordic House in Reykjavik, founded the festival. Ashkenazy wanted an international art festival, while Eskeland wanted a Nordic arts festival. Both ideas were incorporated, and the first festival was held in 1970 and a second one in 1972. It attracted not only local people but also tourists, and it continues to do so. The 1972 festival featured violinist Yehudi Menuhin, Ashkenazy (he's now an Icelandic citizen), Andre Watts, conductor Andre Previn and singer John Shirley-Quirk. Highlights of the 1982 16-day festival were *The Silken Drum*, an opera by Atli Heimir Sveinsson to a libretto by Ornolfur Arnason, and *Edda-Oratorium*, by Jon Leifs. Performers included violinist Gidon Kremer, flutist James Galway, pianist Zoltan Kocsis, bass Boris Christoff and the London Sinfonietta. The arts festival offers performing and visual arts throughout the city. There's music, opera, ballet, theater and art exhibits. By 1974, the third festival, there were 8 art exhibits, 15 drama performances and 24 concerts. It continues to grow and is now international in scope. It is financed through ticket sales and by the Icelandic Ministry of Culture and Education and city of Reykjavik subsidies.

Skagafjordur

ICELAND NATIONAL HORSE MEET SHOW AND RACES

Held once every four years in July, next: 1986
Sports, competition

The Iceland National Horse Meet Show and Races is held at Vindheimamelar in Skagafjordur, about an hour's drive from Reykjavik, the country's capital city. About 600 horses participate in the show. It is held once every four years and always in July. The country's best breeding horses are shown and judged, some with their offspring. The best riding horses are also shown by Icelandic riding clubs. The best racing horses compete in five distinctive gaits: walk, trot, gallop, pace and tolt (a glide-like gait). There are seven races: 250-meter pace, 250-, 350- and 800-meter gallop, 1,500-meter trot, a 200-meter running walk and a pace race for the champions. The four-day show also features a horse market, with horses exhibited and information on each one made available. In the evening, young riders perform varied equestrian acrobatics. The event is financed through entry fees, ticket sales and donations from the breeding farms and riding clubs.

INDIA

Nationwide

FESTIVAL OF LIGHTS

Held annually, October/November, movable date
Religious, New Year celebration

Diwali, or Festival of Lights, is a happy event celebrated all over India. Every village, town and city is lighted by thousands of oil lamps, and electric lights illuminate homes and public buildings. The holiday marks Rama's return from exile, and in some parts of India Diwali marks the start of the Hindu New Year. On the night of the one-day festival, most of India honors Lakshmi, the goddess of prosperity. Eastern India, especially Bengal, worships Kali, the goddess of strength. Statues of Kali are dipped in the river as a sign of respect.

Delhi, Mysore, Kulu, Calcutta

DUSSEHRA/DASEHARA

Held annually, September/October
Folkloric, cultural, legendary

Dussehra or Dasehara is a ten-day festival of plays and music honoring a legendary hero, Rama. It recalls the epic story of the Ramayana and the victory of good over evil. Each region of India celebrates the event differently. In northern India the story is retold in special plays and dance dramas, Ramlila, recalling Rama's heroic deeds. The celebration is considered best in Delhi, where amateur groups produce and act in plays based on the epic story. After nine days of celebrating there's an elaborate procession to the Ramlila grounds, where large fireworks are stuffed into demon effigies and shot by Lord Rama with an arrow. This ignites the effigies, setting off explosions and destroying the evil ones. In the mountains of Kulu, villagers dress up in their best clothes for a week-long dance festival. They also hold processions of local gods and a parade to the accompaniment of pipe and drum music. There is also a community fair. In Mysore, the festival becomes a pageant with the entire city decorated with lights, buntings and arches. In Bengal and the rest of eastern India, it is celebrated as Durga Puja with community music, dancing and drama. On the last day, statues of the warrior-gods are paraded and then immersed in local waters. In the south, the name of the same festival changes to Navaratri, with dolls and possessions arranged and exhibited in tiers by the young girls of the area. Friends and relatives visit each other's homes to exchange greetings.

Delhi Union Territory

New Delhi

REPUBLIC DAY

Held annually, January 26
Patriotic

Republic Day is India's national festival with military parades in all state capitals at which each governor takes the salute. The most spectacular observance, however, is in New Delhi, where there is an impressive parade of the armed forces and civilians, with the president of India taking the salute. The national day is followed by two folk dance festival performances, January 27 and 28, with more than 20 folk and tribal dance groups from all over India participating. Republic Day has been celebrated since 1953, when the Republic of India was established.

Kerala State

Aranmula, Champ Akulam, Kottaya

ONAM

Held annually, August/September, movable date
Harvest, folkloric

Onam is a four-day harvest festival in a very tropical area of India. According to legend, Onam is celebrated to assure good King Mahabali that his subjects are all well and happy. It is highlighted by special feasts, folk dancing and boat races, which are the most exciting part of the festival. Huge black boats with thin high sterns are manned by crews of 60 to 100 men, who compete in the snake boat race in the lagoons of each town. These crews train for several months before the rigorous race. There is also the Vallomkali musical boat race at both Aranmula and Kottaya. Festival events continue into the evening, ending with Nair girls performing a clapping dance around a traditional brass lamp set on the flower-strewn grass.

Rajasthan

Pushkar

PUSHKAR FAIR

Held annually, November
Economic, fair

The Pushkar Fair is held annually on the banks of Pushkar Lake, where the god Brahma is worshipped in a living shrine. The fair attracts thousands of peasants, who gather to buy and sell livestock, mostly camels and horses. Others come to watch the sales, camel races and games of skill, all part of the fair. The camel races are held in a large arena, and the riders on the decorated camels show great speed and skill in moving the animals. Sometimes the riders will perform in a musical chairs presentation of the camels, to the enjoyment of the crowds. Prizes are awarded to the top riders.

INDONESIA

Bali

BALINESE NEW YEAR

Held once every 210 days
Folkloric, New Year celebration

The Balinese New Year is celebrated every 210 days and is an important time in Bali, since it marks the arrival of ancestral spirits who live for five days before and after Galungan in the local descendant's homes. Galungan is for rejoicing, and that can include *legong*, a dance mime by either two or three beautifully costumed young women. It can also include a *baris*, or warriors' dance, performed by very agile middle-aged males. There is a solo dance, *kebyar*, performed by a seated male whose facial expressions and torso and arm movements match the changing music. Also part of the celebrations are the *topeng* performances by masked actors doing historical plays in pantomime. The dialogue is spoken by comic characters wearing halfmasks. These performances are given in the afternoon. Another masked performance, dealing with Ramayana stories, is by *wayang wong*, singers and dancers whose style is like that of shadow puppets.

Jogjakarta (Java-Yogyakarta District)

RAMAYANA DANCE FESTIVAL

Held annually, May/October
Folkloric, religious, cultural

The Ramayana Dance Festival is staged beside an impressive twelfth-century Hindu temple in the village of Prambanan, about a half-hour drive from Jogjakarta. The theme of the festival is taken from the epic story of Rama, dating back to 300 years before the birth of Christ. More than 100 richly costumed players and dancers reenact the epic through traditional dances to the accompaniment of a large gamelan orchestra and to the beat of native bamboo instruments. The dance dramas deal with the adventures of Rama and his wife, Sita, including their encounters with giants, dragons, godlike foes and allies. There is the abduction of Sita and later her rescue by Rama, who allied himself with one of the best in all folklore, the monkey general, Hanuman. The festival of today was started over ten years ago to enable visitors to understand and appreciate it. The Ramayana Ballet is the classical dance drama of the court, in which the dancers perform like shadow puppets. The festival has eliminated some of the subplots of the epic to include more dancing, music and beautiful costumes. The festival is presented on four consecutive nights of each month during the full moon and covers the complete story. If the rainy season should come early, the October performances are canceled. All performances are from 7 to 9 p.m.

IRELAND

Dublin (County Dublin)

DUBLIN HORSE SHOW

Held annually, August
Sports, competition

The Dublin Horse Show is one of the top social and sporting events of the year in Ireland, attracting up to 200,000 spectators from all over the world. More than 2,000 horses, the best of Ireland's bloodstock, are entered in the six-day show, sponsored by the Royal Dublin Society. There are daily jumping competitions, with the chief event being the International Teams Jumping Competition for the Aga Khan Trophy, the Nations Cup and the Grand Prix. All events are held at Ballsbridge. There are both military and civilian jumping events and a grand parade of prize-winning horses and ponies. The auction sale of horse and ponies in the bloodstock paddock attracts hundreds of worldwide buyers. Army bands give daily concerts. Reserved seats are available for the whole show or on a daily basis.

Galway (County Connemara)

GALWAY OYSTER FESTIVAL

Held annually, September
Economic, fish, competition

The Galway Oyster Festival always marks the start of the oyster season in the area with the ceremonial opening of the first oyster of the season, oyster banquets and an International Oyster-Opening Competition. It was started in 1954 by the local chamber of commerce and industry to call attention to the local oyster fisheries of Galway Bay and to attract tourists. It began as a ten-day event but now is held for four days in mid-September. There is a sea angling competition, a pageant complete with Neptunia and her court, ballad singing, dancing and other events. Several thousand attend the event. It is financed by contributions from the oyster fisheries and subsidized by the chamber of commerce and industry. There are admission charges for the banquets and entry fees for the competitions.

Tralee (County Kerry)

THE ROSE OF TRALEE INTERNATIONAL FESTIVAL

Held annually, August/September
Cultural, folkloric

The Rose of Tralee International Festival is host to about 150,000 visitors. It was originally started in 1959 to get all Kerrymen to come home for a visit, a homecoming celebration. The six-day festival began to attract other national groups, adding a new dimension to the celebrations. It still is a showcase for Irish culture. Free Irish folk songs and dance performances are given, and the National Folk Theatre of Ireland also participates. Festival highlight is the selection of the Rose of Tralee, the festival queen for the year. She is always Irish but not necessarily born in Ireland. The crowning takes place at a nearby racetrack to handle the large attending crowds. The entire town is decorated with thousands of rosebuds donated by Irish and European rose growers. There are 20-foot-high heraldic pennants with the crests of historic Kerry clans on view. At dusk, 35,000 multicolored lights brighten Tralee. The event is financed through private donations and admission charges.

Wexford (County Wexford)

WEXFORD FESTIVAL OPERA

Held annually, October
Cultural

The Wexford Festival Opera is known for productions of rare or seldom heard operas, since the first festival in 1951. It has developed into a musical festival of local and worldwide importance, attracting internationally famous performers and thousands of visitors. While the focus is on opera, there are other performing arts, such as drama, band concerts, chamber music, recitals, choral concerts and traditional song and dance performances. There are also fringe events like a mumming performance, a hurling match, late night revues and a festival ball.

In 1982, the 12-day festival presented three operas. One was *La Liggenda di Sakuntala* by Franco Alfano, the composer who completed Puccini's *Turandot*. His opera was destroyed in World War II and rescored two years before the composer's death in 1954. Haydn's *The Desert Island*, shortest of six operas, written between 1777 and 1784, was performed, as was Massenet's *Griselidis*, based on Bocaccio's *Decameron*. The event is financed through ticket sales and private donations and sponsorships.

ISRAEL

Caesarea, Haifa, Jerusalem, Tel Aviv

ISRAEL FESTIVAL

Held annually, September, sometimes May/June
Cultural

The Israel Festival began in 1961 as an international event of music, opera, dance and theater. As it continued, it became an all-Israel festival of native arts and culture. However, guest conductors and performers from other countries do appear from time to time. The three-week festival presents symphony and choral concerts, recitals, opera, ballet and modern dance, theater, jazz, folklore, films and exhibitions pertaining to visual and performing arts. In the past the festival has always been held in July and August, but in 1982 it was changed to September, just prior to the observance of the Jewish New Year, Rosh Hashanah.

Performances are held in a Roman amphitheater in Caesarea and in concert halls and other sites in the other cities. The Israel Philharmonic Orchestra usually performs in Tel Aviv and Jerusalem with guest conductors like Zubin Mehta and Leonard Bernstein. In 1976, when Zubin Mehta conducted an outdoor concert at City Hall Square in Tel Aviv, 30,000 people crowded into the square. Israeli dance groups that participate in the festival program include the Inbal Dance Theater devoted to the Yemenite idiom in its dance performances. The Batsheva Dance Company is on the contemporary level and patterned after the Martha Graham School, and there's the Bat-Dor Company, offering a mixture of the classical and modern in dance. Over the years, the festival has attracted thousands of people to see famous dancers like Rudolf Nureyev and Merce Cunningham and to hear Pablo Casals and Isaac Stern perform. The festival is a member of the European Association of Music Festivals. It is financed through ticket sales, private donations and government aid.

Jerusalem

SPRING IN JERUSALEM FESTIVAL

Held annually, April/May
Cultural, patriotic

Spring in Jerusalem Festival is a twofold event. It celebrates Jerusalem Reunification Day on May 12 and is a cultural event with music, dance and theater with both Israeli and foreign companies and performers. It was started in 1975 as a joint venture of the Jerusalem Theater, the city of Jerusalem and the Israel Festival. Orchestral and chamber music concerts are given in local theaters and concert halls, and there are also street performances of folkloric songs and dances. The Jewish Quarter in the Old City is also a focal point for patriotic and religious ceremonies, street fairs and the rededication of the Quarter. Foreign theater companies that have appeared at this annual event include the Royal Shakespeare Company of Great Britain, the Club Teatro di Roma of Italy and the Arlequin Puppet Theater of Austria. The month-long event is financed through some ticket sales, private donations and help from the city, Jerusalem Theater and the Israel Festival.

ITALY

Florence (Tuscany)

MAGGIO MUSICALE FLORENCE/ FLORENTINE MUSICAL MAY

Held annually, May/July
Cultural

The Maggio Musicale or Florentine Musical May marked its forty-fifth year in 1982. It offers opera, ballet, chamber music, choral and orchestral concert programs. In 1982, the two-month festival honored Stravinsky with performances of *The Rake's Progress*, *Le Rossignol*, and *Le Baiser de la fee*. There were world premieres of Salvatore Sciarrino's *Macbeth* (conducted by the composer) and Romano Pezzati's *The Dreamer*.

Also performed was Prokofiev's *Marriage at the Monastery*, Leonardo Vinci's *Li Zite 'n Galera* (composed in 1772) and a new choreographic work, *Aboriginals*, by Kiri Kylian and performed by the Netherlands Dance Theater to music by Berio, Nordheim and Takemitsu. The two operas, *Macbeth* and *Li Zite 'n Galera*, were also given at the Edinburgh Festival when the Maggio Musicale Company made its debut in Scotland later in the summer. Among famous participants were Zubin Mehta, Riccardo Murti, Hans Werner Henze, Karl Kleiber, Emil Gilels, Jessye Norman, the Yuval Trio and the London Sinfonietta. The festival commissions new opera and dance productions each year, using funds of almost a million dollars given them by the Ministry of Culture. Performances are in theaters and public buildings throughout the city.

Milan (Lombardy)

MILAN TRADE FAIR

Held annually, April
Economic, fair

The Milan Trade Fair dates back to 1920 and was started for economic reasons to show off Italian products and to act as an exchange for other countries to display their products. Milan was selected because of its geographical proximity to the rest of Europe. The ten-day fair has attracted hundreds of thousands of people. In 1981, there were 87 official foreign delegations, represented with 25 countries permanently operating in the Fair Quarter with European jurisdiction. The fair is host to 35,000 manufacturers, with 110 countries exhibiting yearly. Twenty-five of them have their own pavilions. Various Italian regions have their own buildings for the textile industry, graphic arts, leathercraft, jewelry, fashions and ceramics. The fair boosts not only Milan's economy but also that of all Italy. It is financed through exhibit fees, admission fees and help from the government.

Nola (Campania)

LILY FESTIVAL

Held annually, Sunday following June 22
Religious, folkloric

The Lily Festival is a one-day religioius–folkloric event honoring San Paolino, the town's patron saint. It is always observed with great pageantry the Sunday following June 22, the date of the saint's death. The festival is an ancient one that began between A.D. 354 and 431 as a spontaneous welcome home to Paolino upon his return from Africa. He had placed himself in slavery to release a local widow's son from bondage. When Paolino returned to Nola, he was greeted by eight tradesmen (respresenting the whole town), who strewed flowers at his feet. Those original greeters included a farmer, grocer, wine merchant, baker, butcher, blacksmith, shoemaker and tailor. As the one-day festival was continued over the years, the original eight tradesmen were represented at the ceremony by lilies, giving the festival its current name. As the celebration continued, it was decided by the townspeople that only one beflowered stick per trade should be allowed. The lily stick grew longer and more ornate. Today, they are from 25 to 30 meters high, and each weighs 50 tons. Each one is carried by 40 men, and each lily, or *giglio*, is heavily decorated. At its base is an entire live orchestra. A traditional blessing is given. The crowd throws flowers in the air, and then the parade or procession begins in the piazza, led by a boat carrying a statue of San Paolino and a Moor, representing the African king who kept the saint prisoner. This is followed by the eight *gigli* and their own orchestras, going through some very narrow streets. The procession takes three hours and returns to its starting point, the piazza. Then each *giglio* group sings and dances. Work on the festival is on a voluntary basis and includes almost the whole town. It is financed through private donations.

Sassari (Sardinia)

SARDINIAN CAVALCADE

Held annually, Ascension Day; May, movable date
Commemorative, historic, procession

The Sardinian Cavalcade is an annual one-day commemorative event recalling the victory of the allied forces of Pisa and Sardinia over the invading Saracens around the year 1000, occurring on the Feast of the Ascension. It is always observed on that day. Some 3,000 people participate in the cavalcade, or procession. Some parade as singles, others as couples or in small groups. All wear beautifully ornate costumes, often decorated with antique gold jewelry and embroidery. Some paraders ride on horses or in carts pulled by oxen and covered with flowers. The cavalcade includes performers of traditional folk dances accompanied by folk instruments. The Ancient Maritime Republics of Pisa, Genoa, Venice and Amalfi are represented by the various costumed people. Folk groups from all over Italy participate. The event helps to keep the historic event alive and promotes the ethnic heritage of Sardinia. There is no charge to watch the parade. It is financed through local donations. The whole city is involved in the event and preparations for it.

Siena (Tuscany)

PALIO OF SIENA

Held annually, July 2, August 16
Historic pageantry, competition, horses

The Palio of Siena is a historic pageant dating back to the Middle Ages, when Siena was an independent republic and was divided into 17 *contrades*, or wards, each with its own church, homes and military armies. Horse races together with ballgames, fist fights, stone throwing and fencing were pastimes for the soldiers then. *Contrade* members centered their activity around the wild horse race, which only lasted a minute but became a bitter competition among *contrade* members. Though the city is part of Italy and no longer an independent republic, the *contrades* are still very much part of the city. On July 2 and August 16, the horse race for the *palio* (banner) is run on both days around the Piazza del Camp, the city's main square. Today there are ten contrades and a horse and rider for each one (they are usually imported from another city, never Sienese) wearing the colors of each *contrade*. Ten priests in ten churches bless the ten horses before the race, in which only the horses are said to be honest. Bribes and skullduggery are all part of the event. The start of the race is exciting. The horses stand betwen two ropes, in the order selected by lot. The tenth chosen horse is the last to come, entering a space left free by the second rope. The starter activates a mechanism and the race is on. Anything goes, and the purpose is to win the race no matter how it's done. There are flag-waving performances by medieval-costumed flag wavers and parades almost as exciting as the race. After the race, which can be dangerous, the jockey, who rides bareback, is honored. Once the race is won, all 100,000 spectators go completely wild with songs, fights and the blessing of the "Rag," the nickname for the *palio*. There are parades, street feasts and folk dancing. There is a charge for chairs and bleachers along the square where the race is held. The event is financed by each ward and private donations.

Spoleto (Umbria)

SPOLETO FESTIVAL/FESTIVAL OF TWO WORLDS

Held annually June/July
Cultural

The Spoleto Festival or Festival of Two Worlds, started in Spoleto by famed opera composer Gian Carlo Menotti in 1958, does embrace two worlds with the opening of its counterpart in Charleston, South Carolina, U.S.A., in 1977. The month-long festival is still designed to give young performers an opportunity to further their talents by appearing with established artists in the same fields. There are about 14 productions each year, half American and half European. There is ballet, modern dance, English and Italian drama, opera, seminars and workshops. Performances are in two opera houses, one large and the other small, local theaters, an ancient Roman amphitheater and some city buildings. Menotti received early financial help from Countess Alicia Paolozzi, a Boston-born socialite. Today, the festival raises about one-third of an annual budget matched by a grant from the Italian government. Another third comes from New York, through the efforts of the Festival Foundation, Inc., a nonprofit organization that aids the festival and gives scholarships to American students and handles American artists who are invited to perform in Spoleto. The town of Spoleto became internationally famous because of the festival, and there are now more restaurants and hotels, showing how it has benefited the area economically. Several hundred thousand attended the performances. Once it attracted only the wealthy, but now it attracts people from all walks of life and all financial backgrounds. Opening night of the festival is always covered by Italian television.

Venice (Venetis)

FEAST OF THE REDEEMER

Held annually, third Sunday in July
Religious, folkloric

The two-day Feast of the Redeemer began soon after 1575 as a religious celebration of thanksgiving by the Venetians for being delivered from an epidemic. In appreciation, they built the Temple of the Redeemer on the Island of La Giudecca. The architect was Palladio. Every year on the eve of the third Sunday in July, local residents parade to Giudecca over the bridges originally built for that purpose between Venice and the island. When the religious part is over, a huge illuminated barge carrying an orchestra and singers goes down the Grand Canal. It is followed by smaller barges, also carrying musicians and singers, and then by gondolas and by all kinds of boats. Every palazzo is lighted, as are the bridges, boats and floats. All music stops at 10 p.m. for a spectacular fireworks display. The music resumes and continues to 12:30 a.m., when a second fireworks show takes place, but from the Island of San Giorgio. Festivities continue until just before dawn, when it's traditional to go to the Lido to watch the sunrise over the Adriatic Sea. Sunday morning, there's a solemn procession with clergy, city officials, dignitaries and standard-bearers with multicolored flags, costumed torchbearers and crowds of people who cross the pontoon bridges returning to the Temple of the Redeemer for the closing services. The event is financed through private donations.

JAMAICA

Kingston, Montego Bay, islandwide

JAMAICA FESTIVAL

Held annually, July/August
Cultural, competition

The Jamaica Festival is an islandwide cultural showcase of Jamaican art, music and drama. It is a five-day event that begins in late July and ends the first Monday of August, Jamaica's Independence Day. The festival began in 1963 as the Independence Festival of Jamaica, changed a year later to its present name. The festival features competitions in the arts, concerts, exhibits and performances for the general public. Emphasis is on the cultural roots, conservation and revival of traditional art forms by ethnic groups, especially in rural areas. Highlights are the folk dances, folk music and folk games of African origin. The competitive aspect begins as early as May at the parish (local) level, going through regional to national finals, from which the best is selected in different categories. Winners participate in the final festival programs, which include exhibitions, street dances, concerts, costume shows, plays, readings and ceremonial proclamations. In 1977, a film festival was added, and for the first time, lunchtime concerts, featuring festival gold medalists, were given. Since 1963, it is estimated that 14 million people have attended and participated in the festival. It is financed through a grant from the Jamaican government, from contributions from private enterprise and from festival projects. There are admission charges to the main stage productions only.

JAPAN

Hamamatsu (Shizuoka Prefecture)

KITE BATTLES OF HAMAMATSU

Held annually, May 3–5
Tradition, sports, competition

The Kite Battles of Hamamatsu are a more than 400-year-old tradition that attracts up to 2 million visitors to see 60 neighborhood teams of 50 to 100 men compete in a kite-flying competition. Hamamatsu is located midway between Tokyo and Osaka. Huge kites are flown by the teams, who try to cut the strings of their opponents by skillful maneuvering, adding to the excitement of the event. Competing families have been known to spend hundreds of dollars each for the kites, and they entertain the kite fliers with food, drink and parties late into the night. Thousands of kite fliers tug lines along the oceanside Nakatajima Dune, and it's done to the accompaniment of chants, whistles and bugle calls. They continually try to cut down their opponents' kites by sawing the quarter-inch hemp ropes. This event always ends on Boys Day, honoring the town's last-born eldest son, in whose honor the kites are flown.

Kyoto (Kyoto Prefecture)

HOLLYHOCK FESTIVAL OF SHIMOGAMO AND KAMIGAMO SHRINES

Held annually, May 15
Religious, folkloric, legendary, floral

The Aoi Matsuri, or Hollyhock Festival of Shimogamo and Kamigamo Shrines, is probably one of the world's oldest festivals. This one goes back to the sixth century and is always held on May 15. It is based on a legend. In the sixth century, Kyoto was hit by heavy rains, causing flooding. Local residents petitioned the gods to end the flooding. They did, and the people have been celebrating ever since. The pageant depicts the feudal emperor visiting the shrines of Shimogamo and Kamigamo. "Aoi" translates as "hollyhock" but is a different flower, probably wild ginger with heart-shaped leaves and now rare. It is often replaced by other showy flowers. The purpose of the special flower is that it is offered at the shrines as a token of respect and appreciation to the gods for saving Kyoto from the floods. The day's events begin at 10 a.m. with a procession from the Gosho or Imperial Palace. Tickets are made available to visitors to view the procession. The procession or parade includes the imperial messenger and his retinue, who surround a large oxcart, or *gissha*, an authentic lacquered one complete with noisy wheels. Streamers of artificial wisteria or *fuji* flowers cascade from the cart's roof. The paraders are dressed in beautiful brocades and large-sleeved kimonos of the Heian period. The cart is usually pulled by black oxen and covered with a bright orange and silver coverlet complete with silk cords and tassles. Marchers lead the oxen by silken ropes. Other parade features include the large umbrellas, or *furyugasa*, whose weight make them more ceremonial than functional. The umbrellas are covered with large garish artificial flowers. Also part of the procession or parade is a lovely lady carried on a litter. She represents a princess, who in ancient days had to assume the not-so-easy life of a Shinto priestess. Others represent various members of the feudal imperial family and ride on horses with exquisite saddles. There is usually an explanatory session by local guides to acquaint visitors with the various Heian ranks and costumes and the courtiers, guards, warriors and dignitaries in the parade. Paraders move along the route to the accompaniment of flutes, gongs and drums.

Nikko (Tochigi Prefecture)

GRAND FESTIVAL OF THE TOSHOGU SHRINE

Held annually, May 17–18
Religious, folkloric, historic, procession

The Grand Festival of the Toshogu Shrine is a centuries-old event that marks the burial of Shogun Ieyasu at his resting place, Toshogu Shrine, in May 1617. The burial was observed by a long procession that crossed the vermilion-lacquered bridge over the Daiya River, climbed the stairs to the long pathway bordered by cryptomeria trees (Japanese cedar trees) and brought the shogun's body to the shrine. The morning of May 17, descendants of the shogun's family and various selected representatives cross the same bridge to the shrine to make offerings to three deities: Minamoto Yoritomo, Toyotomi Hideyoshi and Tokugawa Ieyasu, founder of the powerful Tokugawa shogunate feudal system. The spirits of the three shoguns, symbolized by metallic mirrors, are taken to three sacred portable shrines to be carried through the Yomelimon Gate (Gate of Sunlight, also called the Twilight Gate) to Futaarsan Shrine, remaining there until the next day's procession of 1,000 persons. Hundreds of thousands of Japanese and foreign visitors gather the next day, May 18, around the Futaarsan Shrine to watch the historic procession. The first horseman comes down the pathway with great clamor to lead 100 armor-clad soldiers with halberds marching in two lines down the avenue of cryptomeria trees. They move along accompanied by costumed samurai guardsmen. Lions in Japanese legend ward off evil along the road, and so as the soldiers pass by there are men with shaggy, shaking manes along the way. Fifty spear carriers, or *yarimochi*, follow, and after them an equal number of men with old matchlock guns and others with bows and arrows, all representing men in the service of the shogun. Next come the warriors with antlered helmets and decorative protective armor, carrying orange shields. Twelve page boys are next, and they wear animal head hats, each symbolizing one of 12 hours of daylight. Marchers, wearing fox masks, follow. They represent phantoms who live in the mountains around Nikko and who are pledged to guard the Toshogu Shrine and the area. The procession includes a larger number of Shinto priests. Some walk with very measured steps. Others are on horseback, and others carry flags and streamers of different colors, designs and sizes. Shinto musicians walk in time to the sonorous beats of great drums and chiming bells. They are followed by men with stuffed hawks, recalling trainers of hawks during the Tokugawa shogunate, who used to catch small birds. The shining sacred *mikoshi*, holding the spirits of the three deified shoguns, add to the procession's solemnity. The portable shrines are returned to the Toshogu Shrine before the day's event ends, with crowds around the shrine to watch the sacred *azuma-asobi* dance. The day usually ends with an arrow-shooting rite or *yabusame*, recalling the Kamakura period competition.

Osaka (Osaka Prefecture)

OSAKA INTERNATIONAL FESTIVAL

Held annually, April
Cultural

The Osaka International Festival began in 1958 to be a meeting of Eastern and Western cultures, attracting both local citizens and visitors. It is still going strong and continues to be a spring cultural offering. However, when the 18-day festival celebrated its twentieth anniversary in 1977, it was held in autumn, and in 1978, cultural programs with artists from past festivals were held April through October. In 1979, the festival returned to April. It always includes one performance of Noh plays in the program, which also features dance, drama, opera and music concerts with both Japanese and foreign performers. The 1982 festival starred the Osaka Philharmonic, the Tokyo Metropolitan Symphony Chamber Music, the Wiener Kammerensemble and more. In 1981, Berlioz's *Damnation of Faust* was performed on opening night, the first time the work had been performed in Osaka. Spanish mezzo-soprano Teresa Berganza sang works by Scarlatti, Pergolesi, Faure and Granados. She also gave a concert of arias with the Osaka Philharmonic Orchestra with Kazuyoshi Akiyama conducting. Other 1981 highlights included a recital by pianist Mark Zeltser, who performed works by Haydn, Moussorgsky and Chopin. There was a concert by cellist Pierre Fournier, accompanied by Michio Kobayashi at the piano, offering Brahms, Bach and Debussy. Among theatrical companies at the festival have been the Comedie

Francaise, Vienna Burgtheater and Theatre de France Renaud-Barrault. Dance companies have included the Ballet Aztlan de Mexico and the New York City Ballet. Performances are in the 3,000-seat Osaka Festival Hall. The event is financed by ticket sales and contributions from private industry.

JORDAN

Jerash

JERASH FESTIVAL

Held annually, August
Cultural

The Jerash Festival is a nine-day visual and performing arts event held amidst the ruins of Jerash, a 2,000-year-old Graeco-Roman city. It is very new as an event with the first festival held in 1981 and attracting more than 180,000 visitors plus thousands of participants. The idea for the cultural festival is credited to Jordan's Queen Noor, who suggested it to Dr. Adnan Badran, president of Yarmouk University. Dr. Badran is chairman of the Festival Executive Committee, aided by Dr. Mazen Al Armouti, festival director. The Queen is very active in the festival planning stages. The event officially opens with a great deal of fanfare by King Hussein and Queen Noor. The ceremony is usually held in the colonnaded city forum where a symbolic flame is lit by the king to open festival events. The program is held in mid-August and includes Jordanian music performances by the Jordanian Armed Forces Band and its Bagpipe Corps, the Radio Jordan Orchestra and several jazz groups and two rock concerts at the Sound and Light Theater. Folkloric dances are performed by five Jordanian groups as well as by other Arabic groups. In 1983, these included the Reda Dance Troupe of Egypt, the Television Popular Arts Troupe of Kuwait, the Folklore Troupe of Yemen, the Folklore Troupe from Algeria and the Popular Arts Troupe of Tunisia. Also performing in 1983 was the famous Lebanese singer, Fairouz, accompanied by 70 dancers and musicians on stage at the Jerash South Theater. The singer, a woman, is well-known in the Arab world. The festival also includes an Arab book fair which in 1983 featured more than 25,000 titles by 100 publishers from 15 countries. Titles were in both Arabic and English. The fair is sponsored by the Jordan Department of Libraries, Documentation and National Archives. There is usually a special section devoted to children's books, educational toys and audio-visual entertainment. Drama is also a vital part of the festival and includes Arabic plays for both adults and children. The dramas are written and produced by Jordanians who also put on puppet shows and offer poetry recitals. There are exhibits of contemporary Jordanian art as well as arts and crafts, displayed in stalls along the ancient Street of Columns. Craftspeople demonstrate and sell their work which includes carpets, ceramics, wood and stone carvings, traditional embroidery, glassware and jewelry. In addition, a variety of films are shown. In 1983 "The Message," or "Al Risala," on the life of the Prophet Mohammed was shown. It stars Anthony Quinn and Irene Pappas and was produced by Mustafa Akkard. While the festival is designed to be a showcase for Jordanian and Arab culture and talent, it also is international in scope. In 1983 there were performances by groups around the world. They included the Hano Acrobacti Troupe from China; the Empire State Institute for Performing Arts; the Hall-Rogers Modern Dance Group and Doyle Lawson and Quicksilver Folk Music, all three from the United States; Sufia Kamal of Chhayanot Troupe from Bangladesh; Salzburger Stierwascher Folklore Troupe from Austria; La Ciamada Missarda Folklore Troupe of France and Pipes and Drums of the Argyll and Sutherland Highlanders of Scotland. Festival goers are brought to Jerash via roundtrip shuttle air service from Amman by the Public Transport Corporation. Other sponsors and participants include the Jordanian Armed Forces, ALIA, the Royal Jordanian Airline, the Ministry of Culture and the Ministry of Tourism and Antiquities. There are ticket sales but many events are free. The festival is supported through government subsidies and the purchase of arts and crafts. In the short existence of the festival which plans to expand in the future, more than a half-million people have attended, aiding the local economy greatly at that time of year.

KENYA

Nairobi

SAFARI RALLY

Held annually, Easter weekend, movable dates
Sports, competition

The Safari Rally is a top racing event, sponsored annually by the Kenya Safari Rally, Ltd., and attracting thousands of spectators and hundreds of entries from other African nations and foreign countries. The rally originally started as part of the celebrations marking the coronation of Queen Elizabeth II and was called the Coronation Rally. Because of the great interest it generated, it was continued and in 1960 was renamed the East African Safari. The auto rally went through the East African countries of Kenya, Uganda and Tanzania. In 1973, Uganda was dropped, and a year later, the safari rally was confined to Kenya. In 1975 the event was renamed Safari Rally. It has been part of the FIA International Calendar since 1957 and was a qualifying event for the RAC World Rally Trophy for Manufacturers from 1964 to 1969. In 1970 it became a qualifying event for the FIA World Rally Championship for Makes. The rally travels over rough terrain and through changes in climate. Within a few hours, the cold of the night changes to tropical heat and humidity. Some areas are extremely dry and dusty, while others are wet and slippery, challenging the skill of the driver, car and crew. The Safari Rally has achieved records, too. In 1959, the rally was literally the "mile-a minute" event, with 3,200 miles to be covered in 3,200 minutes, and was drier than the one in 1967. The 1970 rally was the wettest, and there were 19 finishers out of an entry of 98. In 1971 there was a record entry of 118 cars, a record distance of 6,400 kilometers, a record number of overseas drivers and a record entry of African drivers, with Kenya providing 58 crews. In 1974 the first ever all-African ladies crew was entered. The Safari Rally is financed through entry fees and by sponsorship of Kenyan industries and auto companies.

KOREA, SOUTH

Chinju

NATIONAL FOUNDATION ART FESTIVAL

Held annually, November 1–5
Cultural, fair

The National Foundation Art Festival is a local cultural event of interest. It is marked by traditional processions, exhibits of local products, a country fair and farm tool displays. However, there are also competitions in Chinese poetry, calligraphy, music, art and drama. These are demonstrations, exhibitions and performances. An unusual sword dance is performed by 4 to 8 dancers to music played on traditional Korean musical instruments.

Gochang

MOYANG CASTLE FESTIVAL

Held annually, October
Folkloric, historic, competition

The Moyang Castle Festival is the only castle festival in the country and recalls the completion of the building in 1453. Interestingly enough, the work was done entirely by women and girls. The one-day festival is usually held on the ninth day of the ninth lunar month, or around mid-October on the solar calendar. About 5,000 women and girls dress up in their Korean finery to walk on the castle wall, which is 1,780 meters long and 3.6 meters high. They pray for long life, good health, paradise and ascension into heaven. There is a vocal music competition and an archery match to keep things lively.

Namwon (North Jeolla)

CHUNHYANG FESTIVAL

Held annually, May
Folkloric, cultural, competition

The Chunhyang Festival is a Korean traditional narrative song competition to mark the place where music originated. Chunhyang was a folkloric heroine and symbol of female virtue, marked by exceptional beauty and fidelity. The three-day festival is held on the eighth day of the fourth lunar month to coincide as close as possible with Buddha's birthday, which can be in early May on the solar calendar. Festival programs are held at Kwanghanru Pavilion in Chiri Mountain Park, where legend claims that Chunhyang began her romance with Mongyong. *Pansori*, or narrative songs, started with the romance. The competitions still mark the event.

LUXEMBOURG

Echternach

DANCING PROCESSION

Held annually, May or June, Whit-Tuesday, movable date
Religious, pageantry, procession, folkloric

The Sprangprocession, or Dancing Procession, is a medieval religious custom that has survived the centuries (13 of them) and is still held on Whit-Tuesday, which comes about 50 days after Easter. This procession, however, honors St. Willibrord (St. Wilfred), who came from North England to convert locals to Christianity. He not only did that but he also saved the area from a plague. Legend claims that Willibrord promised that if the people prayed and subjected themselves to physical punishment, the plague would disappear. He taught them to dance or hop to the tune of a jig melody brought from Northumberland. The people hopped up and down until completely exhausted. Eventually the plague disappeared. To this day, the procession is held not to chase away the plague but to honor the saint. It begins at 9 a.m. after a sermon by the bishop of Luxembourg. Participants dance, taking three steps forward and two backward to the same tune played 13 centuries ago. Local bands continually play the same melody. The procession goes through narrow cobblestone streets before entering the Basilica. More than 10,000 watch the procession, and thousands are in it. It is led by priests, boys and girls of the city, then older men and women and pilgrims from Eifel and the city of Luxembourg. The event continues until late afternoon. The procession enters the Basilica, where there is a white marble sarcophagus with the remains of St. Willibrord. The fresco-painted vaults date back to A.D. 1100. The festivities end in the evening with special meals.

Luxembourg City

POTTERY FESTIVAL

Held annually, Easter Monday, March or April, movable date
Folkloric, market

Emaischen is a traditional folkloric festival and market celebrated for a few hundred years in the center of Old Luxembourg. It originally started out as a pottery market. While some pottery is still sold, its main attraction is the sale of small whistling ceramic colorful birds, *Peckvillechen*, and is traditionally a gift exchange between young lovers. The items are sold at Marche-aux-Poissons, or the Fish Market, where children play special games, followed by folk song and dance concerts in the afternoon.

Luxembourg

SHEPHERD'S FAIR

Held annually, August
Folkloric, fair

The Schueberfo'er, or Shepherd's Fair, dates back to 1340, when it was a market for the wool and sheep merchants of middle Europe. Today, it is an amusement fair with carousels, food stands, candy booths and lots of pageantry. It begins with an afternoon parade and the official opening attended by local dignitaries. There is a dance in the evening. The two-week fair usually begins the last Sunday in August. There is also the Marche des Moutons or March of the Sheep, with a herd of sheep decorated with multicolored ribbons and accompanied by shepherds in their own folkloric costumes. They all walk in front of a band that plays fourteenth-century music.

Wiltz

BROOM FLOWER FESTIVAL

Held annually, Whitmonday, May or June, movable date
Folkloric, floral

The Genzefest, or Broom Flower Festival, is a one-day celebration to view the golden blossoms of the gorse or broom plant that covers the Ardennes. There is a parade with floral floats, folk dance groups and bands. There are also concerts, dancing and performances by majorettes. The pageant ends with several evening festival balls.

MACAO

PROCESSION OF OUR LORD OF PASSOS

Held annually, February/March
Religious, procession

The Procession of Our Lord of Passos is only held in Macao. It includes taking in procession a statue of Our Lord from its place on the altar of St. Augustine's Church to the Cathedral of Se. It is a statue of Christ on his way to Calvary. There is an all-night vigil at the cathedral over the statue. The next day it is carried in a solemn procession around Macao before being returned to St. Augustine's. Many miracles have been attributed to the statue. During the procession, it is carried on the shoulders of purple-robed church dignitaries.

MACAO GRAND PRIX

Held annually, November
Sports, competition

The Macao Grand Prix is Asia's top motor racing event, held for ten days in mid-November. Mororcycle, production car and formula cars compete for top prize money in excess of $20,000. The first race was held in 1953. The annual competition has grown in scope and size, attracting thousands of spectators as well. Three races, the Grand Prix motorcycle, Grand Prix and Guia saloon car race, are all international. Other events are restricted to various categories of riders or drivers. The Grand Prix meeting always begins with scrutinizing of entries on both the Monday and Tuesday of the event. Practice sessions are held on a Thursday and Friday, with the week reaching its climax on Saturday and

Sunday with ten events in Formula II racers, saloon cars and motorcycles. Eight prizes are awarded in the Grand Prix, with a sizable cash prize HK $25,000 and the Governor's Cup with the runner-up getting $15,000 and the Carlos da Silva Cup. Third to sixth place win cash prizes and trophies. The first Asian driver home gets $2,000 and a trophy. It is financed through entry fees, ticket sales and sponsorships.

MALAYSIA

Nationwide

NATIONAL DAY

Held annually, August 31
Patriotic

National Day marks the birth of Malaysia, and it is celebrated with great feeling. Towns and buildings are illuminated and beautifully decorated. There are open-air drama shows, parades and music festivals in all 13 states of Malaysia. A highlight is the variety show of Malaysian classical dances and music performed on an open-air stage in the Lake Gardens of Kuala Lumpur. The National Day parade in Kuala Lumpur starts from the Padang opposite the Sultan Abdul Samad building early in the morning. Thousands watch the parade and attend the different shows.

Bachok

BACHOK FESTIVAL OF CULTURE

Held annually, May
Cultural, competition

The Bachok Festival of Culture centers on performances of traditional Menora and Makyong dance drama groups, often along the beach. The two-week festival also includes the *wayang kulit*, or shadow plays, usually only performed for private patrons to celebrate some special or important event like an anniversary or wedding. Also featured are giant top-spinning and kite-flying competitions, open to visitors. The shadow plays involve a puppeteer, To'Dalang, or Father of the Mysteries, who sits within an enclosed bamboo stage. He moves the puppet, whose shadows are cast on a screen directly in front of the audience. The shadow plays presented are based on the Ramayana or Mahabharata epics of Indian origin. The performances are done to the accompaniment of a small band of five or six players, using drums, flageolet, a gong and even a Malay violin.

Penang, Kuala Lumpur, Gaja Berang

THAIPUSAM

Held annually, January/February
Religious

Thaipusam is the yearly celebration by members of the Hindu faith of the birth of Lord Subramaniam. The one-day event is observed with great pomp and circumstance. At the Waterfall Temple in Penang, the faithful with skewers pierced into their bodies, carry the penitent punishment, *kavadi*. At night, a deity is carried in a decorated silver chariot in a procession that goes through the city streets to the accompaniment of instrumental music. In Kuala Lumpur, thousands of Hindus from all over the country participate in a pilgrimage that includes climbing the 272 steps to the Cave Temple at Batu Caves. At Gaja Berang in Malacca, the Hindu faithful meet at the temple to later walk in a procession, carrying the *kavadi* and silver chariot containing the effigy of Lord Subramaniam through the city streets.

Sarawak

DAYAK FESTIVAL DAY

Held annually, June 1–2
Harvest, folkloric

Dayak Festival Day or Gawai Dayak is a festival that celebrates the end of a paddy season after harvest and also invokes blessings on a new paddy-planting season. It falls on the first day of June every year. The Dayaks are mostly farmers and live in all five administrative divisions of Sarawak. The main festival ritual is the *miring* ceremony, conducted by the "bard" of the tribe. The Dayaks all gather together to make offerings of different foods and the traditional rice wine, *tuak*. The bard recites a poem for the occasion, asking for guidance, blessings and long life. While reciting, he holds in his hands a sacrificial white cockerel, which he swings back and forth to drive away evil spirits. Then the blood of the cockerel is smeared over the offerings. Celebrations vary in each area, but always includes the reciting of the *pantuns*, the performance of the *ngajet*, or Dayak war dance, demonstrations of blowpipe skills and cockfights. Each community usually presents a cultural program.

MARTINIQUE, FRENCH WEST INDIES

Fort-de-France

CARNIVAL/MARDI GRAS

Held annually, February or March, movable date
Religious, folkloric

The Carnival or Mardi Gras celebrations in this French Caribbean island and its sister island of Guadeloupe don't end on Shrove Tuesday, the day before Ash Wednesday but go right through the first day of Lent. Carnival celebrations actually begin the Sunday after New Year's, with weekend parades, dances and merriment in the streets of larger towns and cities of both islands. Shortly before Lent, celebrations become wild. The Sunday before Lent, there are daylight parades with marchers in exotic and theme costumes playing instruments and dancing to the beat of the beguine, a refined Congolese ritual dance. On Monday, all stores and offices close, and the local rum is consumed by almost all, followed by singing and dancing all day. Masked balls continue far into the night. Shrove Tuesday is for a parade of children dressed in brilliant red-devil costumes and carrying homemade tridents. They dance in the streets until sundown, when their elders take over. Ash Wednesday is the day of the she-devils, La Fere des Diablesses, with tens of thousands of masked, costumed devils (many are men in drag), marching in the streets. Only two colors are allowed, black and white. Dark faces are smeared with pale ash. For those not in a satan costume, any crazy clothes will do, but they must be the basic black and white. Focal point is the king, known as Vaval, and his alter ego, Bois-Bois ("wood-wood" pronounced "bwa-bwa") who tower over the dancing procession. By now the death notices of King Carnival appear in local papers, and festivities continue as his funeral pyre is being built. When dusk comes, the flames light up the sky, and Vaval's effigy is put on the fire as the dancing reaches a crazy peak then slowly calms down as Vaval's coffin is lowered into the ground at midnight. Crowds sing, "Carnival, don't leave us." The celebration is over.

MEXICO

Guadalajara

FIESTAS DE OCTUBRE

Held annually, October/November
Cultural, ethnic, folkloric, fair, sports

The month-long Fiestas de Octubre or October Fair is a showcase for Mexican arts, crafts, folklore and products. Also called the October Festival, it officially opens with an elaborate parade with floats, bands and dancers, going from the downtown area to Agua Azul Park, site of the fair. There is an international exhibition of handicrafts, an antique bazaar, a world beer festival with free samples and a display of national wines and cheeses. There is a book fair, a Mexican chili cook-off and a photographic exhibit. There are stands selling Mexican regional foods, arts and crafts. Performances are given by the original flying Indians of Papantla, plus fireworks and three operas, ballet performances and folkloric dancing. Sports events include golf, tennis, soccer, water skiing contests and even bicycle races. Bullfights and Mexican rodeo events are also part of the event. The fair attracts close to a million people, both Mexicans and tourists. There is an admission fee to the concerts and performances. The event is financed through admission charges, sale of souvenir booklets, rental fees and grants from the local government.

Guanajuato

INTERNATIONAL CERVANTES FESTIVAL

Held annually, April/May, sometimes October/November
Cultural

The International Cervantes Festival offers three weeks of music, theater, dance, arts, cinema and lectures in the eighteenth-century city of Guanajuato, about four hours from Mexico City. The festival is organized under the personal patronage of the first lady of Mexico, who in 1982 was Mrs. Carmen Romano de Lopez Portillo. The festival is named for Miguel de Cervantes, Spanish novelist and playwright, poet and humanist, famed for his creation of *Don Quixote*. At the opening festival ceremony the statues of both Don Quixote and Sancho Panza are lighted by fireworks. The festival attracts thousands of Mexicans and foreign tourists.

Highlight of the 1982 event included Leonard Bernstein with the Israel Philharmonic, the Mexico City Philharmonic, the European Community Youth Orchestra and more. Among the ballet, dance and folk ensembles were the Boston Ballet with Nureyev, Merce Cunningham, Bejart's XX Century Ballet; Mexico's Ballet Folklorico and groups from Yugoslavia, Egypt, Japan, Thailand, Philippines and Spain. Theater featured companies from Berlin, Poland, Spain, Greece, Italy, the United States, Hungary, Nigeria, Brazil, Cuba and Argentina. Mexican players gave street performances of Cervantes' famous one-act plays. There was an international ballet gala featuring Natalia Makarova–Denys Ganio, Gelsey Kirkland–Frank Augustyn, Valentina Kozlova–Leonid Kozlov, Marianna Tcherkasky–Danilo Radjojevic, Maria Aradi–Sandor Nemethy. The opera company was from Argentina, and a festival production of *Fidelio* was given with the Dallas Symphony Orchestra.

The festival, first organized and held in 1973, is financed by the federal government, Guanajuato State and ticket sales.

Huamantla

RUNNING OF THE BULLS

Held annually, August
Religious, historic, commemorative

The Running of the Bulls is always held on the Sunday following the August 15th Feast of the Assumption Day. It is actually part of the annual feast celebration. This particular running dates back to the time the Spanish conquistadores introduced cattle to Mexico, and within a short time, a crude running of the bulls was being held every year. Then as now the ceremony is a mixture of the Aztec and Christian religions. The event was continued over the centuries but began to fade away around 1700. It was revived in the 1920s by local people as part of the Assumption Fiesta, and it has been held ever since. This Running of the Bulls is considered more dangerous than the famous one in Pamplona, Spain. Unlike the Spanish event, which comes in July, this one releases the bulls from cages in nine separate locations within a nine-square-block area of the city. In Spain, they are all released from one location, rushing headlong on a well-known route to the bullring, which is down one street. People can try to outrun them to the arena, knowing the direction from which they are coming. In Huamantla, the bulls run through a maze of connecting streets, so that local folks have to be very careful, anticipating several groups of onrushing bulls at one time. Homeowners along the nine-block area often invite visitors to use their housetops for viewing. The bulls are rolled into town in their large secure cages by 11 a.m. It takes 45 minutes to get the cages in place, and at high noon they are released. Suddenly a yell of "Here come the bulls" is heard, and everyone in the street starts to run. The opening of the cages and releasing of the bulls is coordinated. The official signal to release them is the firing of a skyrocket, whose sound is often drowned out by the noise raised by the townspeople. Each cage is in sight of one another so that the men atop each one can watch and tell exactly when to raise the doors of their own cage. Once the bulls are loose, there is pandemonium. The bulls run around the streets for four hours and by then are tired. They are lassoed and led back to the cages and taken back to their *rancheros* outside town.

Mexico City, nationwide

INDEPENDENCE DAY CELEBRATION

Held annually, September 15–16
Historic, patriotic

Independence Day Celebration is observed nationwide, but it is especially significant in Mexico City. Traditionally, it is commemorated by the repetition of the "Grito" or "Viva Mexico" or call to arms said by patriotic Miguel Hidalgo on the night of September 15, 1810. Now it is voiced by the president of the republic at 11 p.m. on the same day and from the central balcony of the National Palace before a crowd of a half-million jammed into the Zocalo. This is followed by a spectacular fireworks display, the ringing of the cathedral bells and a very fancy banquet in the palace for about 2,500 members of the diplomatic corps, government officials and other special guests. The next day, September 16, Independence Day, there is a huge military parade lasting three hours. It begins in the Zocalo and continues to the Independence Monument on Paseo de la Reforma. The city's main streets and plazas are all decorated with special lights and displays.

MONACO

Monte Carlo

INTERNATIONAL CIRCUS FESTIVAL

Held annually, December
Economic, circus

The International Circus Festival is a fairly new event that has gained in popularity since the first one was held in December 1974. It was started under the patronage of Prince Rainier to attract tourists during a slack season and to share his love of the circus with everyone. As the name indicates, the five-day festival features circus act performances by world famous performers and circuses. It has expanded every year to accommodate the increasing number of acts demanded by those who attend. More than 16,000 visitors come to the festival, which is covered by both European and American television. It is financed through admission fees and help from the government. Performances are held at Esplanade de Fontveille. Special awards are also given to top circuses and performers by Prince Rainier.

Monte Carlo

INTERNATIONAL FESTIVAL OF ARTS

Held annually, January/April, May
Cultural

The International Festival of Arts started in 1970 as a one-week spring program of ballet, dance and opera. It was organized by the late Princess Grace. Not only did it succeed, but it also expanded to cover the first five months of the year, with famous ballet companies, symphony orchestras and opera performances held several times a week during the five-month period. The festival includes performances by the Philharmonic Orchestra of Monte Carlo at Rainier III Auditorium at the Congress Center. At one time, the festival shifted to July and August, but it failed to attract as many visitors so it was returned to the beginning of each year. It is financed through ticket sales and government subsidy.

Monte Carlo

MONACO AUTOMOBILE GRAND PRIX

Held annually, May/June
Sports, competition

The Monaco Automobile Grand Prix, or Grand Prix Automobile de Monaco, was started in 1929 for economic reasons and was held in early spring but later was changed to late May/June because the weather was better. It is basically the same, with the race course going through the streets of Monaco. Every year it attracts more than 30,000 spectators, many tourists and thousands of competitors. The race features top race car drivers from all over the world. The four-day event ends with a gala evening for awards and festivities at the Monte Carlo Sporting Club. It is a self-supporting event.

MOROCCO

Fez

FANTASIA/HORSE FESTIVAL

Held annually, October
Sports, folkloric, competition, horses

Fantasia or Horse Festival is a display of equestrian skills and a folkloric event. Every October, tents are set up just outside the city to accommodate the hundreds of people who participate in the event. It attracts thousands of spectators, many tourists. Hundreds of riders attired in exceptionally interesting outfits meet to present their mounts. Celebrations get underway with a parade of women of the Zaian tribe on horseback, followed by men whose line of march or riding is determined by the tribe they belong to. The festival features a variety of equestrian riding skills and exciting stunts, accented by thundering hooves and blasting guns by the riders, who gallop fast. They let out shrieks and twirl their muzzle loaders, often throwing them up into the air and catching them as they ride. The horses are brought to an abrupt halt when the weapons are fired simultaneously. There are special foods available and folkloric dance and song performances.

Marrakesh

FESTIVAL OF FOLKLORE

Held annually, May
Folkloric, cultural, competition

The Festival of Folklore features ten days of exotic Moroccan songs, dances and music, usually performed on the grounds of the old Ksar El Badi Palace in Marrakesh, a city founded at the end of the eleventh century. The festival is an annual gathering of tribes from all over the country and is a competitive event. Thousands of tourists come to see the performances.

NEPAL

Patan, Kathmandu

THE CHARIOT FESTIVAL OF MACCHENDRANATH/FESTIVAL OF THE GOD OF RAIN

Held annually, April/May, movable dates
Religious, legendary, pageantry

The Chariot Festival of Macchendranath/ Festival of the God of Rain honors the god, Macchendra, named for a fish (macch), who, according to Nepalese legend, gave birth to the deity. The festival is celebrated in Patan and Kathmandu, lasting for two months, usually April and May but dates can vary. Every few years, the festival is extended through August. The last such grand scale event was in 1980. The event is celebrated mostly by Buddhist Newars, although other sects have participated from time to time. The festival officially begins on the first day of the dark moon of *Baisakh* (April-May) and is based on the ancient fertility rites for rain and a good harvest. However, over the centuries, Hindu and Buddhist symbolism has been added to the event. There are two Macchendras. One is the *Rato* or red Macchendra of Patan. This deity's image is housed in a temple at Tahabal, near Patan's Durbar Square. The other deity is *Setu* (white) Macchendra of Kathmandu. Some believe the two gods are one, while others think they are sisters. Still others have different theories. Hindus worship Rato

Macchendra as Karunamya, the god of mercy. The Buddhists consider him to be the fourth of the five Buddhas, Padmapani, noted for the protection and teaching of the gods, which include Lord Shiva. This god's shrine is in Bunga village where the *Kalash* (holy vessel) containing a god in the form of a bee, was put by King Narendra Deva. The Macchendra in Patan is known as Bunga Dev in the farming regions. He is the god of rain and, with the help of the snake gods, he assures a good harvest and prosperity. He is also known as the patron of the Kathmandu Valley. According to ancient Nepalese legend and folklore, there was a disciple of Macchendra, Gorakh Nath, who visited Nepal where he was ignored. Deeply hurt, he went to Mrigasthali, a deserted hill near the Pashupatinath Temple. He brooded over the bad treatment for 12 years and at the same time sat on all the rain-giving snakes, causing a drought in the Kathmandu Valley. The valley people begged for mercy but Gorakh Nath refused. King Narendra Deva of Bhadgaon, greatly distressed by the drought and Gorakh Nath's refusal of mercy, petitioned the help of the god Macchendranath, who was meditating in the Assam Hills. Macchendranath agreed to visit the valley but in the form of a black bee carried in the Kalash by the King's envoy, Bandhudutt. As soon as the pouting Gorakh Nath learned of Macchendranath's arrival, he left the hill retreat to go down into the valley. This released all the rain snakes and the rains came, turning the valley green once again. King Narendra Deva officially decreed that Lord Macchendranath should henceforth be honored. The honor is a thousands-of-years-old festival which lasts two months and is a three-part event with much pageantry, ceremony and celebration. Bunga village is still the site of the sacred shrine of Macchendranath. The Kalash, containing the Macchendra-bee, is duly worshipped and then carried on a chariot. The Kalash contains the god's spirit and according to legend, as long as the Kalash is filled with the "elixir" of life, the soul of Macchendranath will remain in it. If the Kalash should dry up, the spirit would escape and the statue in Patan would die. The first festival day is devoted to bathing an image of the god, a ceremonial rite performed under a designated tree in Patan. The statue is repainted and dressed in new robes. During the night, the statue is taken from the temple at Tahabala and kept hidden until the first day of the bright lunar fortnight. It is then placed in a beautifully decorated chariot at Phool Chowk. The chariot is no ordinary one. It actually consists of a 50-foot high wooden spire, designed as a throne for the god. It is ornately decorated with evergreens, flowers and paper garlands. The spire is supported by four huge wooden wheels. Each wheel is said to hold the spirits of the four *Bhairavas*. These spirits are credited with frightening away evil spirits when Lord Macchendra was brought back from Assam. In front of the chariot is an ornately carved figure of Karkot Nagaa, the snake god. Legend says that he helped the god from Assam. On the upper part of the snake god are emblems of the moon and the sun. Macchendra's chariot is always traditionally followed by a smaller chariot, occupied by Moon Nath (also called Chakuwa Dev and Karanamaya, or the one who likes offerings of molasses and rice). This god is said to be either Macchendra's son or daughter, a point never really cleared up to this day. On the fourth festival day, the sacred Kalash, enshrined in the chariot, begins its journey from Phool Chowk, going through all city streets and lanes with the faithful pulling the thick ropes of the *rath* (chariot). This is considered a sacred duty that also brings the rope-puller good fortune. They are accompanied by soldiers and military bands. The chariot procession moves slowly, sometimes taking weeks on end, sometimes months, based on the moment when the sun is in the northern sphere. The chariot's destination is the Jawla Khel parade ground. Whenever the chariot stops during the procession, local people give offerings to the god and ask for his *darshan* or blessing. Many rituals, including animal sacrifices, are made to honor the *Bhairavas* in the wheels of the chariot. The festival ends on *Bhoto Jatra*, which can be in May or as late as August, a day declared appropriate for the final ceremony. Thousands from all over Nepal gather at the Jawla Khel parade ground at night. They carry lighted oil lamps and wait for the final ritual which is the display of the jewel-encrusted robe (Bhoto). The people surround the chariot with offerings of fruit, flowers and coins.

This is also the day that the "Living Goddess Kumari" of Patan is carried to the parade ground to see the robe of Lord Macchendra displayed. The King and Queen of Nepal, civil and military officials and dignitaries also attend to pay their homage. The priest from the Banra caste displays the *Bhoto* before the crowd. The priest also drops a copper disc, especially for the attending peasants. The Banra priest climbs to the top of the chariot to drop the disc to the ground. If it falls face down, this is a good omen for the Kathmandu Valley. However, if it falls face up, drought and hunger are predicted. This officially marks the end of the festival and the return of Lord Macchendra to the shrine in Bunga. The return is accompanied by gun salutes and singing crowds. Once in 12 years, the festival is held on a larger and more lavish scale. Since the last big one was in 1980 the next larger scale event will be in 1992. The festival, however, is held every year. It has been held and observed for thousands of years with countless numbers of people participating. It is a religious event, based on legend and is open to visitors who might be in Nepal at the time.

NETHERLANDS

Delft

OLD ART AND ANTIQUES FAIR

Held annually, October/November
Economic, fair

The Old Art and Antiques Fair, the former Delft Antique Mart, is considered to be one of the best of its kind, not only in Europe but also in the world. It is restricted to 31 members of the Vereeniging von Handelaren in Oude Kunst, the cream of dealers in the Netherlands. The exhibits are worth millions of dollars. Antiques for sale include paintings, drawings, prints, furniture, coins, porcelain, silver Delftware made before 1800, clocks and carpets. It is open to anyone who pays the few dollars admission but is designed for serious buyers. The fair is held in the more than 400-year-old Prinsenhof building, once headquarters for William the Silent. The fair or mart was started in 1948 as an experiment to help antique dealers move their merchandise. Although the first year failed to attract many people, it was held again in 1949 with better success. Over the years, more than 40,000 visit the fair, with an impressive grand total of more than a million. The fair is economically a success because record sales are made and because tourists visit Delft, a medieval town, during the off-season.

The Hague/Scheveningen, Amsterdam, Rotterdam

HOLLAND FESTIVAL

Held annually, June 1–23
Cultural

The Holland Festival of music, drama and dance is national and international in scope and the country's annual cultural highlight, dating back to June 15, 1947, when the first festival was held, only two years after the end of World War II. Its purpose is still to offer the Dutch and visitors an opportunity to enjoy "the best possible living art performances by international artists in the main centers of Holland." Since the Netherlands did not have a single composer who could be honored in one town or city, it was decided to have a general festival with a wide range of artistic and cultural activities. The basis for this was two prewar traditions, the summer concerts by the Concertgebouw Orchestra in Amsterdam and the Kurhaus summer series by the Residentie Orchestra in the Hague/Scheveningen. Since many Dutch art institutions were often on vacation between May and September, this festival would bridge the cultural gap. Festival planners also felt that no single Dutch city could provide an audience for such a specialized festival. This led to the larger cities of Amsterdam, the Hague, and later Rotterdam joining with the national government to bring art "at home." The festival continued to be held June 15 to July 15 until 1967, when it was held July 9, continuing for four weeks. It is now held for 23 days, June 1–23. While the festival's more than 150 different programs are held in the large cities, there are spin-off events in smaller cities and towns.

In 1982, the Holland Festival celebrated its thirty-fifth anniversary with a change in dates and an expanded program, May 21 to July 18, and again from August 27 to September 8. It reverted to its regular dates in 1983. Highlight of the anniversary celebration, which also marked the bicentennial of diplomacy between the United States and the Netherlands, was a series of programs dealing with "unknown" American music honoring the 200-year-old friendship. Participants included the 20th Century Players from the California Institute of the Arts, the Percussion Ensemble of the Hague and the Radio Philharmonic Orchestra and Choir and the Arditti Quartet. Operas performed included Mozart's *The Magic Flute* in the first reconstruction of the opera's first performance in Vienna in 1791; Stravinsky's *Oepidus Rex*, Britten's *The Turn of the Screw* and a cartoon opera, *Ape*, by Peter Schat. The dance phase of the festival featured *Aboriginals* by Jiri Kylian and a new work by Pina Bausch. Participants were the Dance Theater of Wuppertal, the Merce Cunningham Dancers of New York, the Bremer Dance Theater and Folkwang Tanzstudio of Eissen. Among the performing ensembles were the Rotterdam Philharmonic, the Netherlands Opera Choir, the Netherlands Chamber Choir, the London Sinfonietta conducted by Hans Werner Henze, the Julliard String Quartet, the Amsterdam University Choir, the Shonberg Ensemble, the Orchestra of the 18th Century and the Amsterdam Philharmonic. In addition, the Abel Gance film *Napoleon*, reedited by Francis Ford Coppola with a new musical score, was shown, as was *The Photographer*, a new work by Philip Glass. The festival contributes to the economy of the cities where programs are held and to the culture of the entire country. It attracts more than 100,000 annually and, over the years, several million. There are ticket sales, but the festival is subsidized by the cities of Amsterdam, the Hague and Rotterdam and by the Dutch Ministry of Culture. The festival is handled in each city by a paid staff who work year-round on festival details. The festival is administered by the Holland Festival, a private foundation with a board of directors. The Holland Festival was among the founder-members of the European Association of Music Festivals, created under the auspices of the European Cultural Foundation in Geneva, under the direction of Denis de Rougemont.

Lisse

KEUKENHOF

Held annually, March/May
Economic, floral, horticultural

The Keukenhof is now a world famous exhibition of millions of bulb flowers in a 70-acre park in Lisse, located between Haarlem and Leiden. It was started by Dutch bulb growers in 1949. Its purpose was to call attention to the country's leading product, the bulb flower. Although first planned to be a showcase for Dutch bulb growers, it became much more. The park has a roofed-in garden, a show glasshouse with more than 500 tulip varieties, a separate amaryllis hothouse and a special plot of ground for the cultivation of heath plants. There is an authentic corn mill from Groningen and several restaurants and terraces for relaxing and viewing. There is a collection of sculptures by Dutch artists who exhibit together with the flowers. Flower arrangement demonstrations are given in the Queen Juliana Pavilion. The popularity of the park exhibit is evident in the growing number of visitors, both Dutch and foreign. In 1950, 236,000 came. In 1973 there were more than 840,000, and in 1982, over 1 million. There is an admission fee to the exhibit park. The exhibit is financed by the more than 10,000 Dutch bulb growers who exhibit there.

NEW ZEALAND

Auckland

AUCKLAND FESTIVAL

Held biennially, even-numbered years, March/April; next 1986, 1988
Cultural

The Auckland Festival is a performing and visual arts event dating back to 1949. It offers music concerts, opera performances, theater, poetry, art exhibitions and dance recitals. It is a self-supporting event with monies coming from ticket sales and private donations.

Christchurch

CHRISTCHURCH ARTS FESTIVAL

Held biennially, even-numbered years, March; next: 1986, 1988
Cultural

The Christchurch Arts Festival is actually international in flavor since it does headline both international and New Zealand performers. It focuses on opera, music, ballet, drama, literature, crafts and plastic arts, with special events for children. Performances and exhibits are held at different city locations. The two-week festival dates back to 1965 and was introduced to fill a cultural void. It has continued with relative success. It is financed through ticket sales and help from the Christchurch Town Hall Board of Management, Queen Elizabeth II Arts Council and local Christchurch groups.

NORWAY

Bergen

BERGEN INTERNATIONAL FESTIVAL

Held annually, May/June
Cultural, folklore

The Bergen International Festival is Norway's top cultural event, keyed to music, drama, folklore, opera and ballet, with world famous orchestras, soloists and foreign opera and ballet companies. It has been held annually since 1952 with performances in Bergen's Viking Castle, Haakon's Hall (built in 1250) and the 1,500-seat Grieg Concert Hall opened in 1978, at Trollhaugen, Grieg's home, now a museum, and finally at Lysoen, the island home of the world famous composer and violinist Ole Bull. The purpose of the festival is to bring cultural experience to as many people as possible and to educate the world about the Norwegian composer Grieg, his works and other Norwegian music, drama and folklore. The festival also serves to bring foreign culture to Norwegians and is an exchange of cultures. Although the first festival only goes back to 1952, it was based on an idea of famous composer Edvard Grieg, who wanted such an event back in 1898. He is considered to be the first festival founder. He actually sponsored a festival then, and Norway was considering the formation of an annual event, but World War II postponed it. The festival continues to offer orchestral and solo recitals, classical music, jazz, organ concerts, military band performances, folklore opera and drama. Sometimes films and art exhibits are also featured. The festival has more than 100 different events in both the performing and visual arts.

In 1982, the festival offered Menotti's *The Medium* and a musical fantasy, *Animalen*, by Tage Danielsson and Lars Johan Werle. Festival performances included those by the Mormon Tabernacle Choir, the Peking Opera, the Cracow Philharmonic Orchestra and Mixed Choir, the Swedish Cullberg Ballet, I Solisti Veneti, the New Music Ensemble, the Kroumata Percussion Ensemble, the Story Theater of Goteborg, Gospel-Jazz of New Orleans and the Kodaly Quartet. The festival continues to play to audiences of thousands, with the number increasing every year. It is financed through ticket sales, private contributions and government help.

Oslo

HOLMENKOLLEN SKI FESTIVAL

Held annually, March
Sports, competition

The Holmenkollen Ski Festival is the highlight of the winter sports season in Norway, attracting 100,000 spectators to watch the world's best skiers compete in downhill, slalom and giant slalom, cross-country ski races and jumping at the Holmenkollen ski area. The Norwegian king and royal family always attend the event, which dates way back to 1892, when it was started to promote skiing. The first jumping event in 1892 at Holmenkollen measured 71 feet. The hill has been changed radically several times. The first tower was built in 1914, and the present one in 1951 for the 1952 Winter Olympic Games in Oslo. The Holmenkollen ski competitions were opened up to foreigners in 1903. A Norwegian won every year except 1939, when a Swede took honors in the jumping contest. Skiers from more than 18 countries, including the United States, now compete during Holmenkollen Week. No one is permitted to use the ski jumping tower until the festival itself. This is designed to give everyone a fair chance. Only the very best skiers may enter. The jumping tower is 184 feet high and its top is 1,350 feet above the fjord, overlooking Oslo. The hill has a built-in museum, restaurant and post office. In 1976 two new events were added. The festival officially opens now with Children's Holmenkollen Day, a cross-country ski race for 3,000 children. The festival ends with the Holmenkollen Ski Marathon, a cross-country ski race for women and men, amateur and expert. The trail is 42 kilometers long, mainly in Nordmarka, a park surrounding Oslo. The race ends at Holmenkollen. The different ski events offer special trophies, with the most coveted being the King's Cup, going to the skier who wins the combined 15 kilometer cross-country race and jumping competition. Silver cups are awarded in each class. The highest distinction in the ski world is the Holmenkollen Medal, presented at the Holmenkollen prize ceremony. The festival is financed by admission and entry fees and by private donations. The Holmenkollen Ski Jumping Hill is owned and operated by the Society for the Promotion of Skiing.

PANAMA

Boquete

COFFEE FAIR AND FLOWER FESTIVAL

Held annually, April
Economic, fair, harvest, floral

The Coffee Fair and Flower Festival is a four-day event in late April, usually at coffee harvest time and when flowers bloom in abundance in the area. The Coffee Fair is a marketplace for the coffee bean. There are also floral arrangement displays and competitions, handicrafts exhibits, a queen's coronation, parades, folk dancing and fun contests like greased pole climbing. The first event was held in 1966, started by the local people to show off their products and to attract visitors to the area. About 20,000 attend each year making a grand total of almost half a million. Work on the fair and festival is by local residents. It is financed by grants from both the government and private industry and by admission fees and sales. The event is held on special exposition grounds within the city limits.

David

INTERNATIONAL FAIR OF SAN JOSE

Held annually, March
Economic, fair, folkloric

The International Fair of San Jose is a combination industrial, commercial and agricultural fair with exhibits, displays and competitions. It is also a folkloric festival that honors St. Joseph. It was organized by local residents and cattlemen as a showcase for local achievements and as a way of preserving local folk music, song, dance and arts and crafts. The first fair was held in 1950, and it has continued with as many as 150,000 attending annually. The most popular fair events include the cattle and horse shows, the handicrafts and different social programs. There is also a Queen Pageant with a number of contestants from other Central American countries. Local government officials usually preside at the opening fair ceremonies. It is financed by government subsidies and private contributions. There are admission fees. The ten-day fair is always held to include the Feast of St. Joseph on March 19. Events are held at local fairgrounds just outside the city.

Macaracas

CANAJACUA FOLKLORE FESTIVAL

Held annually, January
Folkloric, cultural, competition

The Canajacua Folklore Festival was started in 1972 to preserve local folk music and dances. Basically, competitions are held to encourage young people to continue to perform the dances and sing and play the music. There are also cockfights, bullfights and other events staged by local committees. This four-day festival always centers around the town's patron feast, the Feast of the Three Kings, or Epiphany, on January 6, also gift-giving day. About 5,000 people attend. Work is done by local volunteers a month before the actual festival. It is financed by grants from the local government and private businesses. There is no admission charge. Events are held throughout the town.

Ocu

COUNTRY FAIR

Held annually, January
Economic, fair

The Country Fair dates back to 1966, when it was organized to exhibit the agricultural and livestock produce of the area as well as the arts and crafts. Other events include folk dance performances, bullfights, a rodeo and religious services. It is always held to include January 20, the Feast of San Sebastian, the local patron saint. The fair attracts more than 20,000 persons every year. Popular aspects of the fair include the folkloric programs, which many top Panamian government officials attend. The fair is helped by the government and local industry. There are admission charges.

Panama City, nationwide

CARNIVAL

Held annually, before Ash Wednesday, February or March, movable date
Religious, folkloric

Panama's Carnival celebration takes place four days before Ash Wednesday ushers in the Lenten season. Festivities are nationwide but especially festive and interesting in Panama City. Carnival, celebrated since colonial days, wasn't official until 1910, when it was better organized. Celebrations begin the Saturday before Ash Wednesday, when the Queen and her court enter Panama City in the morning to be greeted by Momus, God of Gaiety. Walking bands, *murgas*, play music for the Queen as she leads a parade through the city streets. Events reach a climax with festive evening street dancing. On Sunday, there is another parade, more music and Pollera Day, with all the women wearing exotic hand-embroidered *pollera* dresses. These appliqued dresses are multilayered, brilliantly colored and accented by handmade jewelry and hair ornaments, *tembleques*. It takes a whole year to make one of these dresses, which become family heirlooms. The ladies in their *polleras* meet at Belisario Porras Plaza Sunday afternoon and from there gracefully parade through the streets. At night, the dresses are washed, pressed and put away until next year. Monday festivities feature the *comparasas*, precision dance groups dressed in dazzling costumes. They compete for three prizes, which vary each year. On Tuesday, the day before Ash Wednesday, all the groups who either paraded or performed on previous days join for a huge Grand Parade of floats, music, costumes, confetti, walking bands and dancers.

Crowds move along with the parade as it goes back and forth throughout the city, starting at 3 p.m. It doesn't end but moves into open-air dance halls, social clubs and hotel ballrooms, with festivities ending at dawn. At dawn, the ceremonial "burial of the fish" takes place, officially ending carnival. The carnival attracts hundreds of thousands. The event is subsidized by the government and private industry. There are admission charges to sit in the stands to watch the parades and to attend the balls.

Portobelo

FESTIVAL OF THE BLACK CHRIST

Held annually, October 21
Religious, legendary

The Festival of the Black Christ has been celebrated for more than 300 years, starting when the city was among the world's great trading centers of the Spanish colonial empire. Every year the once splendid city comes alive October 21, when the town's people honor their patron saint, El Jesus Nazarene, whose life-size wooden statue is called the Black Christ. There is a procession of the faithful, who march in the streets as they carry the statue and say prayers. When the statue is returned to its place in the church at the far end of town, the people celebrate with folk dancing, music and songs into the night and the next morning. The festival attracts thousands of pilgrims from all over Panama, coming by car and boat. The 6 p.m. tolling of the church bells officially begins religious sevices in the church, and the procession follows at 8 p.m. El Anda, the platform on which the statue is carried, is decorated with flowers and lighted candles. About 80 men carry the statue and platform on their shoulders. These bearers take two steps forward and one step backward in unison and to the accompaniment of violin music. The priest moves along, giving a blessing to the crowd, and women carrying pots of burning incense follow behind the priest. The people sing a low mourning chant as they move into the procession. The effect is strange and almost hypnotic. There are two legends connected with this annual observance. One deals with a cholera epidemic on the Isthmus. Local people saw a strange crate floating on the water near the beach. Some fishermen went out in their boats, or *cayucos*, to bring it ashore. Upon opening the box, they discovered a statue of a black Christ carrying a crucifix. The statue was brought to the local church, and from that day on, the cholera began to disappear. Within a few days, it completely disappeared from Portobelo, while it still raged in the rest of the Isthmus. This miracle was attributed to the presence of the statue. Immediately, the Black Christ was declared patron saint of the city. The other legend tells of the Catholics of Spain sending the black Christ statue as a gift for a church in Cartagena, Colombia. The ship carrying the statue stopped in Portobelo, as all ships did in those days for fresh supplies and water. When the ship was loaded with provisions and put out to sea, a sudden storm arose, forcing the ship back to Portobelo. This happened five times, so finally the crew decided that the statue should stay in Portobelo. They threw the crate containing the statue into the bay. Local residents were shocked at this disrespect for a holy statue. They pulled the box out of the water and put it in a place of honor in the local church. The statue is credited with thousands of cures and miracles and for helping the city to win the national lottery. The image of the Black Christ is life-size, made of coco-bolo wood and is dark brown. The face reflects sadness and resignation. The eyes are turned up to heaven, and the forehead is stained with blood from the wounds inflicted by the crown of thorns. The Black Christ is wearing clothing of the seventeenth century, similar to the kind Europeans wore then. Artists of that period often clothed religious figures in the clothing of that era. It is estimated that more than 30,000 people attend the festival, which is supported by the local church and by contributions from worshippers and visitors.

PERU

Arequipa

FOLK FESTIVAL

Held annually, August
Folkloric, cultural

The Festidanza, or Folk Festival, is a showcase for many Central and South American countries. It features performances by folkloric groups coming from Brazil, Bolivia, Colombia, Costa Rica, Chile, Ecuador, Mexico and Venezuela. It of course includes Peruvian folk song and dance groups. Its purpose is to be an exchange of customs and cultural achievements, which for the time being are Central and South American. It is financed through admission fees and subsidies from the government.

San Antonio de Pichincha, Cuzco, Andahuaylas and Apurimac valleys

INTI RAYMI FIESTA/SUN FESTIVAL

Held annually, June 24, St. John the Baptist Day
Religious, legendary, pageantry

The Inti Raymi Fiesta or Sun Festival is an ancient Incan festival that honors the Sun God. It coincides with the Feast Day of St. John the Baptist, June 24, and the winter solstice. The seasons are reversed south of the equator. In some areas, the fiesta continues for a week. The ancient residents of the area believed that the sun regulated the universe and controlled the life of plants, animals and man. These ancient people felt that their land was in the center of the earth and so honored the sun god, Inti-Raymi at the southern foot of La Marca Hills. Today's astronomers and geological scientists have confirmed that the dividing point of the earth is only a few meters to the south of these very hills. This is marked by the Equatorial Line Monument, located and built under the direction of geographer and engineer, Luis G. Tufino, in 1936. The Incans, though Christians, still believe that the sun and moon are mystic persons, capable of helping or punishing man. The sun and moon are man and wife and the evening and morning stars, guardians. The Milky Way is a cemetery of beautiful women. Legend, according to the older Indians, claims that the great rock at the top of the same hill of La Marca served as an altar for animal sacrifices to the sun god. These sacrifices were performed by the shaman priest when the sun reached its zenith. This was accompanied by lots of noise and the drinking of *chicha*, made of germinated corn that is ground and fermented. Special dances recalled an ancient battle. Participants were dressed in feathers of macaws and wild turkeys. They also wore masks and brightly colored scarves around their necks. Even today they carry long lances of hardwood palm, usually in their right hands. The dances are performed in rhythmic leaps that resemble elliptical figures, gradually rounding out in the direction of the sun. As the performers leap and dance, they shout "Inti-Raita" or Father Sun, interpreted as shouts of joy and veneration. The dancing is accompanied by the music of the *pinquillo* or bamboo flute and lambskin drums. Bonfires are still lit across the Andes to mark the rebirth of the sun in the Andahuaylas and Apurimac valleys. Residents burn their old clothes as a symbol of destroying poverty and marking the end of the harvest cycle. In Cuzco, there is a special procession and sham sacrifice to the sun, held at Sacsayhuaman Fortress outside the city. Over the years, younger Indians have been taking more of an interest in the ancient festival. Events are financed locally and are open to the public. Usually in Cuzco, it is a week-long event that includes folkloric performances, regional arts, crafts, tours of archeological ruins, colonial houses and churches. There are also exhibits of popular, pre-Columbian and colonial art.

PHILIPPINES

Nationwide

PHILIPPINE CHRISTMAS SEASON

Held annually, December 16–January 6
Religious, folklore, Christmas

The Philippine Christmas season is 22 days long and is said to be the world's longest event, beginning December 16 and ending on the Feast of the Epiphany or Three Kings, January 6. The first day begins with dawn masses at 4 a.m. in every city and *barrio* with church bells ringing out. For nine days prior to Christmas Day, early morning masses, *simbang gabi*, are held. After mass, the people go to small native stands set up at each church to buy steaming cups of ginger tea and some rice cakes to eat and chase away the morning chill. After midnight mass on Christmas Eve, families gather for a special holiday dinner, *noche buena* (good night). Star of Bethlehem lanterns, symbols of Christmas in the Philippines, consist of bamboo sticks covered with thin paper of different colors and used for decorations in steets, plazas, business offices and homes. They are called *parols*, and in San Fernando in Pampanga Province (45 miles from Manila) they are part of a special Christmas Eve celebration. Various *barrios* compete in a giant lantern display parade, the Cavalcade of Stars. Some lanterns (usually placed on trucks) can be as high as 100 feet, decorated with multicolored bulbs and powered by generators. Wayside stands sell native fruits and holiday foods. Choirs of boys and girls sing Christmas carols to the accompaniment of guitars. In the town of Imus in Cavite Province, Christmas Eve is celebrated with a pageant, *panuniuluyan* (seeking shelter), a reenactment of Joseph seeking shelter for Mary about to give birth to the Christ Child. In Mexico and other Latin American countries this *posada*, or procession, is usually held two weeks prior to Christmas. Here, the procession on Christmas Eve consists of *carrosas* (carriages) carrying patron saints around the town. Along the way, the procession stops to ask for shelter. The procession ends at the local church, where there is singing and rejoicing, followed by Christmas midnight mass. The Christmas holiday officially ends January 6. In Manila, in the northern Luzon province of Neuva Ecija and in Gason City on the small island of Marinduque, gift-bearing Three Kings arrive on horseback. Each king is dressed in full regal costume to participate in the pageant of giving gifts to the Christ Child and then to the crowds.

Akland Province (Panay Island)

Kalibo

ATI-ATIHAN FESTIVAL

Held annually, January
Religious, folkloric, commemorative, historic

The three-day Ati-Atihan Festival centers around the feast day of Santo Nino (Holy Child Jesus), patron of the town. It also celebrates the peace pact made more than 700 years ago between the native Negritos and the Malays from Borneo settling there. For the festival, local people, called Ati-Atihan, still cover their bodies with charcoal soot and paint their faces red, blue and white. They wear strange native costumes made from bamboo and abaca (a plant used to make rope). Non-Atis dress like a clown, jester, gypsy or an ape. Often visitors' faces are smudged with soot by the more spirited Atis as an act of friendship. Wild shouts of "Hala Bira, puera pasma!" or "Go on despite the strain" fill the air. Church bells ring as the Atis beat their drums. Everyone parades down the town streets, singing, dancing and forming a Mardi Gras–type parade. The Spanish added the religious note to the event, since the Feast of the Holy Child comes on the same day that the Atis celebrate Ati-Atihan. The final festival day, a Sunday, is marked by religious services and processions.

Marinduque Province (Marinduque Island)

Boac, Gasan

MORIONES FESTIVAL

Held annually, Good Friday to Easter Sunday, March or April movable dates
Religious, folkloric, legendary

The Moriones Festival is a Lenten play about the miraculous cure of the blind eye of Longinus, a Roman centurion who speared the side of Christ on the cross. A drop of blood fell on the Roman's blind eye and restored sight in it. Legend says he proclaimed a miracle and his belief in Christ. The play ends with his beheading. The play was first presented more than a 100 years ago in Mogpog, a small town in the island province. It spread to nearby towns and finally to the province capital city of Boac, which is today's center for the religious festival. Festival participants are called *moriones*. They wear Roman costumes and wooden masks after purchasing festival licenses for a few centavos. The licensed *moriones* join the town's *masquerados* as a form of penance to fulfill some vow or promise. They rove through the towns of Boac, Gasan and Mogpog for four days. On Easter Sunday, they attend the reenactment of the story of Longinus and take part in the chase and capture of the Roman. Festival main events take place on the dried river bed just outside Boac, where shelters are built for visitors to view the activity. The event is financed by private donations.

Quezon Province (Luzon Island)

Manila

FIESTA BLACK NAZARENE

Held annually, January 1–9
Religious, folkloric

Fiesta Black Nazarene honors the Quiapo district of Manila's patron saint, to whom local people attribute many miracles. Starting on New Year's Day and ending January 9, fiesta events include religious services, folk music, songs and dances presented in the Plaza Miranda with fireworks added to each evening's celebrations. Nightly religious services are held in the historic Quiapo Church, where the image of the Black Nazarene was placed. It was taken to the Philippines from Acapulco, Mexico, by Franciscan friars and placed in the original Quiapo Church built of nipa and bamboo in the late sixteenth century. Today, the Black Nazarene is on public display year-round in the church, now a great building. The climax of the fiesta is the procession from the church on January 9 in mid-afternoon and returning in the evening. The life-size statue is taken from its place in the church and carried in a gigantic procession. Barefoot men dressed in undershirts or stripped to the waist carry the full weight of the statue on their shoulders. Thousands of onlookers rush to touch the statue, adding to the burden of those carrying it. Often spectators join the procession of hundreds and carry lighted candles.

Quezon Province

Pulilan, San Isidro, Angono, Sariaya

CARABAO FESTIVAL

Held annually, May 14–15
Harvest, folkloric, pageantry

The Carabao Festival is a harvest celebration, one of the oldest in the Philippines. The earliest inhabitants worshipped gods of harvest, which changed with the coming of the Spaniards and Christianity. Pagan gods were displaced by patron saints, and local farmers eventually adopted San Isidro as their patron, who became responsible for producing an abundant harvest. In Pulilan, San Isidro and Angono, the Carabao Festival is held May 14. Hooves of the *carabao* (water buffalo) are washed and cleaned, and the animals are decorated with floral garlands for the annual parade. The animals pull pretty decorated carts containing crops and farmers dressed in their best clothes. There are also *carabao* races in local fields. Brass bands and pretty ladies lead the parade that goes through the main streets. When passing a church, the *carabaos* are trained to genuflect. The next day, May 15, there is a more formal procession of townspeople and farmers. Celebrating in the towns of Sariaya and Lucban takes place May 15. Houses and fences fronting the parade route in both towns are decorated with bananas, sugar cane, biscuits, candies, cooked food (crab, fish, *lechon*, or roast pig) and multicolored *kipings*, or thin wafers. The farmers' bounty is hung from windows or from bamboo trellis, lowered only when the parade passes by. Later in the afternoon, residents from both towns wait for the procession in which the statue of San Isidro is carried by local men followed by marching bands and floats with pretty girls. Spectators follow the procession to the church, where a thanksgiving service is held.

POLAND

Warsaw

WARSAW AUTUMN/INTERNATIONAL FESTIVAL OF CONTEMPORARY MUSIC

Held annually, September
Cultural

Warsaw Autumn or International Festival of Contemporary Music was launched in 1956 to focus on contemporary music in Poland. It was the idea of several composers, T. Barid, K. Serocki, W. Lutoslawski, W. Kotonski and A. Dobrowolski. Right from the beginning it was to be international in scope to bring other East European as well as West European countries together on a musical basis. The festival has featured famous composers as well as unknown ones. The event is always held in fall since this is prior to the start of the Philharmonic season and makes it easier to book orchestras for the festival. While the emphasis is on contemporary music, dance is sometimes included in the programs. There are also choir performances and soloists. The festival has been responsible for the start of the Polish School of Composition and has gained a high place in international music circles. It features a wide range of modern musical expression, from the "classics" to the avant-garde and experimental music. There are symphony concerts, opera, chamber music and ballet featuring Polish artists and internationally famous ones. The first year's festival attracted an audience of 9,000. By 1976 that number increased to 20,000, with each succeeding year adding a larger audience. Work on the festival is by a special program committee meeting once a week year-round. The event is financed through ticket sales and is subsidized by the government. Performances are in the Concert Hall of the Philharmonic Building and concert areas of the Conservatory.

PORTUGAL

Castro Verde-Beja

OCTOBER FAIR

Held annually, October
Economic, fair

The nine-day October Fair has been held here since 1636. It continues to provide a meeting place for people from the Alentejo and Algarve regions. As many as 60,000 attend one day's events at the local fairgrounds. It is basically a cattle show and market for farming materials and equipment. It has a handicraft bazaar selling woolen blankets, shawls of Castro Verde, sheepskin clothes, baskets, mats and oak furniture. Some of the arts and crafts sold are also demonstrated by visiting artisans. There is entertainment and a circus plus the usual food and drink stands. There is an admission fee, which helps support the fair, which also charges rentals for booths and stalls.

Funchal (Madeira Island)

INTERNATIONAL BACH FESTIVAL

Held annually, June
Cultural

The International Bach Festival only dates back to 1979, but it has gained prominence. It features world famous performers, conductors, ensembles and soloists. It was started to give the island a special event that would attract tourists during its so-called off-season. It attracts thousands. Concerts are given in Funchal's fifteenth-century Se Cathedral and at its eighteenth-century Municipal Theater. The festival, under the direction of Yuval Waldman, stars such international artists as Jean Pierre Rampal, Anthony Newman, Julius Baker, Gerald Schwarz and Elly Ameling.

In 1982, the festival featured not only Johann Sebastian Bach but also Mozart, Telemann and Vivaldi and had an anniversary tribute to Haydn. Festival highlights included Bach's *St. John's Passion* and six Brandenburg Concertos and seven Vivaldi concertos, including *The Four Seasons*. Ensembles included the Berlin Radio Choir, the New York Trumpet Ensemble, the Orlando String Quartet and the Utrecht Symphony Chamber Orchestra. The event is financed by ticket sales, private donations and government grants.

Ponta Delgada (Sao Miguel Island, Azores)

CELEBRATIONS OF THE HOLY GHOST

Held annually, August
Religious, folkloric, legendary

The Celebrations of the Holy Ghost have been observed here since the fifteenth century, when the observance was brought from the continent by the first settlers. The medieval ceremonial of the "empires" has remained intact, with the coronation of the little "emperor" at the domestic altars with the silver crown and sceptre. There is also a procession with floats decorated with symbols of the Holy Ghost and from which a "pension" is distributed to the "brothers of the empire" and the poor. Folias, composed of costumed musicians and singers, sing medieval ballads at different balls and parties. There are Holy Ghost theaters where ancient plays are presented.

Vila Franca de Xira

FESTIVAL OF THE RED WAISTCOAT

Held annually, July
Folkloric

The Festival of the Colete Encarnado, or Red Waistcoat, is an annual summer folk festival centering around the *campionos* (Portuguese cowboys), who wear red waistcoats or vests, green stocking caps and black trousers. The *campionos*, who tend to herding of the the bulls in this area, demonstrate their horsemanship skills and dancing abilities when they perform the *Ribatejan fandango*, a competitive dance for men only. This festival is also the Portuguese version of the running of the bulls in the streets, but with a difference: no one gets hurt, and it's against the law in Portugal to kill the bull. Both amateur and professional bullfighters take turns at bullfighting, which is both exciting and comic. There are other folk dance performances, fireworks and a market. Vila Franca de Xira is about 20 miles from Lisbon.

ROMANIA

Borsa (Maramures County)

PRISLOP ROUND DANCE FESTIVAL

Held annually, second Sunday in August
Folkloric

Hora de la Prislop, or the Prislop Round Dance Festival, at Mount Prislop has been observed for more than a century and still begins with a parade featuring folk costumes of Moldavia, Maramures and Transylvania counties or provinces. It is an annual get-together to enjoy picnics, folk songs and dances. It ends with the Hora or round dance with more than 50,000 people trying to dance it at once. Lately the event has been attracting a record number of tourists, helping the local economy.

Husi (Vaslui County)

DIONYSIAD

Held annually, first Sunday in October
Folkloric, economic, wine

Dionysiad is a tribute to local wines and grapes. The area is noted for ottonel and muscat wines. This is simply a grape gathering event with suitable folk songs and dances. There are also sports contests, including barrel-rolling and competitions in prose and humor in honor of the local wines. Local comedians also perform. The evening ends with a banquet in a local wine cellar, highlighted by special wine tasting sessions.

Mamaia, Efore, Sinala (Constanta County and Black Sea Coast)

NATIONAL FOLKLORE FESTIVAL

Held annually, August
Folkloric, competition

The National Folklore Festival is a month-long competitive and entertainment event alternatively held at Mamaia, Efore and Sinala, all Black Sea Coast resort cities. The dances, songs and national costumes represent all regions of Romania. There are special foods and arts and crafts available. The festival is a competition in song and dance, with winners of this event competing in a larger folkloric event in Yugoslavia. It is supported by the resort cities and government.

SINGAPORE

BIRTHDAY OF THE MONKEY GOD

Held annually, February and September/October, movable dates
Religious

The Birthday of the Monkey God (T'se Tien Tai Seng Yeh) is celebrated twice a year in several Chinese temples in Singapore, with the most popular one being Soon Thian Keng Temple on Bukit Permei. Mediums with skewers pierced through their cheeks and tongues go into a trance during the ceremony and write out special charms in their blood. *Wayang* (Chinese Opera) and puppet shows are performed in the temple courtyard, and processions are held at the temples on Eng Hoon Street and Cumming Street. Chinese parents usually ask the Monkey God to be godfather to their children. They believe the children will grow up tough and strong like the Monkey God who also cures the sick and frees the hopeless.

MID-AUTUMN MOONCAKE FESTIVAL

Held annually, September
Folkloric, commemorative, historic, food

The Mid-Autumn or Mooncake Festival is another major festival in the Chinese calendar and is celebrated by all Chinese communities around the world. It is also called the Mooncake Festival because of the special cakes that are eaten at this time. The cakes recall an uprising against the Mongols in the fourteenth century, when the call to revolt was written on pieces of paper and placed in cakes smuggled out to compatriots. Today, the cakes are filled with a mixture of ground lotus and sesame seeds or dates and sometimes a duck egg. The cakes are usually sold with brightly colored lanterns in the shape of a different animal before the festival begins. Mooncakes in Singapore are filled either with a sweet bean paste or with melon and lotus seeds. Orange peel, egg yolks and spices are added for flavor. On the night of the one-day festival, children all over Singapore stage spontaneous parades, and they carry their lighted lanterns of all shapes and sizes. The festival features lantern-making contests and a historical Chinese costume-making competition. There are also lion and dragon dances and concerts.

NATIONAL DAY

Held annually, August 9
Patriotic

National Day marks the anniversary of Singapore's independence with a variety of events. The traditional parade was decentralized in 1979 to six parade centers to allow greater participation by civilian and cultural groups and organizations. There are military-style parades and also cultural performances in all six parades. Each parade lasts 75 minutes and is reviewed by a senior minister of the government. During the evenings, there are 45-minute firework displays along the waterfront.

SINGAPORE ARTS FESTIVAL

Held annually, December
Cultural

The Singapore Arts Festival was started in 1978 by the Ministry of Culture to give local residents a chance to enjoy drama, music and dance. It also helped attract tourists at this time of year as well. While the festival started out as a local one keyed to Singapore cultural performances and performers, it soon took on an international look. Past international guests have included the world famous Vienna Boys Choir. The three-week festival offers Asian arts, ballet, choral and instrumental music. Both Chinese opera and English plays are presented at the Victoria Theater and at the Cultural Centre. The Singapore Symphony Orchestra also is part of the festival program, and there is an Asian photographic salon at the National Museum Art Gallery. Dance programs include performances by college and dance academy students. There are also many free outdoor programs. The festival is sponsored by the Ministry of Culture and financed through ticket sales and private donations.

SOUTH AFRICA

Inanda

SHEMBE/ZULU FESTIVAL

Held biennially, Sunday nearest July 25
Religious, folkloric

The Shembe or Zulu Festival dates back to 1909 and is a religious event of the Nazarite sect , founded by Isaiah Shembe, an African prophet and faith healer.

The event is held every two years. The festival actually begins a week before, but the Sunday nearest July 25 is the day the religious dance rituals are open to the public. The festival and dances combine ancient pagan ceremonies with the teachings of the Old Testament of the Bible. The July event is a major celebration. There is a minor one in January, but it is not open to outsiders. Both events are held at Ekuphakemeni Shembe's Shrine. The dances are performed by excited and noisy performers. The dances are interesting and include Zulu women, who are divided into age groups. They do a dance of thanksgiving and of rejoicing. The Zulu accept the Old Testament because they can relate to the Biblical military traditions. The event is spontaneous and is the climax of a pilgrimage to Shembe's grave.

Johannesburg

RAND SHOW

Held annually, April/May
Economic, fair

The Rand Show, formerly the Rand Easter Show, is like a state fair in the United States. This one has agricultural, industrial and livestock exhibitions and displays. The livestock include cattle, sheep, goats and pigs. The fairgrounds have national pavilions and a main area for equestrian shows. There is also an amusement park. The fair goes back to March 1895, when it was held during Easter holiday school vacations. However, school vacations have changed and so has the Rand Show to coincide with the new school holidays. The show is sponsored and handled by the Witwatersrand Agricultural Society and is considered to be the country's most important fair of the year. Close to a million people attend each year, and exhibitors number in the hundreds including overseas exhibitors. The most popular fair feature is the consumer goods display. The show also attracts celebrities, and in 1947 it was officially opened by King George VI of England. The fair is financed through admission fees and rentals. The fair is held at Milner Park.

SPAIN ───────────────────────────────────────

Barcelona (Barcelona Province)

INTERNATIONAL MUSIC FESTIVAL/ BARCELONA FESTIVAL

Held annually, October
Cultural

The International Music Festival or Barcelona Festival was launched in 1963 to encourage young Catalan composers and performers to develop their talents. It was started by the already famous. Each year the month-long festival is the setting for 180 world premieres of works by local Catalan composers. The festival was not held in 1975 for political reasons. It was later reestablished, and its continuance and organization is assured by Madrid authorities. The festival, a member of the European Association of Music Festivals, is now international in scope, with musicians and famous artists from other countries featured. The festival is always held in October, as part of the Fiestas de la Merced honoring the city's patron saint, Our Lady of Mercy.

In 1982, there were 27 concerts, some honoring both Haydn and Stravinsky during their special anniversaries. There was a world premiere of a work commissioned by the festival, Leonardo Balada's chamber opera, *Hackland, Hackland*, based on a cowboy theme. Performing ensembles included the Israel Philharmonic, the Chorus and Orchestra of La Scala, Milan, the Madrigal Chorus and Opera Orchestra of Budapest and the Melos Quartet. Among the soloists were Ton Koopman, harpsichordist, Marta Argerich and Jorge Demus, pianists, and tenor Rene Kollo. The festival attracts more than 25,000 people with a grand total of half a million. It is financed through ticket sales and grants from the city government. Performances are given in churches and concert halls throughout the city.

Cadiz (Cadiz Province)

JEREZ DE FRONTERA FESTIVAL

Held annually, September
Harvest, economic, wine

The Jerez (Sherry) de Frontera Festival is a sherry wine harvest celebration that only began in 1948 to call attention to the quality and importance of sherry wines. It was started by the sherry wine industry of the area. Each year, the festival is dedicated to one of the countries that imports Jerez wine. It begins with the blessing of the grapes and the first wine of the season before the statue of Saint Gines de la Jara, patron saint of the region's wine growers. A cavalcade or parade follows, with a festival queen and her court officiating. There is a flamenco festival, a competition of farming skills and literary contests hailing the excellence of the sherry wines. There is also a livestock show, exhibition of horses and bullfights. Some of the sherry exporting companies sponsor folkloric programs. The event attracts thousands of visitors, who are always impressed with the Andalusian costumes worn by marchers in the cavalcade. The event is financed and sponsored by all the local vintners.

Granada (Granada Province)

INTERNATIONAL FESTIVAL OF MUSIC AND DANCE/GRANADA FESTIVAL

Held annually, June/July
Cultural

The International Festival of Music and Dance or Granada Festival was first held in 1952 to call attention to Spanish cultural achievements and to act as an exchange of cultural experiences with other countries. It was started by the Ministry of Fine Arts under the direction of D. Antonio Gallego Burin. Because of Granada's significant history, the city was selected as the setting for the music and dance programs. Performances are still held in the courtyards, gardens and salons of the Alhambra Palace and the Manuel de Falla Center of Granada. World famous conductors, soloists, ballet companies and ensembles appear every year.

The 1982 festival began with a piano recital by Rosa Sabater in the Palacio de Carlos V. Festival highlights included a concert in tribute to Stravinsky by the Ensemble Contraste and a concert by the National Orchestra and Chorus of Spain, conducted by Jesus-Lopez Cobos. Among other famous participants were the mezzo-soprano Christa Ludwig, tenor Jose Carreras, the Philharmonic Orchestra of Leningrad, the National Clasical Ballet and the London Festival Ballet. The festival is a member of the European Association of Music Festivals. It is financed by ticket sales and help from the national government.

Pamplona (Navarra Province)

SAN FERMIN FESTIVAL/RUNNING OF THE BULLS

Held annually, July
Folkloric

The San Fermin Festival or Running of the Bulls, made famous by Hemingway, is observed every July for ten days. It was first held way back in 1591. It celebrates Saint Fermin Day on July 7, patron saint of the city. The running of the bulls in the streets is by far the most spectacular part of the festivities. Events officially begin with the firing of a gun by the president of the Fomento Committee from the balcony of City Hall. This is followed by *txistularis*, or Basque music bands, and marching bagpipe players performing songs that actually announce the running of the bulls to be fought that afternoon. The town's young men, dressed in Pamplona costumes, and lots of tourists run through the streets toward the bullring where the fights are held. There is a great deal of risk involved, with some getting badly hurt or killed. Others wander through the streets, singing, dancing and drinking all day and night. Other events include firework displays, livestock fairs and performances by more than 100 *txistularis*, or Basque flute players, who belong to the Basque-Navarra Association. Pamplona is at the foot of the Pyrenees. The festival is both culturally and economically successful, attracting thousands of visitors to the area. At times, the festival has gotten so wild that it has been canceled. It is financed by local contributions and the city government.

Santander (Santander Province)

INTERNATIONAL FESTIVAL OF MUSIC AND DANCE/SANTANDER MUSIC FESTIVAL

Held annually, July/August
Cultural, folklore

The 37-day International Festival of Music and Dance or Santander Music Festival, dating back to 1951, is a showcase for Spanish-American folklore, opera, recitals, chamber music, ballet and theater. It also offers a symphonic and choral cycle, medieval and Renaissance music, theater and an international piano competition. Performances are given in the tent-covered Plaza Porticada. In 1982, the London Philharmonic Orchestra performed under the direction of Jesus-Lopez Cobos and Maurice Bejart's Ballet of the 20th Century was featured. In the past, the festival has presented folk dance groups from Senegal and Czechoslovakia. The festival is a member of the European Association of Music Festivals. It is financed through ticket sales and government grants.

Seville (Sevilla Province)

APRIL FAIR

Held annually, April
Folkloric, economic, fair

The week-long April Fair usually follows Easter celebrations, unless Easter comes in March. Originally, the fair was a livestock market that gradually added festive events until it became more colorful and exciting. All city streets are decorated with multicolored lights, and booths are set up to sell food, drink and handicrafts. There are all-day folk dances, *Sevilanas*. There is an impressive parade of decorated carriages and the carrying of religious statues. Most local women wear traditional folk costumes of shawls and polka-dotted dresses. During the fair, several bullfights with the most famous fighters featured are held at the Plaza de la Maestranza Ring. Tickets are needed for the bullfights, but most events are free. The fair is financed by contributions from local industry and the city government.

Valencia (Valencia Province)

ST. JOSEPH'S BONFIRES

Held annually, March 12–19
Religious, folkloric

The Fallas of San Jose, or St. Joseph's Bonfires, originated in the sixteenth century with the local carpenters. They often worked well into the night by candlelight or oil lamps placed on large makeshift wooden candelabra. With the coming of spring and longer days, the lights were no longer needed. The eve of St. Joseph's Day (patron of carpenters) was the last evening of the year when the candles and lamps were lighted, making it a time for a celebration. These carpenters enjoyed burning the *parot*, or wooden candelabrum, in front of their shops. They also swept their workshops clean of debris, throwing it into the fire—a sort of spring cleaning. It soon became a fiesta with music, dancing and fireworks. One year, the *parot* was dressed to resemble a local gossip, whose effigy was burned to the amusement of spectators. Eventually the *parots* became large papier-mache and wooden tableaux satirizing national and international personalities, conditions and events, with themes ranging from the high cost of living to modern art or political situations at home or abroad. All of this evolved over the centuries, with today's event basically the same as it was during the middle of the nineteenth century. Today, the figures are several stories high, beautifully colored by artists and skilled technicians, who spend several months preparing them in complete secrecy and under tight security. The tableaux are erected in the different city plazas a few days before the festival begins. All, but one, the *ninot* or grand prize winner, will eventually be burned. Week-long festivities include parades, folk dancing, concerts, theater, sports and the burning of the tableaux.

SRI LANKA (CEYLON)

Nationwide

NATIONAL NEW YEAR/SINHALA AND TAMIL NEW YEAR OBSERVANCE

Held annually, April; movable date
Traditional, New Year

The National New Year Observance or Sinhala and Tamil New Year is based on the Sakha calendar. It is the first day of the Sinhala month of Bak and the Tamil month of Chittrai. The two-day event is a nationwide celebration, with folk dancing, elephant races and racing chariots pulled by dwarf bulls. The New Year of the Sinhalese and Tamils, native peoples of the country, is always in April after the harvest season. While there are public events, the festival remains a family event with special meals and ceremonies, like lighting the hearth and anointing with oil at astrologically auspicious times. Holiday foods include oil cakes, or *kokis* (biscuit-like wafers fried in oil). Young girls dressed in their best holiday clothes usually play together in groups, and a favorite pastime is riding on swings. In most rural villages, there is the playing of *rabanas*, or large bass drums, which are placed over hot coals. Women sit around them to beat out ancient rhythms and sing humorous songs.

Kandy

ESALA PERAHERA

Held annually, July/August, movable date
Religious, pageantry, procession

The Esala Perahera or Mahanuwara Esala Dalada Perahera is a ten-day and ten-night religious festival held in the lunar month of Esala, whose exact dates are determined by the Temple astrologers, according to ancient traditions, and in keeping with the phases of the summer moon. Kandy was the last citadel of the Sinhala kings and a hill capital of Sri Lanka. It is a religious event that dates back to the third century. It is held to honor the Sacred Tooth Relic of the Buddha and is pageantry in its highest form. The *perahera*, or procession, is held nightly. Festivities begin each evening at dusk when the old cannon booms out over the city. Whip throwers and crackers demonstrate their skill at clearing the path for the *perahera*. While torch spinners light the way with fiery jugglery, they add to the glow of the braziers of burning coconuts and the moonlight. Braying conchs echo and re-echo through the hills with cries of "Sadhu," a form of thanksgiving. Thousands of dancers in crimson, white and silver leap and whirl. Chieftains in full regalia, with 40 yards of muslin draped around their waists, follow. Drums roll. Oboes wail. Eighty elephants follow, each different and all draped in silk finery entwined with gold and silver threads and semi-precious stones, wearing tinkling bells and carrying *howdahs*. The Maligawa Tusker, elegantly clad, carries the golden relic casket. The elephant moves gracefully on white cloth laid on the road to avoid stepping on the dirt. The elephant moves with such poise that the golden relic never moves from beneath the huge canopy protecting it. The high point of the procession for spectators is to see the golden relic (Sacred Tooth Relic of Buddha), a symbol of rebirth. The procession is repeated each night, growing larger and larger until the final night. Excitement grows too. There's always the heavy scent of jasmine and burning incense in the background. The festival's last day ends with a morning parade. This observance is said to have been started by the ancient kings of Sri Lanka, starting with King Kirthisiri Meghawanna, who ruled in the ancient capital of Anuradhapura from A.D. 303 to 331. The observance continued, but over the centuries it waned until it was revived and expanded by King Kirthisiri Rajasinghe in 1775. The expansion incorporated Hindu rituals in the original Buddhist theme. It is always held in either July or August because this is spring harvest time for the area, which observes a different calendar. The observance helps to keep the area's cultural traditions and artistic expressions alive. It attracts more than 100,000 people. Preparations are made only three weeks in advance of the festival, which is supported by local contributions and the ancient system of land tenure.

SWEDEN

Nationwide

SANTA LUCIA FESTIVAL

Held annually, December 13
Folkloric, religious, pageantry

The annual Santa Lucia Festival is a nationwide celebration based on a religious legend. St Lucy was born and lived in Sicily, Italy. On the eve of her wedding, she donated her entire dowry to the poor of her village and confessed that she was a Christian. She was accused of witchcraft and was burned at the stake, December 13, A.D. 304. She was later cannonized as Santa Lucia. Sweden has traditionally always recognized her as the Queen of Light and holds a celebration December 13 to honor the return of light after the dark winter. While the winter solstice, the shortest day of the year, is December 22, the original celebration was held when the Julian calendar was still used. When the Lucia tradition began, December 13 was then the winter solstice. Sweden adopted the Gregorian calendar in 1753 but still celebrated the return of light, Santa Lucia Day, on December 13. It is a family event, but recently it has become a community one and is observed in offices, factories and schools. Each Swedish community elects its own Lucia, and the election is usually sponsored by a local newspaper. A Lucia Parade is combined with the election as a fund-raising event for a needy charity. The biggest public celebration is held in Stockholm, where hundreds of girls compete for the Stockholm Lucia title. The final election is by popular vote and is among ten girls already selected by a special jury. The evening of December 13, the Stockholm Lucia and her attendants and followers parade in the city streets riding in decorated carriages. Hundreds watch as the parade ends at City Hall. In homes and local churches, Santa Lucia wears a long white gown and on her head a crown of lighted candles set in a green wreath of lingonberry sprigs. Saffron buns are traditionally served everywhere. Often gingerbread cookies and a hot cup of *glogg*, a spicy wine punch, a Swedish Christmas season drink, are also served.

Drottningholm (near Stockholm)

DROTTNINGHOLM COURT THEATER SEASON

Held annually, June/August
Cultural

Opera and ballet performances are given every year in the eighteenth-century rococo Drottningholm Court Theater, Europe's oldest theater still in use with its original paintings and stage mechanisms. The event is known simply as the Drottningholm Court Theater Season. The theater was built in 1776 by Queen Lovisa Ulrika, sister of Frederick the Great of Prussia, to bring continental culture to Scandinavia. It was built as an addition to the summer royal palace in Drottningholm, about ten-miles from Stockholm. A year later it passed to King Gustav III, who for 15 years made it the country's center for theatrical and musical entertainment. When the king was assassinated in the new opera house in Stockholm (immortalized by Verdi in *Un Ballo in Maschera*), the theater was not used and fell into neglect. It was forgotten for 130 years. A young librarian, Agne Beier, found it by accident. It was dusty and filled with junk but still intact. Now every summer it is the setting for opera and ballet featuring world famous companies and performers. The theater itself is interesting. The stage, orchestra pit and seats are within one large room decorated with painted woodwork gilded to look like marble and gold. The theater has 470 seats and a huge stage 62 feet deep. It originally was meant only for the king and queen and their retinue. Two-hundred-year-old marks on the blue benches show where the noblemen, the king's guard and "His Majesty's Second Valet," sat. Tiny electric lights in the crystal chandeliers indicate the twentieth century, but nothing else has changed. Ushers and musicians wear powdered wigs and period costumes, all original. Even the orchestra's conductor is costumed. The costumes and settings are actually from the theater's own eighteenth-century collection. The 1982 season featured the ballet *Two Harlequins* and the operas *Montezuma* by Roger Sessions, *La Cenerentola* by Rossini and *The Magic Flute* by Mozart. The theater is financed through ticket sales and by the Swedish government, which pays about three-quarters of the cost. For every front row ticket sold, the national, county and state governments contribute twice its price.

Jokkmokk (Lapland)

GREAT LAPP WINTER FAIR

Held annually, February
Economic, fair

The four-day Great Lapp Winter Fair was started more than a 100 years ago for trading purposes among the Lapps and for the exchange of ideas, as well as for some dancing, drinking and eating. The Lapps display and sell handicrafts made during the rest of the year. Special Lapp foods are served. The fair is always held at this time of year because all of the Lapps and their reindeer are in the area. The event also helps introduce visitors to the Lapp culture and brings tourist dollars to the area. As many as 10,000 attend. The most popular fair features are the reindeer roundup demonstrations and the marking of the reindeer. Work on the fair is by volunteers from among the Lapps. The event is financed by each Lapp who attends. Eveyone pays their own expenses, and there is no admission charge to the fair. The fair is held in an open field with a marketplace for selling goods in tents.

SWITZERLAND

Appenzell (Commune of Urnasch)

SWISS NEW YEAR'S EVE CELEBRATION

Held annually, January 13
Folkloric, New Year

The Swiss New Year's Eve Celebration in Appenzell is still celebrated January 13 by local residents, who continue to follow the Julian calendar and have done so since 1582. Dressed in unusual costumes and silly headgear and wearing huge clanking cowbells, these "Sylvesterklaeuse" jump, dance and make noise as they go from house to house. According to legend, they are driving out evil spirits so that the New Year will be good and safe. The Julian calendar dates back to 45 B.C. and in comparison with the presently used Gregorian calendar is 13 days behind. The Protestants of Appenzell still observe the Julian New Year's Eve on January 13. It's a festive time with yodeling and carrying on. The villagers whose homes are visited repay the Sylvesterklaeuse with coins, wine and presents.

Lausanne (Vaud Canton)

INTERNATIONAL FESTIVAL OF LAUSANNE

Held annually, May/June
Cultural

The International Festival of Lausanne offers two months of opera, concerts, ballet and jazz with famous performers who appear in the Palais de Beaulieu Convention and Exhibition Center. The center contains the 1,900-seat Theater Congress Hall, the 730-seat Cinema and Festival Hall.

The 1982 season opened with a program of Negro spirituals sung by the Davis Sisters and closed with Verdi's *La Traviata* with Katia Ricciarelli as Violetta. Other operas included Mozart's *Lucio Silla* and *Idomeneo*, Smetana's *The Bartered Bride*, Janacek's *Cunning Little Vixen* and Dvorak's *Rusalka*. Also performing were the Festival Strings of Lucerne, the Orchestra and Chorus of the Suisse Romande, the Chamber Orchestra of Lusanne, the Zurich Opera, the State Opera of Brno with Claudio Arrau, pianist, and violinist Gidon Kremer. The London Sinfonietta was conducted by the Hans Werner Henze. Ballet companies from Hamburg, Geneva, Marseilles and the Paris Opera performed, and Jack DeJohnette's *Special Edition* was given in a jazz recital. The festival began in 1955. It is financed by ticket sales and by private donations.

Lucerne (Lucerne Canton)

INTERNATIONAL FESTIVAL OF MUSIC/ LUCERNE FESTIVAL

Held annually, August/September
Cultural, economic

The International Festival of Music or Lucerne Festival was launched in 1938, when the city president, Dr. Jakob Zimmerli, persuaded Arturo Toscanini to conduct a concert at the Tribschen estate, once the home of composer Richard Wagner. The city had purchased the estate in 1933 and turned it into the Wagner Museum. In the same year, the city opened a new art gallery and Congress Hall, with a Museum of Art and a house that became the concert hall for the music festival. Because the festival began shortly before the start of World War II, it actually filled a cultural void during the war years and also attracted famous conductors and performers, all war refugees. Dr. Zimmerli had help in persuading Toscanini to come to Lucerne from Ernest Ansermet, the founder of the Orchestre de la Suisse Romande, who members, under Ansermet's direction, gave a concert July 1938 in the Kursalla. In addition to Toscanini, other famous personages in the early days of the festival included Bruno Walter, Willem Mengelberg, Fritz Busch, Wladimir Horowitz, Walter Gieseking, Arthur Schnabel, Pablo Casals, Bronislaw Huberman, Adolf Busch and Rudolf Serkin. Sergei Rachmaninov played his Rhapsody for Piano and Orchestra, Opus 43, in 1939 under Ansermet's baton. In 1943 the Swiss Festival Orchestra was formed by Ernest Ansermet, Fritz Busch and Bruno Walter. It is a vital part of each year's festival and consists of the best musicians from Swiss orchestras and can only be heard at this festival. Each year's event is themed to the music of a different country. In 1982, the theme was "Music in Britain." Each year's event attracts more than 30,000, and to date, the total is well over a million. The festival is financed through ticket sales, donations from individuals and subsidies from the local government. Performances are held throughout the city in concert halls, in churches and in the open air. The festival is a member of the European Association of Music Festivals.

Montreux (Vaud Canton)

MONTREUX INTERNATIONAL MUSIC FESTIVAL/MONTREUX JAZZ FESTIVAL

Held annually, July
Cultural

The 17-day Montreux International Music Festival or Montreux Jazz Festival was first held in 1966 to create a medium for the expression of jazz around the world. It continues to attract top performers in jazz, offering a variety of styles. Most concerts are given in the Montreux Casino, overlooking Lake Geneva. The 1982 festival featured new music from Brazil, reggae and jazz bands from both Purdue University and Western Michigan University from the United States. There also were rock music concerts plus a blues marathon, a salute to Lionel Hampton and on the last day a tribute to Detroit, Michigan, U.S.A. There is now a Montreux–Detroit Jazz Festival in Detroit every September, started about two years ago. In the past, the Swiss festival has honored the Newport Jazz

Festival and other worldwide jazz events. This annual program has also featured folk and country music and soul tunes. It is financed through ticket sales and sponsorships by various businesses.

Montreux–Vevey (Vaud Canton)

FESTIVAL OF MUSIC MONTREUX-VEVEY

Held annually, August/October
Cultural

The 38-day Festival of Music Montreux–Vevey started in September 1946 as the September Musical to attract culturally minded tourists in the off-season to the neighboring resorts of Montreux and Vevey on Lake Geneva. The festival, a member of the European Association of Music Festivals, offers five weeks of concerts and soloists with world famous ensembles and artists. Festival performances are held in the Montreux Congress Hall, the Theatre de Vevey, the Church of St. Martin, the Montreux Palace, the Chateau d'Aigle and the Castle of Chillon.

The 1982 event featured the Sofia Philharmonic, London Symphony, Rotterdam Philharmonic, New Orleans Philharmonic, Academy of St. Martin in the Fields, I Musici, Camerata Bern, Ensemble Instrumental de France, Johann Strauss Ensemble of Vienna, Cologne Chamber Orchestra, Vienna Bach Ensemble, Yuval Trio and London Early Music Group. Participants included conductors Eugene Ormandy, Claudio Abbado and Philippe Entremont (as conductor and soloist), Maurice Andre, trumpeter, Jean-Pierre Rampal, flutist, Edith Mathis, soprano, Radu Lupu and Claudio Arrau, pianists, and Andre Segovia, guitarist. Ticket prices ranged from $11 to $55 per person. This helps finance the annual event, as do private donations and grants from each resort city.

Vevey (Vaud Canton)

WINE GROWERS' FESTIVAL

Held once every 25 years, in August; next: 2002
Pageantry, folkloric, wine

The Fete des Vignerons, or Wine Growers' Festival, is a once in a lifetime event. It is held four times a century, or every 25 years. The last one was in 1977, so the next will be in the twenty-first century. Sometimes there are only 20 years between festivals, which honor the local winegrowers in the Canton of Vaud. The 16-day August festival attracted several million visitors, who not only watched several huge parades complete with floats, but also attended the festival pageant at the local amphitheater, which seats 15,000. The festival pageant themed to the seasons of the year was performed 12 times a day during the spectacular folk festival. More than 4,000 townspeople participated in the pageant, which also included singers and dancers from all over Europe. The pageant was staged by Maurice Lehmann, managing director of the Paris Opera. Each performance continued the age-old tradition of crowning the winegrowers with wreaths of gilded vine leaves. The last festival had four parades with 4,000 costumed marchers, 750 musicians, singers and animals. The festival dates back to 1797, staged by the Brotherhood of Winegrowers (Confrerie des Vignerons) in the canton of Vaud, where the first grape vines were planted by monks during the Middle Ages. The 1977 festival was entirely different from the 1955 one. There was a new score, a new libretto and new costumes. The Confrerie paid for half the cost of each person's costume, which was not to exceed $25, but many people spent more. They were reimbursed by the profits realized from the festival. This event is partially financed by the Confrerie des Vignerons, who donated $100,000 from their treasury, with another $300,000 coming from business, local and cantonal governments and private individuals, followed by local banks advancing the rest. The production costs more than $1 million. Gross receipts realized from festival ticket and parade sales totaled $1.5 million. After the Confrerie reimbursed all the townspeople for their costume expenses, there was a clear profit of $300,000. Part of this was donated to charity and the balance for vinicultural research and for a trust fund for the next festival. While the festival is a huge success in every way, it is only held once every 25 years because of the expense and work involved in producing it.

Zurich (Zurich Canton)

INTERNATIONAL JUNE FESTIVAL

Held annually, May/early July
Cultural

The International June Festival, originally the Zurich May Festival, dates back to May 1909 and was patterned after the Bayreuth Festival, with the first program being the entire "Ring" production. It was started to give Switzerland a cultural event of prominence, and it has succeeded. It was also started to give singers and actors more work, since the opera season in 1909 usually ended in April. While basically an opera festival, today it also offers concerts, ballet and recitals, headlined by famous performers. The 1982 season offered opera performances of *Carmen, Der Rosenkavalier, Fidelio, Werther, Lohengrin, Lucio Silla* and *Idomeneo* as well as concerts by the Pittsburgh Symphony under Andre Previn, the Tonhalle Orchestra under Christoph Eschenbach and the Zurich Chamber Orchestra under Edmond de Stoutz. Also appearing were pianists Murray Perahia and Claudio Arrau, violinist Nathan Milstein, trumpeter Maurice Andre, tenor

Alfredo Kraus and soprano Jessye Norman. The festival was founded by the then director of the Zurich Opera House, Alfred Reucker, who later became director of the Dresden State Opera House, 1921–33. The festival also offers exhibitions and plays, with all major Zurich cultural groups and institutions participating and guest performances by top foreign theatrical companies and orchestras. The festival attracts up to 150,000 annually, and since 1909, several million. In recent years, the festival has added some free performances and free museum days. Work on the festival is by a special festival organization with paid staffers. It is financed by ticket sales and by sponsorship of the Cultural Department of the city of Zurich. Performances are held throughout the city in theaters, museums and concert halls. Exhibits in city museums are keyed to the annual festival, and master classes in music are also offered.

THAILAND

Nationwide

LOY KRATHONG FESTIVAL/FESTIVAL OF LIGHT

Held annually, November
Religious, folkloric, legendary, pageantry

The Loy Krathong Festival or Festival of Light is a thanksgiving to Mae Kongkha, goddess of all rivers and waterways. It is a thanksgiving for her gift of the waters to mankind. It is celebrated throughout the country but is especially significant in Sukhothai, the first capital of Thailand and where Lady Nopphamat created and launched the first *krathong*. Loy Krathong signifies that all life depends upon water. *"Loy"* or *"loi"* usually is a Thai word for "to float," and *"krathong"* is "leaf cup" or "bowl," usually made from a banana leaf or colored paper in the shape of a lotus blossom. The festival is observed by fashioning these bowls and placing in each one a candle and four joss sticks with some flowers. A small coin and a bit of betel nut and leaf are sometimes added. Loy Krathong is observed by the floating of these leaf cups and bowls along Thailand's rivers, streams and canals as an act of worship to Mae Konghka for her bounty. When the full moon rises, thousands carry their *krathongs* to the edge of the water. The candle and joss sticks are lighted, and the bowls are set on the water's surface. It is a spectacular sight. The *krathongs* float slowly and far out of sight. The festival is of Brahminical origin. Legend claims that Nang Noppamas, the daughter of a Brahmin priest at the court of King Phra Ruang during the country's Sukhothai period of more than 800 years ago, originated and set sail the first *krathong*. Today, the festival also includes a beauty contest to select a Nang

Noppamas. The winner represents the daughter of the Brahmin priest throughout the festival, which varies in length throughout Thailand, ranging from one to three days. It is festively celebrated in Bangkok and Chiang Mai. Many temples also observe a three-day full moon of the twelfth lunar month, or Ngan Duan Sipsong. There are also country fairs and night bazaars at the Golden Mount Temple in Bangkok and Phra Pathom Chedi in nearby Nakhon Pathom.

Bangkok

KITE FLYING SEASON

Held annually, February/April
Sports, folkloric, competition

The Kite Flying Season is a three-month contest held at Sanam Luang in front of the Grand Palace weekday afternoons. Contestants with elaborate kites attempt to knock down opponents through the manipulations of their own kite strings. In conjunction with the competitions, there are dance and music performances every weekend afternoon in the National Museum Compound at the corner of Sanan Luang. It is sponsored by the country's Fine Arts Department.

Paklat, Bangkok, Chiang Mai, nationwide

WATER FESTIVAL

Held annually, April 13–15
Traditional, folkloric, New Year

The Songkran, or Water Festival is the traditional Thai New Year's Day celebration that marks the assumed entrance of the sun into Aries. It is a folk festival of throwing or sprinkling water on Buddha images, monks or elders of the family. It is the time also when captive fish and birds are set free. There are colorful processions and traditional games in Chiang Mai. April 13 is a public holiday throughout the country. In the mornings, people go to monasteries with offerings of rice, meat and fruit to the monks. In the afternoons, there are purification rites when everyone is sprinkled with holy water. Sometimes parents are sprinkled with perfumed water by their children. It usually results in a free-for-all, with everyone pouring water on everyone else. Water-filled plastic bags are sold so that everyone can do some dousing. And this can happen to tourists, too. This is the holiday when presents are usually towels.

Surin

ELEPHANT ROUNDUP

Held annually, third weekend in November
Sports, economic, folkloric, competition

The Elephant Roundup started out in 1961 as a one-day overnight package deal developed by the Tourist Organization of Thailand to arouse interest in an area where elephants are hunted, captured and trained for use all over Thailand. Some 100,000 elephants still work in the country's teak forests. Surin is about 250 miles from Bangkok and an overnight train ride. Surin's residents, members of the Suay tribe, have been handling elephants for the last six generations, and it is they who hold the Elephant Roundup, a sort of elephant rodeo event that attracts thousands of tourists annually. It has gotten so popular that it has been extended to two days during the third weekend in November. The roundup is held in an outdoor arena, and the show begins with a procession of more than 200 very large gray elephant bulls, cows and calves. This is followed by a roundup of wild elephants and surprising demonstrations of the elephant's dexterity, obedience and work. There are elephant races and a tug of war between a hundred men and one elephant, who easily wins. There is a soccer match between the elephants that is so well done that the crowds are soon cheering on their favorite team. The roundup finale is a mock battle featuring war elephants in combat panoply carrying brilliantly costumed warriors on their backs and shaking the ground when they charge. During the roundup there are folk dances performed by local residents dressed in traditional Thai costumes. Each dance is accompanied by its own style of music. An especially popular dance is one in which a young couple skillfully dance weaving in and out of two long poles clacked together by a man on each end. Surin streets are closed for elephant rides after the day's roundup is over. There is also a country fair and night bazaar.

TRINIDAD & TOBAGO

Port-au-Spain

THE TRINIDAD & TOBAGO CARNIVAL

Held annually, Monday and Tuesday before Ash Wednesday, February or March, movable dates
Pageantry, competition

While it is called the Trinidad & Tobago Carnival, all frenzied activity centers in Port-au-Spain on Trinidad. On the Monday before Ash Wednesday, the start of the Lenten season, the bacchanal begins at dawn with the "Joovay" from *jour overt* or "opening day" with merrymakers parading and dancing through the streets to strains of steelband music. The crowds all gather or try to at Independence Square where "Carnival" is officially declared. King Carnival is welcomed and there is the parade of bands on city streets, various carnival competitions in the afternoon and evening both at indoor and outdoor centers. The Carnival continues through Tuesday with marchers and spectators staying up for 48 consecutive hours. There is a second parade of bands and more competitions leading to the "las lap," a final, frenzied jump-up in the streets. By midnight, it's all over for another year. If all this sounds tame, it isn't. These two round-the-clock festive days are preceded by nine days of special events which include the Children's Carnival competition; the crowning of Junior Carnival Queen; "Ole Mas" competition; the steelband finals; the Jaycees "Carnival Queen" Show and the Dimanche Gras Show (Sunday evening before the two Carnival days) when the "Queen of Carnival," "King of Carnival," and "Calypso King" are crowned. The two carnival day parades are a spectacle, one not easily forgotten for those lucky enough to see at least one. There are from 25 to 30 costume bands with about 2500 costumed marchers for each band and each with its own King and Queen. The persons finally selected as "King and Queen of Carnival" preside over all the festivities. The costumes are magnificent.

For example in 1983, the reigning King of Carnival wore a butterfly costume, designed by Peter Minshall, who dressed the "Papillon" (French for butterfly) band to symbolize the spirit of carnival: birth, death and resurrection. The 1983 King's butterfly costume had a wing spread of 20 by 25 feet, created from fiberglass, fishnet and 224,400 metallic sequins. And still the King was able to dance his way across the stage during the competition. It is a carnival stipulation that marchers wear costumes that will not interfere with their parading across the reviewing platform. They must do this unassisted. Minshall's handmade costumes for the 2500 marchers in the band involved the fantastic numbers of one and a half million sequins, 15,329 yards of taffeta, 989 yards of organdy, 125 Oriental blinds and several miles of fiberglass. More than 70 people worked on them. Over the years, many of the artists who have designed the costumes and composed the calypso tunes, the two biggest Carnival attractions, have gone on to fame and fortune. Trinidad calypsonian, The Mighty Sparrow, gained fame in 1956 for his carnival tune, "Jean and Dinah." Costume designer Wayne Berkeley was asked to create costumes for the Paris Lido and Moulin Rouge as a result of his carnival designs. In 1982, he used the theme of "Victory at Trafalgar," showing in costume the final defeat of Napoleon's forces by Britain's Horatio Nelson. Costumed marchers portrayed the heroes and Nelson's battleship with a 40-foot mast and flying the Union Jack. Once the Carnival is over, all costumes are displayed so that the intricate design and work can be appreciated by visitors. Work on these costumes is almost a year-round activity with real activity beginning soon after Christmas and New Year's Day. Many costumes are displayed in costume shops at this time. Steelbands and calypso composers begin their work in calypso "tents" and "panyards." Carnival structures begin to take shape around the Savannah, the city's 200-acre park, the competition site. Victorian cottages, workplaces for the small costume shops, are set up and the steelbands put the finishing touches to their compositions in the city's panyards. All are open to the public. The calypso "tents" are not tents but concert halls that seat hundreds every night as the calypsonians compete for the "Calypso Monarch" title. They sing their newest works late into the night. They write their own music and lyrics which can relate to politics, local gossip, neighbors and so on. Some are funny but always clever, based on the ancient word of mouth communication. One of these songs will be selected as the "Road March" of the Carnival, a great honor for the singer/composer. The costume workshops, called "mas camps" are where the beautiful ornate costumes are produced. "Carnival costumes are the ultimate symbols of our liberation," says Trinidad-born Geoffrey Holder, famous as a dancer, choreographer, costume and set-designer. "Once a year, any man or woman, the poorest person in the street, can dress in the most fanciful costume and vie for the coveted 'King' or 'Queen of Carnival' title." Up to 75 men and women work together in the small Victorian cottages to create these intricate costumes. Costume bands can consist of as many as 5,000 marchers each. They are divided into different sections to portray a single overall theme selected by a designer for that year.

The history of Trinidad & Tobago Carnival goes back more than 200 years when Trinidad was under Spanish rule. In 1783, when the French assumed control, they launched a gala season from Christmas to Ash Wednesday. They introduced bands as masked and disguised individuals, accompanied by musicians. These bands walked in the streets, stopping to visit homes of friends. They often attended holiday balls. The Amerindians did not participate and Negro slaves were banned by law from participating. However, with the emancipation of the slaves in 1833, the Carnival underwent many major changes with all those previously excluded joining in and dominating the street bands. The French stayed in their homes. Today, every person of this multi-racial island is an active part of the Carnival. The excitement begins after New Year's Eve and doesn't end until midnight when Ash Wednesday and Lent begins. During Carnival days, vendors sell some very exotic foods and drinks to carnival goers. For example there are spicy aromas of *callaloo*, a Creole soup of dasheen leaves, okra and even crab. There's *roti*, a pastry filled with curried beef, chicken, goat or shrimp, bread and *bulljol* (salt codfish) and tree oysters. This is all washed down with the famous local rum punch and coconut milk. The Carnival is best described by native son, Geoffrey Holder: "This is our grand release. We sing, dance, laugh and boogie for two days and nights. We are purified and revitalized through Carnival." Millions have attended and participated. It is financed by the participating individuals and help from the local government, the sale of souvenirs, food and special tickets where needed.

TUNISIA

Carthage (North Tunis Region)

INTERNATIONAL FESTIVAL OF CARTHAGE

Held annually, July/August
Cultural, economic

The International Festival of Carthage was started in 1963 by the Tunisian Ministry of Cultural Affairs to bring the culture of the West to Tunisia and to share Tunisian culture with the West in one celebration. It was also introduced to attract more foreign tourists in the off-season, and allows its own citizens to express their own creative talents and abilities. The festival features classical music, jazz, folk music and dance, theater, films and ballet. Tunisian theater, dance and music performers appear together with foreign artists at the Roman amphitheater. Among foreign countries that have participated over the years are France, Germany, Spain, the Soviet Union and various other Eastern European countries. About 50,000 attend each year, making a grand total of close to a million, many tourists. The festival has headlined such personalities as James Brown, Joan Baez, Ray Charles, Cab Calloway and various famous Arabic and French stars. Modern music and jazz are very popular. Work on the festival is by a paid staff, who work intensely for eight months prior to the festival and then all through the two-month event. It is financed through ticket sales and a subsidy from the Tunisian government.

Douz (The South Sahara Region)

SAHARA NATIONAL FESTIVAL

Held annually, November/December, movable date
Folkloric, harvest, economic

The Sahara National Festival is a one-week date harvest event and a time for the gathering of nomads and Bedouins from all over the country. The time of the festival varies, depending upon weather conditions, to ensure harvesting. Douz is considered the gateway to the Sahara Desert, and during the festival, which is open to visitors, tribesmen compete in camel races and perform traditional music. There is also a poetry contest, a traditional wedding ceremony and greyhound racing. Since this is the harvest time for the date palm, there is also a date marketplace set up during the festival. Fresh dates together with *lagmi* (the juice of the palm, fermented in the sun) are sold as well as camels, incense, ebony, copper items, rugs, desert sand flowers, caftans, white wire birdcages and Berber tapestries. The market is usually held on a Thursday and is open to anyone with money. This festival has been held for centuries and has attracted hordes of tribesmen and, in modern times, an equal horde of tourists. Work on the festival is by local residents, who volunteer their time and prepare details about two months before the festival. There is no admission charge to the festival. All competitions and performances are free. It is financed through marketplace sales and is subsidized by the government and National Tunisian Tourist Office.

Hammamet (Nabeul Region)

INTERNATIONAL FESTIVAL OF HAMMAMET

Held annually, July/August
Cultural, folkloric, economic

The International Festival of Hammamet was organized in 1963 by the Tunisian Ministry of Cultural Affairs and shares its performers and events with the International Festival of Carthage. It was started to introduce Tunisians to Western culture and to encourage young Tunisians to pursue the arts, their own and Western. It was also aimed at giving tourists something to enjoy. It has attracted hundreds of thousands of people over the years. It offers drama, folkloric songs, dances, music and art. Performances are at the open-air theater of the city's International Cultural Center, the former home of the American architect Sebastian. He gave his home to the city government for the purpose of establishing a cultural center. The festival is financed through ticket sales and grants from the Tunisian Ministry of Cultural Affairs.

TURKEY

Edirne

WRESTLING GAMES OF KIRKPINAR

Held annually, June
Sports, folkloric, competition

The Wrestling Games of Kirkpinar are not only a Turkish national sports event but also an annual reenactment each June of a military training exercise introduced by Sultan Murat I more than 600 years ago. The training took place on the palace grounds in Kirkpinar outside Edirne (not far from Istanbul). It was designed to keep the troops in a fighting mood just before their raids into Eastern Europe. Today's oil wrestling techniques, ornately decorated leather breeches and nonstop wild Turkish music are all part of an unbroken tradition handed down from father to son and practiced through 33 sultanates and 4 republican presidencies. The wrestling is held in a one-acre field covered with grass up to six inches high. Fifty men wrestle at one time, and there is no time limit. All the wrestlers are covered with olive oil (one and a half tons of it are used during the matches). Rules allow for a wrestler to pick his oppponent up off the ground with his head facing down and turn him around in a complete circle. Or a wrestler can pick an opponent up and carry him three paces or turn him over so that two-thirds of his stomach faces the sun. Or a wrestler can always pull his opponent's trousers down. Kicking, punching and strangling are frowned on but not really forbidden. Wrestlers mostly stand with arms clasped around each other's necks, pushing and straining. Folk dancing and music provide some intermission and also have a cheerleading effect on the wrestlers. The games are held for a week.

Istanbul

FESTIVAL OF ISTANBUL

Held annually, June/July
Cultural

The Festival of Istanbul attempts to follow the philosophy of Mustafa Kemal Ataturk, father of the Turkish Republic, that of Turkey being the bridge between East and West. The festival is the bridge between Eastern and Western cultures. It has become an international event, with world famous composers, conductors, performers, theater, ballet performances of foreign and Turkish works and art exhibits. Since the first festival was held in 1973, it has attained major importance in the festival world. It is a member of the European Association of Music Festivals. The festival marked its tenth year in 1982 with "Nights of Sultan Ahmet," a reenactment of traditional Ottoman entertainment with shadow plays, Turkish commedia dell'arte, music and dances. Mozart's *Abduction from the Seraglio*, staged by the Romanian State Opera, was performed on the grounds of Topkapi Palace. Other participants included I Solisti di Zagreb, the London Festival Ballet, the Trinidad Dance Group, La Goya Guitarists, the Bartok Quartet, the Argentinian Dance Ensemble, the Haydn Trio, the Warsaw Quartet, Leila Gencer, soprano, Emil Gilels, pianist, and the State Opera and Ballet of Ankara. Tickets cost from $1 to $5 per person per performance. The festival was originally organized by the Istanbul Foundation for Culture and the Arts. It continues to offer traditional and contemporary theater, dance and music. Performances are held at Rumelihisar Open-Air Theater, a fifteenth-century Ottoman fortress accommodating up to 1,000 persons and at the fourth-century Byzantine basilica,

St. Irene's Church, seating 1,200. Performances are also held at the 4,000-seat Harbiye Open-Air Theater and at a Byzantine fortress, Yedikule Open-Air Theater, with room for 2,500. The festival continually seeks the advice and help of foreign embassies, and cultural offices. The festival attracts as many as 70,000 persons, many tourists. The festival is financed through ticket sales, private donations and government subsidy.

Izmir

INTERNATIONAL FAIR

Held annually, August/September
Economic, fair

The International Fair is a major annual fair with commercial exhibits of Turkish products and products from around the world. There are arts and crafts displays and demonstrations as well as special fine art exhibits and cultural programs of opera, ballet and drama. There's folk dancing in the city squares and other entertainment and special foods available. The fair is financed through admission and rental fees and a subsidy from the city government.

Konya

FESTIVAL OF MEVLANA

Held annually, December
Religious

The nine-day Festival of Mevlana centers on the ritual performances of the Mevlevis, or whirling dervishes, in the afternoons and evenings. This religious group was founded in the thirteenth century by Mevlana Celaleddin Rumi, a Turkish poet and mystic. The ritual dances were banned earlier in this century, but in 1954, Konya was allowed to hold them again. They are performed to the accompaniment of chanting and music of the flute, zither and drum. The dervishes turn or whirl in a dance that is supposed to be a mystical talk with the Divine. There are also special Seljuk art exhibits and lectures on the Mevlevis. The art works date back to the eleventh century.

UNION OF SOVIET SOCIALIST REPUBLICS

Leningrad

WHITE NIGHTS FESTIVAL

Held annually, June
Cultural

The nine-day White Nights Festival is an annual June event centering on classical ballet and folk dancing as well as musical theater and opera. It takes its name from the fact that the sun shines round the clock in the area at this time of year. The festival offers the best in productions with performers, winners of national and international competitions in the various arts, presented. The emphasis, however, is more on Soviet performers and companies like the Kirov Opera and Ballet Theater and performances by the students of the Leningrad Choreographic School named for A. Vaganova, considered the best in Russian ballet circles. Concerts are given by the Leningrad Symphony Orchestra, and performing artists from several Soviet Union republics are featured during the festival. This event was started in 1964. About 250,000 attend each year's programs, and this includes a large number of tourists. The festival is handled and subsidized by the USSR Ministry of Culture, Soyuzconcert and various Soviet and theatrical institutions.

Moscow

MOSCOW STARS FESTIVAL

Held annually, May
Cultural

The nine-day Moscow Stars Festival attracts nearly half a million people, which includes tourists. It is a festival of the arts covering opera, ballet, symphonic, instrumental and vocal music, with both Russian, Soviet and foreign composers featured. It is primarily concerned with prize-winning creative works from national and international competitions. Performing groups are selected based on proposals made to the festival organizers. Performances are held throughout the city, including the main stage of the Bolshoi Theater, Kremlin Palace of Congresses (seats 6,000) and at the Stanislavsky and Nemirovich-Danchenko Musical Theater. Among Russian participants are the Ensemble of Violinists of the Bolshoi Theater, the Moscow Philharmonic Chamber Orchestra and young Soviet artists. The festival was started in 1964 to offer a spring cultural event. It is financed by the USSR Ministry of Culture, Soyuzconcert, Soviet concert and theater associations and different republic ministries of culture.

Moscow

RUSSIAN WINTER FESTIVAL

Held annually, December/January
Cultural, folkloric, New Year

The Russian Winter Festival focuses in on Russian national arts and that of all the republics of the USSR. Theater, music and the dance are covered. This could be called the theater season in Moscow. The three-week festival also covers the Romany Theater, called "world's only Gypsy theater," the Moscow Circus, choral dances and a variety of theater performing groups. In addition, the festival also includes New Year's Eve celebrations, with the traditional dancing around the New Year tree with the fabled Snow Maiden and Grandfather Frost. There are troika (sled) rides and more. Attendance at the various events is claimed to be more than a half million people from all over the USSR. The first festival was held in 1964 to bring winter arts programs and events under one festival umbrella. The event is financed through ticket sales but is largely subsidized by the USSR Ministry of Culture, Soyuzconcert and various theater and cultural groups.

URUGUAY

Durazno

NATIONAL FESTIVAL OF FOLKLORE

Held annually, January
Folkloric, ethnic, cultural, competition

The National Festival of Folklore is a three-day event of folkloric programs of the songs and dances of the country and neighboring countries. Competitions for the best Latin American groups are held, and there are exhibits and demonstrations of the different countries' arts and crafts, with many for sale. The festival attempts to preserve Latin folk culture for future generations and to educate non-Latins about the rich folklore of the Central and South American nations. Performances are held in the city's open-air theater. The event is financed by paid admissions, entry fees and grants from the federal and local governments.

Montevideo

SUMMER FESTIVAL OF THE LAKE OF RODO PARK

Held annually, January/March
Cultural

The Summer Festival of the Lake of Rodo Park is a three-month cultural event during the country's summer season, January to March. This is a performing arts festival offering programs in music, opera, drama, ballet and modern dance. From time to time, artists and performing groups from other countries participate, and this can include countries from all over the world. The programs are given in the open-air theater of Rodo Park. The entire festival has been sponsored by the Ministry of Education and Culture since 1976. Attendance is in the thousands. The festival was started to give local people cultural events to enjoy during the summer.

VENEZUELA

Barcelona (Estado Anzoategui)

EASTERN FESTIVAL OF THEATER

Held annually, movable dates
Cultural

The Eastern Festival of Theater is a ten-day event keyed to experimental drama and independent laboratory theater in the country's eastern states. These states include Anzoategui, Bolivar, Monagas, Nueva Esparta and Sucre. A special committee selected by all the theaters in these states reviews, the different companies and makes the final selection. This selection makes up the festival presentations. No definite date is set in advance because the selection of the participating drama groups takes quite awhile. The festival was started in 1976 to encourage the development of experimental theater and to help aspiring playwrights. It is financed by paid admissions and grants from the government.

Caracas

INTERNATIONAL THEATER FESTIVAL

Held biennially, during even-numbered years; next: 1986, 1988
Cultural

The International Theater Festival was first held in 1973 and 1974 but then biennially because preparations for the event required more time. The festival was started to encourage the growth of the Latin American theater and to abet the "free" theater movement. Theater groups from all over the world, selected on recommendation of certain groups and people known to the Festival Committee, have performed and continue to do so. Among some of the international groups who have performed are Denmark's Odin Teatret, Spain's Nuria Espert Company and Poland's Teatre Stu. Participating theater companies take care of their own travel expenses to Venezuela, but once there, the Festival Committee takes care of all other expenses, including sightseeing. Performances are held throughout Caracas in concert halls, open-air parks, theaters and community centers. The festival, whose dates are movable, attract thousands of people. The festival's meager budget is heavily subsidized by the government.

YUGOSLAVIA

Dubrovnik (Croatia)

DUBROVNIK SUMMER FESTIVAL

Held annually, July/August
Cultural, economic, folkloric

The Dubrovnik Summer Festival dates back to 1950 and was started to revive the cultural aspect of the city and to attract more tourists during the summer. It offers drama, opera, music, ballet and folklore, featuring famous Yugoslav and foreign performers and orchestras. Since the first festival, an estimated 2 million have attended festival programs. In 1982, a total of 112 different performances were given. They included Rossini's *The Barber of Seville*, Orff's *Carmina Burana* and Cherubini's Requiem in C Minor. Among festival participants were the Hungarian National Symphony Orchestra, the Belgrade Philharmonic Orchestra, the Croatian National Theater Ballet Company, the Australian Dance Theater, I Soloisti di Zagreb, the Cleveland Quartet, pianist Martha Argarich and tenor Peter Schreier. Performances are at 40 open-air stages in parks, squares, castles, churches and along the medieval city's seashore. The festival is a member of the European Association of Music Festivals. Over the years more than 34 foreign countries, including the United States and covering five continents, have actively participated in the festival. In 1978, the festival included Shakespeare, Sophocles and Goldoni productions and pantomime groups from Czechoslovakia and Poland. The festival is financed by 30 percent of the box-office receipts, and the balance is taken up by the government.

Ljubljana (Slovenia)

LJUBLJANA SUMMER FESTIVAL

Held annually, June/August
Cultural

The Ljubljana Summer Festival marked its thirtieth anniversary in 1982 and a record number of attendees, more than 100,000. The event is a well-integrated festival of drama, dance, mime, opera, ballet, folklore and chamber and orchestral music featuring both well-known Yugoslav and foreign performers and companies. Performances are citywide and usually in the outdoor Summer Theater, the courtyard of the Crusaders' Church, the Knight's Hall and Tivoli Sports Palace.

In 1982, several visiting opera companies performed in a large variety of operas, ranging from Verdi's *Macbeth* by the Belgrade Opera to Smetana's *The Bartered Bride* by the Brno National Opera. Anniversary highlights included Haydn's *Der Apotheker*, the Broadway musical *Ain't Misbehavin'* and performances by the New Danish Ballet. Performing ensembles included the Fires of London, Orchestre du Capitole of Toulouse, Camerata Amsterdam and the Hungarian National Orchestra. There were also special films, exhibits and puppet shows and the eighth Yugoslav Opera Biennial with roundtable symposium and awards. This festival is also a member of the European Association of Music Festivals. It is financed by paid admissions and help from local and federal governments.

Split (Croatia)

SPLIT SUMMER FESTIVAL

Held annually, July/August
Cultural, economic

The Split Summer Festival was first held in June 1954, when it was known as the Summer Events of Split. Its name was changed in 1968 to simplify it. The festival was started by local citizens active in the arts to give everyone a chance to enjoy theater, opera, ballet and concerts in the summer and to attract tourists. The festival hosts up to 70,000 people, many tourists, and has gained prominence in the arts festival field. It won the Award of the City of Split and one from FIDOF (Federation Internationale des Organisateurs de Festivals) for promoting a cultural event and showcasing young talent. Yugoslavian drama, ballet, opera and music groups perform, as do international companies. In 1982, two Verdi operas, *Nabucco* and *Aida*, were presented together with a series of organ recitals and a performance by the Australian Dance Theater. Performances are held in Diocletian's Palace and the fortified estate of the Capogrosso family. From time to time, the festival also includes a songwriter's and singer's competition. Work on the festival is by a special committee and is a year-round job. The event is financed by contributions from the Split City Town Hall, the republic of Croatia and partly by the federative government. There are admission charges to the different programs.

Zagreb (Croatia)

INTERNATIONAL FOLKLORE REVIEW

Held annually, July
Folkloric, cultural

The International Folklore Review was launched in July 1966 to give a cultural vehicle for preserving not only Yugoslavian folklore but also that of all foreign countries. It was also started to attract summer tourists. Local Yugoslavian experts in folklore are responsible for the event, which has continued so well that a few million have already attended the festival and several thousand have participated. The review includes competitive folk song and dance performances with the performers dressed in appropriate folkloric costumes. This includes about 200 performers from all parts of Yugoslavia and an equal number from other countries. Additionally, there are folkloric musicians who play authentic music. Special foods of the different countries are exhibited and sampled by those attending the event. There are arts, crafts, exhibits and ethnic film showings plus fireworks and a torchlight procession late at night in the city's Upper Town. Events are citywide and are open-air performances, weather permitting. The last festival day is devoted to a special awards ceremony. The review is financed by various folklore organizations and subsidized by the city and federal governments.

ZAMBIA

Lealul Knoll, Mongu (Western Province)

KU-OMBOKO CEREMONY

Held annually, February or March
Folkloric

The Ku-Omboko Ceremony is a century-old Lozi festival whose dates depend upon the rise of the Zambezi River in the Barotse flood plains of the country's Western Province. "Ku-omboko" means "getting out of the water" and is the time when local residents escape from the floods, going to higher grounds until the waters go down. This is celebrated with a regatta of thousands of boats and canoes, led by the paramount chief with his royal barge oared by 60 or more chanting paddlers to the accompaniment of drums and xylophones. Once dry land is reached, then traditional ceremonies and tribal dances are performed, celebrating the safe arrival of the chief and his people. The event attracts thousands of curious visitors.

Lusaka, nationwide

INDEPENDENCE DAY

Held annually, October 24
Patriotic

Independence Day celebrations nationwide mark the country's independence in 1964. Parades and special events are held throughout the country, but the most festive are in the country's capital, Lusaka. There is a traditional parade of the military, labor and youth organizations, dance groups and marching bands. At Independence Stadium, there are tribal dance performances representative of all the country's provinces. Children perform gymnastic drills, and the Independence Soccer Trophy final game is played before an audience of 70,000.

CALENDAR OF FAIRS AND FESTIVALS

Unless otherwise noted, events are held annually.

Antigua

January
  New Year's Day Street Dancing, Steelbands, Masquerades, January 1
April
  Sailing Week, local waters
May or June
  Whitmonday Spear Fishing Competition, local waters, movable date
July
  Midsummer Carnival, islandwide, through mid-August
August
  Police Week Festival, St. John's, through early September
November
  Independence Day Celebration, islandwide, November 1

Argentina

January
  International Folkloric Festival, Cosquin
February or March
  Carnival, nationwide, movable date
March
  Fishing Festival: International Trout and Salmon Fishing Tournaments, Chubut Province
  International Regatta Season, Tigre River, Buenos Aires

National Festival of the Grape Harvest, Mendoza
May
- National Anniversary of The Cabildo Abierte, nationwide, May 25
- Opera Season, Buenos Aires, through September

June
- Flag Day, nationwide, June 20
- Gaucho Week, Salta

July
- National Cattle Show, Bueno Aires
- National Day of Argentina: Independence Day, nationwide, July 9
- Snow Festival, Bariloche, through August
- Snow Festival and Ski Tournament, Los Molles Vallecitos, Mendoza Province, through August

August
- Anniversary of General San Martin, Liberator of Argentina, nationwide, August 17
- Dorado Fishing Season and International Fishing Tournament, National Park of Iguazu, through November

September
- Arts Exhibitions, Buenos Aires, through October
- Fiesta Del Sonor y La Virgen Del Millagre, Salta

October
- Columbus Day or Race Day, nationwide, October 12
- National Yachting Championship, Olivos, Buenos Aires

November
- International Fishing Contest, Bariloche

Aruba

February or March
- Carnival/Mardi Gras, Oranjestad, movable date

April
- Queen's Birthday Celebration, islandwide, April 30
- Watapana Folkloric Festival, Oranjestad, through mid-December

June
- Aruba Sports Union Olympiad, islandwide
- St. John's Day and "Derramento di Gai" Folkdancing, Oranjestad, June 24

Australia

January
- Dragon Class Yachting: World Championships, Hobart, through early February

CALENDAR OF FAIRS AND FESTIVALS 191

    Hahndorf Scheutzenfest: German Festival, Hahndorf
    International Chess Tournament, Adelaide, through February
    Perth Cup: Horse Race, Perth
February
    Festival of Perth, Perth, through early March
    Festival of the Arts, Adelaide, through early March, held biennially, even-numbered years only
    National Agricultural Show, Canberra
March
    Ballarat Begonia Festival, Victoria
    Canberra Week, Canberra
    Moomba Festival, Melbourne
March or April
    Royal Easter Show, Sydney, coincides with Easter observance, movable date
April
    Anzac Day: Honors All War Dead, nationwide, April 25
    Australian National Boomerang Championships, Albury
    Barossa Valley Vintage Festival, Barossa Valley, Tanunda, held biennially, during odd-numbered years only
    Sydney Cup: Horse Race, Sydney
May
    Bangtail Muster, Alice Springs
    Camel Cup: Camel Racing, Alice Springs
June
    Beercan Regatta, Darwin
    Skiing Season, New South Wales, Victoria, Tasmania, through early October
August
    Pacific Festival, Townsville
    Royal Adelaide Show, Adelaide, through early September
    Royal National Show, Brisbane
September
    Carnival of Flowers, Toowoomba, through October
    Perth Royal Show, Perth, through early October
    Royal Melbourne Show, Melbourne
    Warana: People's Festival, Brisbane, through early October
October
    Royal Hobart Show, Hobart
    Waratah Spring Festival, Sydney
    Wine Bushing Festival, McLaren Vale
November
    Great Barrier Reef Islands Festival, Queensland
    Melbourne Cup: Horse Race, Melbourne
December

Festival of Sydney, Sydney, through January
Sydney-Hobart Yacht Race, Sydney Harbor, December 26
Tasmanian Fiesta, Hobart, through January

Austria

January
  Mozart Week, Salzburg
  Opera Season, Vienna, Graz, through June, also September-December
February
  Vienna Operetta Festival, Vienna
March
  International Spring Fair, Vienna
  Opera Ball, Vienna
March or April
  Easter Music Festival, Salzburg, movable date
  Film Festival, Vienna
April
  Marionette Theater, Salzburg, through September
May
  Gauderfest: Folklore Festival, Ziller Valley, Tyrol
  Vienna Festival, Vienna, through June
June
  Carinthian Summer Festival, Ossiach, Villach, through August
  Corpus Christi Lake Procession, Traunkirchen, Hallstatt, movable date
  Operetta Performances, Baden, through September
July
  Bregenz Festival, Bregenz, through mid-August
  Salzburg Festival, Salzburg, through August
  World Youth Festival of the Performing Arts, Vienna
August
  Austrian Danube Festival, Grein, Lower Austria, through September
  Chamber Music Festival, Stift Altenburg, Lower Austria, through September
  Festival of Early Music, Innsbruck
  International Folk Festival, Krems, Lower Austria, through September
  Philharmonic Week, Salzburg
September
  Autumn Festival, Millstatt, Carinthia, through October
  Beethoven Festival, Baden, Lower Austria
  International Autumn Fair, Vienna
  International Bruckner Festival, Linz, through October
  International Film Festival, Bludenz
  International Organ Contest, Innsbruck

Vintage Festival, Retz, Lower Austria
October
  Styrian Autumn, Graz, Styria, through early November
November
  "Christkindlmarkt" Traditional Christmas Market, Vienna, through mid-December
December
  New Year's Eve Fanfares at City Hall and Imperial Ball, Vienna, December 31
  St. Stephen's Day, nationwide, December 26
  "Silent Night, Holy Night" Celebrations, Hallein, Oberndorf, Wagrain, all of Salzburg, December 24

Bahamas

January
  Supreme Court Opening, Nassau
February
  Frankie Brown Billfish Tournament, Bimini
  Nassau Cup Yacht Race, Nassau
March
  His & Hers All Billfish Tournament, Chub Cay
April
  Calcutta Golf Classic, Freeport
  Community Track & Field Meet, Nassau
  Family Islands Regatta, Exuma
  Hemingway Billfish Tournament, Bimini
May
  Regatta, Long Island
  Tuna Tournament, Bimini
June
  Bahamas Jr. National Tennis Championship, Nassau
  Bahamas National Amateur Golf Championship, Freeport
  Pro-Am Golf Classic, Freeport
July
  Bahamas Goombay Holiday, Freeport, Nassau, through August
  Commonwealth Exhibition and Fair, Nassau
  Regatta Week, Green Turtle Cay
August
  Fox Hill Day, Nassau, second Tuesday
  Invitation Scramble Golf Classic, Nassau
September
  Lyford Cay Golf Classic Foursomes, Nassau

October
  Bahamas Bonanza Bone-Fishing, Exuma
  Captains Cup Golf Classic, Freeport
  Discovery Day, all islands, October 12
November
  Adam Clayton Powell Memorial Wahoo Tournament, Bimini
December
  Junkanoo Parade and Festival, Freeport, Nassau, Family Out Islands, December 26, January 1

Barbados

January
  Horse Shows, Bridgetown
  Yacht Club Regattas, Bridgetown, through August
May
  Amateur Golf Championships, Sandy Lane Golf Club
June
  June Corp-Over Festival, Bridgetown, islandwide, sometimes in July

Belgium

February or March
  Carnival, Binche, movable date
March
  Automobile Festival, Namur
April
  Brussels International Fair, Brussels, through May
  Flanders Festival, Antwerp, Bruges, Brussels, Ghent, Kortrijk, Leuven, Mechelen, through October
  Golden Egg Celebrations, Kruishoutem
May
  Cat Festival and Parade, Ypres, second Sunday
  Holy Blood Procession, Bruges, always on Ascension Day
  International Rowing Matches, Ostend
June
  International Drum Band Festival, Ostend
  Whit-Monday Market and Festivities, Diksmuide, movable date
July
  Festival of Folkdancing, Schoten

CALENDAR OF FAIRS AND FESTIVALS 195

    Procession of the Witches, Beselare, last Sunday
August
    Begonia Festival, Lochristi
    Festival of the Canals, Bruges
    Festival of the Giants, Ath
    Grand Nautical Festival, Berlare
    International Speed Roller Skating Competition, Ostend
September
    Air-Balloon Contest, Sint-Niklaas
    October Beer Festival, Wieze, through early October

Bermuda

January
    Bermuda Festival, Hamilton, through February
    Bermuda International Marathon and Ten Kilometre Race, Hamilton
    Bermuda Square and Round Dance Festival, various sites
February
    Invitation Rendezvous Bowling Tournament, Warwick
    Round-the-Town Road Race, Hamilton
March
    Bermuda College Weeks, Hamilton, St. George's, through mid-April
    Bermuda Dog Show International, Paget
    Bermuda Goodwill Tennis Tournament, Hamilton
    Bermuda Hockey Festival, Prospect, through April
April
    Bermuda Heritage Fair, Warwick
    Peppercorn Ceremony, St. George's, April 23
    St. George to Somerset Road Relay, St. George's
May
    Bermuda Day, islandwide, May 24
    Bermuda Spring Music Festival, Hamilton
    Game Fishing Tournament, local waters, through November
June
    Cup Match Cricket Festival, Sandys Parish

Bonaire

February or March
    Carnival, islandwide, movable date
April

Coronation Day, islandwide, April 30
June
 Celebration of Dia de San Juan: St. John's Day, islandwide, June 24
 Celebration of Dia de San Pedro: St. Peter's Day, islandwide, June 28
October
 International Regatta, Kralendijk
December
 Kingdom Day, islandwide, December 15

Brazil

January
 Nosso Senhor Do Bomfim: Our Lord of the Happy Ending Festival, Salvador, Bahia
 "Repentista" Tournament: Brazilian Folkloric Competitions, Olinda
 Southern Brazilian Hang-Gliding Championship, Florianopolis
 Summer Festival, Petropolis, through February
February
 Brazilian Formula I Grand Prix-Car Racing, Rio de Janeiro
 Festival of Iemanja, Salvador, February 2
 Itapua Costume Festival, Salvador
February or March
 Carnival, Rio de Janeiro, movable date
March
 Brazilian Film Festival, Gramado
April
 National Holiday and Founding of Brasilia, Brasilia, nationwide, April 21
May
 Fishing Season in the Araguaia Valley, Sao Miguel do Araguaia, Ila do Bananal, Aruana, through October
 Grand Sweepstake Horse Race, Sao Paulo, first Sunday
June
 Amazon Folklore Festival, Manaus, through July
 June Festivals, Sao Luis, month-long
 Winter Festival, Petropolis, through August
July
 Dragao do Mar: Raft Regatta, Fortaleza
 International Music Festival, Gramado
August
 Brazilian Grand Prix-Sweepstake Horse Race, Rio de Janeiro
 Folklore Week, Sao Luis
September
 Rodeo, Caruaru

Sport Fishing Season, Manaus, through December
October
  Art Festival, Sao Cristovao
  Challenge Cup: International Dourado Fishing Open Contest, Foz do Iguacu
  "Cirio" Procession of Our Lady of Nazareth, Belem

British Virgin Islands

February
  Aquatic Sports Events, all islands
March or April
  Easter Monday Picnics, Fairs, Sports, all islands, movable date
June
  Sovereign's Birthday Observance, all islands
July
  International Billfish Tournament, local waters
August
  Tortola Festival, Tortola
October
  St. Ursula's Day, all islands, October 21

Bulgaria

January
  Winter Carnivals, Pamporovo, Borovets, Vitosha
February
  International Graeco-Roman Wrestling Tournament, Sofia
  International Skiing Competitions, Borovets
March
  International "March Music Days" Musical Festival, Rousse, through April
  Spring Festival, Kyustendil
April
  Canoe-Kayak Balkaniad for Men and Women at Pancharevo Lake, near Sofia
May
  International Spring Fair, Plovdiv
  National Humor and Satire Festival, Gabrovo
May/June
  International Music Festival, Sofia
  Rose Festival, Kazanluk
June

Golden Orpheus, Slunchev Bryag
International Book Fair, Sofia
International Music Festival, Varna, through July
July
International Surfing Regatta, Michurin
August
Sea Week, Black Sea
September
International Automobile Rally, Plovdiv
International Chamber Music Festival, Plovdiv
Silver Amphora International Underwater Fishing Tournament, Primorsko

Canada

Alberta Province

January
Winter Carnival, Jasper
February
North American Snowmobile Races, Wetaskiwin
March
Canadian Western Superrodeo, Edmonton, through early April
Rodeo Royal, Calgary
May
Festival of the Arts, Banff, through August
June
Highland Games, Red Deer
National Horse Show, Calgary
July
Calgary Exhibition and Stampede, Calgary
Hot Air Balloon Race, Grande Prairie
International Folk Festival, Red Deer
Klondike Days Exposition, Edmonton
Ukrainian Pysanka Festival, Vegreville
August
Folk Festival, Calgary
Folk Music Festival, Edmonton
North American Chuckwagon Races, High River
North American Indian Classic Rodeo, Hobbema
September
Masters Horse Show, Calgary
October
Western Canadian Hungarian Folk Dance Festival, Calgary

CALENDAR OF FAIRS AND FESTIVALS 199

November
  Canadian Rodeo Finals, Edmonton

British Columbia

February
  Canadian Open Dog Sled Championships, Fort Nelson
  Cariboo Cross-Country Ski Marathon, 100 Mile House
  Snowgolf Championship, Prince George
  Winter Carnival, Vernon
March
  Labbatt's Brier Men's Curling Championship, Victoria
  World Cup Downhill Week, Whistler
May
  Children's Festival, Vancouver
  Swiftsure Race: Sailboats, Victoria
June
  Folkfest, Victoria, through July
July
  Bathtub Race, Nanaimo to Vancouver
  Canadian Open Sandcastle Competition, White Rock, through August
  Pow Wow, Mission
  Regatta, Kelowna
  Sea Festival at English Bay, Vancouver
  Stampede, Williams Lake
August
  International Air Show, Abbotsford
  Pacific National Exhibition, Vancouver, through early September
  Peach Festival, Penticton
September
  Septober Wine Festival, Okanagan-Similkameen, through early October

Manitoba

February
  Festival du Voyageur, Winnipeg/St. Boniface
  Kinsmen Winter Carnival, Thompson
  Northern Manitoba Trappers' Festival, The Pas
  Winter Farewell and the Canadian Power Toboggan Championship Races, Beausejour
March
  Royal Manitoba Winter Fair, Brandon

June
  Manitoba Marathon, Winnipeg
  Maple Leaf International Air Show, Gimli
  Provincial Exhibition of Manitoba, Brandon
  Red River Exhibition, Winnipeg
  Trout Festival, Flin Flon, through early July
July
  Call of the Wild Mountain Music Festival, Boggy Creek
  Canada's National Ukrainian Festival, Dauphin, through early August
  Highland Gathering, Selkirk
  Manitoba Stampede and Exhibition, Morris
  Manitoba's Thresherman's Reunion and Stampede, Austin
  Nickel Days, Thompson
  Winnipeg Folk Festival, Winnipeg
August
  Folklorama, Winnipeg
  Icelandic Festival, Gimli
  Pioneer Days, Steinbach
September
  Oktoberfest, Winnipeg
October
  Ag-Ex: Rodeo, Livestock Show, Brandon, through early November

New Brunswick

February
  Winter Carnival, Dalhousie
March
  Atlantic Stage Band Festival, Saint John
  Festival of Music, Moncton, through early April
  Festival of Music, Sackville
April
  Festival of Cultures, Dalhousie
  National Broomball Championships, Moncton
May
  Acadian Heritage Festival, Moncton
  Cathedral Festival of the Arts, Fredericton
  New Brunswick Motocross Championship Series, Riverglade
June
  Bitowa Outdoor Festival, Tracadie
  Chamber Music and All That Jazz, Fredericton
  Crab Festival, Le Goulet, through early July
  Miramichi Folk Song Festival, Newcastle

    Potato Festival, Grand Falls, through early July
    Salmon Festival, Campbellton
    Scallop Festival, Richibucto, through early July
    Summerfest, Fredericton, through July
July
    Brussels Sprout Festival, Rogersville, through early August
    Clam Festival, Saint-Simon
    Corn Festival, Saint-Leolin, through early August
    International Festival of Baroque Music, Lameque
    Lobster Festival, Shediac
    Loyalist Days, Saint John
    Strawberry and Bluegrass Festival, Woodstock
    Summer Festival, Paquetville
    Western Rodeo, Saint Isidore, through early August
August
    Acadian Festival, Caraquet
    Atlantic National Exhibition, Saint John, through early September
    Canadian Marathon Canoe Championships, Fredericton
    Harvest Festival, Saint-Andre
    Lumberjack Festival, Edmundston
    Miners Festival, Nigadoo
September
    Exhibition and Provincial Livestock Show, Federicton
October
    Friendship Festival, Riviere-du-Portage
    Maritime Winter Fair, Moncton
    Oyster Festival, Maisonnette

Newfoundland and Labrador

March or April
    Drama Festival, provincewide and during Easter, movable date
June
    Conception Bay Folk Festival, Carbonear, through July
July
    Fish, Fun and Folk Festival, Twillingate
    Labrador Heritage Festival, Happy Valley/Goose Bay, Labrador
    Summer Festival of the Arts, St. John's
August
    Blueberry Festival, Springdale
    Newfoundland and Labrador Folk Festival, St. John's
    Regatta on Quidi Vidi Lake, St. John's

Northwest Territories

March
  Arctic Winter Games, Yellowknife
  Caribou Carnival, Yellowknife
  Winter Carnival, Fort Resolution
  Wood Buffalo Frolics, Fort Smith
March or April
  Top of the World Ski Meet, Inuvik, during Easter, movable date
April
  Toonik Tyme, Frobisher Bay, through early May
June
  Folk on the Rocks, Yellowknife
  Midnight Sun Golf Tournament, Yellowknife
July
  Northern Games, Inuvik and local areas
September
  Fall River and World Championship Fiddling and Jigging Contest, Hay River
October
  Delta Daze, Inuvik

Nova Scotia

February
  Music Festival, Halifax
  Winter Carnival, Dartmouth
  Winter Carnival, Halifax
March
  Maple Syrup Festival, Kenzieville, through April
May
  Annapolis Valley Apple Blossom Festival, Annapolis Valley Region, through early June
  Festival Acadien d'Halifax, Halifax
  International Festival of Clowning, Dartmouth
  Scotia Festival of Music, Halifax, through early June
June
  Bluenose Rally: Motorcyles, Kentville, through early July
  Glooscap Summer Festival, Canning
  Nova Scotia Tattoo, Halifax, through July
July
  Craft Festival, Lunenburg

CALENDAR OF FAIRS AND FESTIVALS 203

    Highland Games, Antigonish
    Lobster Carnival, Pictou
    Maritime Old Time Fiddling Contest, Dartmouth
    Nova Scotia Bluegrass and Oldtime Music Festival, Ardoise
August
    Blueberry Harvest Festival, Amherst
    Downeast Old Time Fiddling Contest, Sackville
    Nova Scotia Gaelic Mod, St. Ann's, Cape Breton
    Nova Scotia Provincial Exhibition, Bible Hill, Truro
    Scallop Days, Digby
    Western Nova Scotia Exhibition, Yarmouth
September
    Eastern Nova Scotia Exhibition, Antigonish
    Harvestfest, Truro
    International Air Show, Shearwater
    Joseph Howe Festival, Halifax
    Nova Scotia Fisheries Exhibition and Fishermen's Reunion, Lunenburg
October
    Annapolis Valley Fall Harvest Festival, Wolfville, Kentville
    Atlantic Film Festival, Halifax

Ontario

January
    Bon Soo Winter Carnival, Sault Ste. Marie
    Export "A" Cup Ski Jumping Championships, Thunder Bay
    Kawartha International Snowmobile Races, Peterborough
February
    Winterlude, Ottawa
April
    Spring Festival, Guelph, through early May
May
    Festival of Spring, Ottawa
    Shaw Festival, Niagara-on-the-Lake, through October
June
    Caravan, Toronto
    International Air Show, London
    International Freedom Festival, Windsor, through early July
    Stratford Festival, Stratford, through October
July
    Caribana, Toronto, through early August
    Festival Ottawa Opera Plus, Ottawa
    Gemboree, Bancroft, through early August

National Hot Air Balloon Championship, Barrie
August
　Canadian National Exhibition, Toronto, through early September
　Glengarry Highland Games, Maxville
September
　Niagara Grape and Wine Festival, St. Catharines
October
　Oktoberfest, Kitchener-Waterloo
November
　Royal Agricultural Winter Fair, Toronto

Prince Edward Island

February
　Winter Carnival, Charlottetown
May
　Maritime Championship Drag Races, Oyster Bed Bridge, through August
June
　Charlottetown Festival, Charlottetown, through September
July
　Lobster Carnival and Livestock Exhibition, Summerside
　Maritime Craft Festival, Georgetown
　Northumberland Provincial Fisheries Festival, Murray River
　Potato Blossom Festival, O'Leary
August
　Oyster Festival, Tyne Valley
　Provincial Plowing Match and Agricultural Fair, Dundas
　Summerfest, Summerside

Quebec

January
　Quebec International Bonspiel, Quebec City
February
　Canadian Ski Marathon, Lachute to Hull
　Carnaval-Souvenir de Chicoutimi, Chicoutimi
　Quebec Winter Carnival, Quebec City
April
　Maple Festival, Plessisville
May
　International Book Fair, Quebec City
June

CALENDAR OF FAIRS AND FESTIVALS 205

    Canada Grand Prix, Montreal
    International Jazz Fest, Montreal, through July
    Shrimp Festival, Matane
July
    Fun Fest, Lac St.-Jean
    International Regatta, Valleyfield
    Summer Festival, Quebec City
    World Folk Festival, Drummondville
August
    Expo Quebec, Quebec City, through mid-September
    Grand Prix, Trois-Rivieres, through early September
    Lac Saint-Jean Blueberry Festival, Mistassini
    World Film Festival, Montreal
September
    International Marathon, Montreal
    Western Festival, Saint-Tite
October
    Fall Festival, Rimouski
    Festival of the Snow Geese, Montmagny

Saskatchewan

February
    International '250 Snowmobile Race, Regina
    Winter Festival, Prince Albert
March
    Winter Festival, La Ronge
April
    Folkfest, Melville
    Bronc Rodeo, Swift Current
May
    Kinsmen International Band Festival, Moose Jaw
    Vesna Festival, Saskatoon
June
    Northern Pike Festival, Nipawin, through August
    Saskatchewan Air Show, Moose Jaw
    Western Canadian Agricultural Fair, Regina
July
    Buffalo Days, Regina, through early August
    Old Time Fiddlers Contest, Carrot River
    Pioneer Days, Saskatoon
    Saskatchewan Handicraft Festival, North Battleford
August

Folkfest, Saskatoon
September
Western Canadian Old Tyme Fiddling Championships, Swift Current
November
Canadian Western Agribition, Regina

Cayman Islands

May
Discovery Day, islandwide, movable date
Flower Show, George Town, Grand Cayman, through June
June
Queen's Birthday Celebration, islandwide
July
Constitution Day Sailing Regatta, George Town, Grand Cayman
October
Pirate Week Festival, George Town, Grand Cayman

China, Republic of (Taiwan)

January or February
Chinese Lunar New Year, nationwide, movable date
February
Lantern Festival, movable date
March
Flower Season at Yangmingshan Park, Wulai, Wushe, Taroko
Youth Day, nationwide, March 29
April
Buddha Bathing Festival, April 8
April or May
Brithday of Matsu, Goddess of the Sea, movable date
June
Dragon Boat Festival
September
Mid-Autumn Moon Festival
October
Double Tenth National Day, October 10

Colombia

January
Black and White Carnival, Pasto

International Fair and Coffee Festival, Manizales
February or March
  Carnival, Barranquilla, movable date
March
  Festival of Caribbean Music, Cartagena
March or April
  Holy Week Observances, Popayan, movable date
April
  International Festival of the "Vallenato" (Musc) Legend, Valledupar
  International Film Festival, Cartagena, sometimes in June
May
  International Festival of Culture, Tunjas, Boyaca
June
  Festival of Bambuco, Neiva
  National Art Festival, Cali
  National Folk Festival, Ibague
  Tango Festival, Medellin
July
  Handicraft Fair and Exposition, Sagamoso
  National Cotton Pageant, Cattle Fair and Exposition, Buga
  Festival and Queen of the Caribbean Pageant, Santa Marta
August
  Flower Fair, Medellin
  Kite Festival, Villa de Leyva
September
  Drum Festival, Tamalameque
  Folklore Festival of the Pacific Coast, Buenaventura
  Indian Handicrafts Fair, Bucaramanga
  Salt Fiesta, Manaure
October
  Coal Festival, Barrancas
  National Coffee Pageant and Cultural Week, Armenia
November
  Quadrilles of San Martin, San Martin, November 11
December
  Festival of the Colombian Song, Villavicencio
  International Sugar Cane Fair, Cali, through early January

Cyprus

January
  Feast of the Submersion of the Holy Cross, local waters, January 6
February

International Ski Competition, Troodos
February or March
   Carnival, Limassol, movable date
March
   Greek National Day, nationwide, March 25
April
   Procession of the Icon of St. Lazarus, Larnaca
May
   Anthesticia Flower Festival, Paphos
   International Fair, Nicosia
June
   Beer Festival, Nicosia, through July
   Curium Festival, Curium/Limassol, through July
   International Art Fair, Limassol, through July
August
   Folk Art Festival, Paphos
   Open Tennis Tournament, Troodos
September
   Wine Festival, Limassol

Czechoslovakia

April
   Maypole and burning of the Witches Festival, Postupice, through early May
   North Bohemian Slalom Canoe Race, Decin
May
   International Festival of Songs: LYRA, Bratislava
   International Music Festival, Marianske Lazne, through July
   Prague Spring Music Festival, Prague
   The Ride of Kings: Celebration of Summer Solstice, Vlchnov, Moravia
June
   Folklore Festival, Straznice, Moravia
   Horehronic Songs and Dances Festival, Helpa, Slovakia
   Janosik Folklore Festival, Terchova, Slovakia
   Music Summer, Trencanske Teplice, through July
   Piestany Festival, Piestany, through July
   Spartakiade, Prague, held once in every five years
   The Ethnographic Festival, Svidnik, Slovakia
   Znojmo Feast, Znojmo, through September
July
   Folklore Festival Under Polana, Detva, Slovakia
   Parade of the Best Folklore Ensembles of Czechoslovakia, Vychedna
August

Chodsko Festivities: Folk Songs and Dances, Domazlice, Bohemia
Chopin's Festival, Marianske Lazne
Folklore Festival, Cerveny Kostelec
September
Autumn Music Festival, Teplice v Cechach, through October
Dvorak's Autumn Music Festival, Karlovy Vary
International Music Festival Brno, through October
October
Bratislava Music Festival, Bratislava, Slovakia
International Jazz Festival, Prague

Denmark

April
Scandinavian Gold and Silver Fair, Copenhagen, through early May
May
NUMUS Festival: Nordic Festival of Contemporary Music, Aarhus
June
Riverboat Festival: Jazz, Silkeborg
Roskilde Festival of Rhythmic Music, Roskilde, through July
Song Festival, Skagen, through July
Viking Festival, Frederikssund, through July
July
Central Funen Festival, Ringe
Hans Christian Andersen Festival, Odense, through August
Jazz Festival, Copenhagen
Rebild Festival of Fourth of July Celebration, Aalborg, Rebild, North Jutland, July 4
Sonderborg Tilting Tournament, Sonderborg
Summer Festival, Copenhagen, through August
August
Folk and Jazz Festival, Tonder
September
Aarhus Festival Week, Aarhus
International Jazz Festival, Holstobro, through October

Ethiopia

January
Genna: Christmas Celebration, Addis Ababa, January 7
April

Ethiopian Easter Observance, nationwide, movable date
September
    Ethiopian New Year Observance, nationwide, movable date
    Maskal Festival, Addis Ababa, September 27

Finland

January
    Arctic Rally, Rovaniemi
    January Market, Hamima
    Snow Sculpture Contest, Helsinki
February
    Finlandia Ski Race, Hameenlinna-Lahti
    International Short Film Festival, Tampere
    Snow Rally, Helsinki
March
    Arctic Circle Skiing, Rovaniemi
    Lahti Games, Lahti
    Ounasvaara International Winter Games, Rovaniemi
    Pirkka Ski Race, Niimisale-Tampere
    Reindeer Driving Competitions, Imari, Rovaniemi, Kemijarvi, through April
April
    Hetta Music Days, Hetta Village, Enontokio
    Lapponia Ski Race Week, Muonio
    Marathon in Ice Fishing, Oulu
May
    Finlandia Marathon, Jyvaskyla
    International Folk Dance and Music Festival, Tampere
June
    Dance and Music Festival, Kuopio
    International Puppet Theater Festival, Vaasa
    Jyvaskyla Arts Festival, Jyvaskyla, through July
    Midsummer Eve, nationwide, June 22
    Music Festival, Naantali
July
    Folk Music Festival, Kaustinen
    Kuhmo Chamber Music Festival, Kuhmo
    Pori Jazz, Pori
    Savonlinna Opera Festival, Savonlinna
August
    Helsinki Festival, Helsinki, through early September
    International Organ Festival, Lahti
    Maritime Festival and Sea Shanty Festival, Kotka

Tampere Theater Summer, Tampere
Turku Music Festival, Turku
September
Porridge Feast, Kesalahti

France

January
Battle of Flowers, Cannes, January 1
February or March
Mardi Gras Celebration, Nice, movable date
March or April
Easter Festival of Sacred Music, Lourdes, movable date
April
Paris Opera Season, Paris, through June
May
Gypsy Pilgrimage, Saintes-Maries-de-la-Mer
International Film Festival, Cannes
May International Musical, Bordeaux
Paris Marathon, Paris, third Saturday
June
Auto Race, Le Mans
D-Day Observance, Normandy, June 6
International Festival of Lyon, Lyon
International Music Festival, Strasbourg
Paris Air and Space Show, Paris, held once every two years.
July
Bastille Day, nationwide, July 14
International Festival of Opera and Music, Aix-en-Provence, through early August
Pablo Casals Festival, Prades, through August
Summer Festival of Paris, Paris, through September
August
Festival of the Blue Fishing Nets, Brittany
Grand Prix: Horse Race, Deauville
September
Besancon International Music Festival, Besancon
Festival of the Nativity of the Virgin, Lourdes, September 8
International Show of Contemporary Art, Paris
October
Gastronomic Fair, Dijon, through early November
November

Les Trois Glorieuses: Three Days of Glory, Beaune, Meursault, Nuits-St. Georges

Germany, Federal Republic of

January
    International "Green Week," West Berlin, through February
    International New Year's Ski-Jumping, Garmisch-Partenkirchen, Bavaria, January 1
    International Sledge Dog Races, Todtonoos/Black Forest
January/February or March
    Carnival: Fasching Events, Rhineland, Baden-Wurttemberg, Bavaria, Hesse, Munich, Cologne, movable date
February
    Film Festival, West Berlin
    International Black Forest Ski Marathon, Schonach-Hinterzarten/Black Forest
March
    Almond Blossom Festival, Gimmeldingen/Palatinate
    International Sky-Flying Week, Oberstdorf
April
    Blossom Festival and Parade, Koblenz, through early May
    Historic Shepherds' Dance and Hans-Sachs Plays, Rothenburg/Tauber
    International Curling Tournament, Oberstdorf
    International Rowing Regatta, Mannheim
    Walpurgis Night Festivities in the Harz Mountains, April 30
May
    Ballet Festival, Hamburg
    Franconian Festival Week, Bayreuth, through early June
    German Mozart Festival, Augsburg
    International May Festival, Wiesbaden
    International German Tennis Championships, Hamburg
    May Fair and Folk Festival, Mannheim
    Oberammergau Passion Play, Oberammergau, through mid-September, held once every 10 years
    Ruhr Festival, Feuchtwangen, through August
    European Weeks Festival, Passau, through July
    Film Festival, Munich, through July
    Handel Festival, Gottingen
    International Music Festival, Bad Bramstedt
    Landshut Wedding 1475, Landshut, Bavaria, held once every three years, through July
    Mozart Festival, Wurzburg
    Open-Air Festival, Dinkelsbuhl, through August

Regatta Week, Kiel
July
  Antiques Market, Munich, through August
  Bayreuth Festival/Richard Wagner Festival, Bayreuth, Bavaria, through August
  Folk Festival, Lubeck
  Folk and Marksmen's Festival, Dusseldorf
  Hummelfest Folk Festival, Hamburg, through August
  International Choral Festival, Koblenz
  Master Draught Pageant, Rothenburg/Tauber
  Opera Festival, Munich, through August
August
  German Grand Prix-World Championship Race for Formula I Cars, Nurburgring
  Heather Blossom Festival, Amelinghausen/Luneburg Heath
  International Fair, Frankfurt/Main
  Rhenish Vintners' Festival, Nierstein/Rhine
  Wine Festival, Trier/Moselle
September
  Berlin Festival, West Berlin, through October
  Berlin Marathon, West Berlin
  Franconian Wine Festival, Crailsheim
  Oktoberfest, Munich, through early October
  Sausage and Wine Festival, Bad Durkheim
October
  Book Fair, Frankfurt
  Indoor Horse Show, Mannheim
  International Organ Festival, Gottingen
  Six Days Bicycle Race, West Berlin
  Wine Festival, Boppard/Rhine
  World Fair of Photography, Cologne
November
  Christmas Market, Nurnberg, Cologne, Lubeck, through mid-December
  International Art Market, Colgne
  Jazz Festival, West Berlin
December
  Christmas Market, West Berlin
  Intersport Ski-Jumping Tournament, Oberstdorf

Gibraltar

January
  Three Kings' Cavalcade with Bands, Floats, January 6

March
  Flower Show
April
  International Shark Angling Competition, City Wharf, through May
July
  Deep Sea and Pier Fishing Competition

Great Britain

England

January
  Antiques Fair, London
February
  Crufts Dog Show, London
  International Spring Fair, Birmingham
February or March
  Pancake Race, Olney, always Shrove Tuesday, movable date
March
  All England Badminton Championship, London
  Antique and Collectors Fair, London
  Chelsea Antiques Fair, London
April
  Festival of Country Music, London
  International Youth Music Festival, Harrogate
  London Handel Festival, London, through May
  Royal Shakespeare Company/Shakespeare Festival, Stratford-upon-Avon, Warwickshire, through December
May
  Bath Festival, Bath
  Brighton Festival, Brigton, East Sussex
  Chelsea Flower Show, London
  Chimney Sweeps Procession, Rochester, Kent, May 1
  Dickens Festival, Rochester, Kent, through June
  Glyndebourne Festival Opera Season, Glyndebourne, through August
  International Folk Festival, Eastbourne, East Sussex
  Jermyn Street Festival, London
May/September
  Chichester Festival Theater Season, Chichester, West Sussex
June
  Aldeburgh Festival, Aldeburgh, Suffolk
  Dickens Festival, Broadstairs, Kent
  Henley Royal Regatta, Oxfordshire, through early July

CALENDAR OF FAIRS AND FESTIVALS 215

    Ludlow Festival, Ludlow, Shropshire, through July
    Stour Music Festival, Boughton Aluph, Kent, through July
    The Derby: Horse Race, Epsom, Surrey
    Trooping the Colour—The Queen's Official Birthday Parade, London, movable date
    Wimbledon Lawn Tennis Championships, London, through early July
    York Festival and Mystery Plays, York, Yorkshire, through July, held once every three years
July
    Festival of Flowers, Salisbury, Wiltshire
    Festival of the City of London, London, held biennially, during even-numbered years
    International Festival of Music, Cheltenham, Gloucestershire
    King's Lynn Festival, King's Lynn, Norfolk
    Mystery Plays, Coventry, West Midlands, through August
    Regatta Week, Cowes Isle of Wight, through early August
    Summer Music Festival, Chester, Cheshire
August
    Battle of Flowers, St. Helier, Jersey, Channel Islands, second Thursday
    International Folklore Festival, Sidmouth, Devon
    Three Choirs Festival, Gloucester, Hereford, Worcester, alternating in each city each year
September
    Crab Fair, Egremont, Cumbria
    Hereford Festival of British Music, Hereford, Worcester
    International Aerospace Exhibition and Flying Display, Farnborough, Hampshire
    International Boat Show, Southampton, Hampshire
October
    Delius Festival, Bradford, West Yorkshire
    Goose Fair, Nottingham, Nottinghamshire
November
    Craft Fair, London
    Lord Mayor's Procession and Show, London
December
    International Show-Jumping Championships, London

Scotland

January
    The Famous Grouse Scottish International Badminton Championships, Edinburgh, Lothian
February
    Scottish Curling Championships, Perth, Tayside

March
  Music Festival, Inverness, Highland
  Scottish Antiques Fair, Edinburgh, Lothian, through early April
  Snow Fun Week, Glenshee, Tayside, through early April
April
  Edinburgh Folk Festival, Edinburgh, Lothian
  Folk Festival, Inverness, Highland
  Pitlochry Festival Theater Season, Pitlochry, Tayside, through September
May
  Perth Festival of the Arts, Perth, Tayside
  Shetland Folk Festival, Lerwick, Shetland
June
  Highland Games, Ardressan, Strathclyde
  Royal Highland Agricultural Show, Edinburgh, Lothian
July
  Dundee Highland Games, Dundee, Tayside
  Dunvegan Castle Chamber Music Festival, Dunvegan Castle, Isle of Skye, Highland, through August
August
  Aberdeen International Youth Festival, Aberdeen, Grampian
  Edinburgh Festival, Edinburgh, Lothian, through September
  Flower Show, Ayr, Strathclyde
  Perth Highland Games, Perth, Tayside
September
  Pitlochry Highland Games, Pitlochry, Tayside
  Royal Burgh of Peebles Highland Games, Peebles, Borders
  Royal Highland Gathering, Braemar, Grampian
October
  National Gaelic Mod, Inverness, Highland
November
  Scotland's Whiskey Festival, Aviemore, Highland
  Winter Antiques Fair, Edinburgh, Lothian

Wales

March
  Cardiff Festival of Choirs, Cardiff, South Glamorgan
April
  Llantille Crossenny Festival of Music and Drama, Llantille Crossenny Abergavenny, Gwent
May
  St. David's Cathedral Bach Festival, St. David's, Dyfed
  Welsh Boat Show, Swansea, West Glamorgan
June

Llandaff Festival of Music, Llandaff, Cardiff, South Glamorgan
July
   International Musical Eisteddfod, Llangollen, Clwyd
   Music Festival, Fishguard, Dyfed
   Summer Festival, Aberystwyth, Dyfed, through August
August
   Royal National Eisteddfod, North and South Wales, alternating each year between the two regions

Greece

January
   Feast of St. Basil, nationwide, January 1
   Feast of the Epiphany, nationwide, January 6
March
   Independence Day Celebrations, nationwide, March 25
April
   Sound and Light Performances, Athens, Rhodes, Corfu, through October
   The Feast of Saint George, Lemnos, Arahova, Assi, Gonia, Cos, April 23
May
   Anastenaria: Traditional Firewalking Performances, Sorres, Thessaloniki
   Dora Stratou Greek Folk Dance Performances, Athens, through September
   Labor Day and Flower Festival, nationwide, May 1
June
   Athens Festival, Athens, through September
   Corfu Festival, Corfu
   Epidaurus Festival, Epidaurus, through September
July
   Aegean Sailing Week, Athens
   Wine Festival, Rethymon, Crete
August
   Dormition of the Virgin Mary, nationwide, August 15
   Epirotika Cultural and Artistic Events, Ioannina
   Hippokrateira Festival, Cos
   Olympus Festival, Katerini
   Prose and Art Festival, Lefkas
September
   International Trade Fair, Film and Song Festival, Thessaloniki, through mid-October
October
   Festival of Demetria, Thessaloniki

Guadeloupe (French West Indies)

January
    Epiphany, islandwide, January 6
February or March
    Shrove Tuesday or Mardi Gras Celebrations, Pointe-a-Pitre, through Ash Wednesday, movable date
March or April
    Easter Monday Picnics and Sports, islandwide, movable date
June
    Floral Routes, islandwide
July
    Bastille Day: islandwide, July 14
    Schoelcher Day: Celebrates Freedoom from Slavery, islandwide, July 21
August
    Fete des Cuisinieres or Cooks' Festival, Pointe-a-Pitre, Saturday nearest August 10

Hong Kong

January
    Hong Kong Arts Festival, through February
    International Marathon
January or February
    Chinese New Year's Day Celebration, movable date
February
    Lantern Festival, movable date
March
    Flower Exhibition
    Hong Kong Schools Music Festival
April
    Birthday of Tin Hau
    Hong Kong International Film Festival
May
    Birthday of Lord Buddha/Tam King Festival, movable date
    Cheung Chau Festival or Festival of the Bun Hills
May or June
    Dragon Boat Festival, movable date
    International Boat Races
July
    Birthday of Lu Pan
August

Maiden Festival
September
　Birthday of Confucius, September 22
　Mid-Autumn Festival
October
　Festival of Asian Arts

Hungary

May
　International Spring Fair, Budapest
June
　Beethoven Concert Season, Martonvasar, through August
　Open-Air Festival at Margaret Island, Budapest, through August
　St. Jacob's Summer Night: Music, Drama, Kapesvar, through August
August
　Guitar Festival, Esztergom
　National Floral Carnival, Debrecen, August 20
September
　Musical Weeks, Budapest, through early October

Iceland

March
　Lava Loppet: Open International Cross-Country Ski Tournament, Blafjoll near Reykjavik
June
　National Holiday-Independence from Denmark, nationwide, June 17
　Reykjavik Arts Festival, Reykjavik, held biennially, during even-numbered years only
　Seamen's Day, nationwide, June 6
July
　Iceland National Horse Meet Show and Races, Skagafjordur, held once every four years

India

January
　Floating Festival, Madurai, through February
　Pongal/Sankranti: Harvest Festival, Tiruchirapalli, Madurai in Tamil Nadu, Andhra, Pradesh, Karnataka

Republic Day, New Delhi, Delhi Union Territory, January 26
Vasant Panchami; Spring Festival, nationwide, through February
February
Holi Spring Festival, Mathura and northern India, through early March
Shivratri Religious Festival, nationwide, through March
March
Gangaur: Honors Parvati, Consort of Lord Shiva, Udaipur, Jaipur, through early April
Jamshed Navroz: Parsi New Year's Day, Maharashtra, Gujarat
April
Id-uz-Zuha (Bakr-Id): Commemoration of the Sacrifice of Abraham, nationwide, through early May
Pooram: Temple Festival, Trichur, through May
Spring Festival, Kashmir, through May
July
Rath Yatra Temple Festival, Puri, Varanasi, Serampore, Jagannathpur
Teej: Women's Festival, Jaipur, through early August
August
Onam: Harvest Festival, Aranmula, Champ Akulam, Kottaya, Kerala State, through early September
September
Dussehra or Dasehara: Festival of Plays and Music, Delhi, Mysore, Kulu, Calcutta, through October
October
Diwali or Festival of Lights, nationwide, through early November
November
Pushkar Fair, Pushkar

Indonesia

Movable date
Balinese New Year, Bali, held once every 210 days
January
Temple Festivals, Bali, through December
April
Bull Races, Madura, East Java, through December
May
Galungan Festival, Bali
Ramayana Ballet Festival, Yogyakarta
Waicak Day: Birth of Buddha, Central Java, movable date
June
Toba Lake Festival, North Sumatra
July

Tumplak Wajik: Ritual Preparing of Rice Mounds at Palace, Yogyakarta
August
Independence Day, nationwide, August 17

Ireland

March
  Limerick Civic Week, Limerick
  St. Patrick's Week Festival, Dublin
April
  International Opera Season, Dublin
May
  Cork Choral and Folk Dance Festival, Cork
  Fleadh Nua: Irish Traditional Music, Song and Dance, Ennis
June
  Festival of Music in Great Irish Houses, Dublin, nationwide
  Irish Sweeps Derby: Horse Race, Curragh
July
  Irish Open Tennis Championships, Dublin
  Race Week, Galway
August
  Rose of Tralee International Festival, Tralee, County Kerry, through early September
September
  Oyster Festival, Galway
October
  Cork Jazz Festival, Cork
  Dublin City Marathon, Dublin
  Dublin Theater Festival, Dublin
  Wexford Festival Opera, Wexford

Israel

January or February
  Tu B' Shevat: New Year of the Trees, nationwide
March or April
  Easter Sunday Procession along Via Dolorosa, Jerusalem, movable date
March
  Feast of Purim, Feast of Lots, nationwide
April
  En Gev Festival, Sea of Galilee area, coincides with Passover observance
  Holocaust Remembrance, nationwide

International Flower Show, Haifa
Passover Observances, nationwide, movable date
April or May
Spring in Jerusalem Festival, Jerusalem
Independence Day Celebrations, nationwide
May
Citrus Festival, Netanya
Israel Festival, Jerusalem, through mid-June. Also in September, Caesarea, Haifa, Jerusalem, Tel Aviv
Jerusalem Day, Jerusalem, movable date
July
Sea of Galilee Festival, Tiberias
Youth Capital, Jerusalem
September
Rosh Hashana: New Year Observances, nationwide
September or October
Yom Kippur or Day of Atonement, nationwide

Italy

January
Feast of St. Agnes, Rome, January 21
New Year's Day Festival, Capri, January 1
Toys and Pastries Fair, Rome
February
Madonic Trophy-National Cross-Country Ski Contest, Pinao Battaglia, Palermo
Purification of the Virgin Mary and Presentation of Jesus in the Temple Observance, Altomonte, Cosenza, February 2
February or March
Carnival, nationwide, movable date
March
Almond Blossom Festival and International Folklore Festival, Agrigento
Feast of St. Joseph, Rome, March 19
March or April
Explosion of the Cart, Florence, Easter Sunday, movable date
April
International Handicrafts Fair, Florence, through early May
Milan Trade Fair, Milan, Lombardy
St. Mark's Feast Day, Venice
May
Cricket Festival, Florence, always on Ascension Day, movable date
Festival of St. Efisio, Cagliari, May 1-4
International Iris Flower Competition, Florence

Maggio Musicale Florence/Florentine Musical May, Florence, through July
Race of the Candles, Gubbio, May 15
Sardinian Cavalcade, Sassari, Sardinia, always on Ascension Day, movable date

June
Flower Festival, Genzano
Lily Festival, Nola, Campania, Sunday following June 22
Medieval Costumed Football Match, Florence, June 24, 28
Shakespeare Festival at Roman Theater, Verona, through September
Spoleto Festival/Festival of Two Worlds, Spoleto, Umbria, through July
Wagner Festival, Ravello

July
Feast of the Redeemer, Venice, third Sunday
Opera Season at Baths of Caracalla, Rome, through August
Opera Festival, Verona, through August
Palio of Siena, Siena, July 2, August 16

August
Joust of the Quintana Ascoli/Piceno, first Sunday
Palio of the Gulf, La Specia, second Sunday

September
Joust of the Quintana, Foligno, second Sunday
Joust of the Saracen, Arezzo, first Sunday
Living Chess Game, Marestica, held biennially, even-numbered years only
Parade of Carnival Floats, Boats and Neapolitan Song Competition, Naples, September 7-8

October
Sagra Musical Umbria, Perugia
White Truffle Fair, Alba

December
Opera and Ballet Season at La Scala, Milan, through June

Jamaica

January
Pantomine Shows, Kingston, through March

February or March
Carnival, Kingston, Montego Bay, movable date

March or April
Yachting Regatta, Montego Bay

May
International Marlin Tournament, Ocho Rios
International Table Tennis Tournament, Kingston
Manchester Horticultural Show, Mandeville

June
  Reggae Sunsplash Festival, Montego Bay, islandwide
July
  Jamaica Festival, Kingston, Montego Bay, islandwide, through August
August
  Independence Day and Week Festival, islandwide, first full week
  National Pushcart Derby, Discovery Bay
October
  International Marlin Tournament, Port Antonio, second week

Japan

January
  Adults' Day, nationwide, January 15
  New Year Parade of Firemen, Tokyo, January 6
February
  Bean-Throwing Festival, nationwide, February 4
  National Foundation Day, nationwide, February 11
  Snow Festival, Sapporo, February 1-5
March
  Doll Festival, nationwide, March 3
  Vernal Equinox Day, nationwide, March 20 or 21
April
  Cherry Dances, Kyoto
  Emperor's Birthday Observance, nationwide, April 29
  Flower Festival and Buddha's Birthday, nationwide, April 8
  Osaka International Festival, Osaka
May
  AOI Matsuri or Hollyhock Festival, Kyoto, Kyoto Prefecture, May 15
  Children's Day, nationwide, May 5
  Constitution Memorial Day, nationwide, May 3
  Cormorant Fishing on the Nagara River, Gifu, May 11-October 15
  Grand Festival of The Toshogu Shrine, Nikko, Tochigi Prefecture, May 17-18
  Kite Battles of Hamamatsu, Hamamatsu, Shizuoka Prefecture, May 3-5
June
  Rice Planting Festival at Sumiyoshi Shrine, Osaka, June 14
July
  "Bon" Festival or Feast of Lanterns, nationwide, July 13-16
  "Gion Matsuri" of Yasaka Shrine, Kyoto, July 17
  Tanabata or Star Festival, nationwide, July 7
  Wild Horse Chase and Roundup, Haramachi, Fukushima
August

Awa Odori Folk Dance Festival, Tokushima, August 12-15
Peace Festival: Memorial Rites, Hiroshima, August 6
Star Festival, Sendai, August 6-8
September
Autumnal Equinox Day, nationwide, September 22 or 23
Respect for the Aged Day, nationwide, September 15
Yabusame: Target Shooting on Horseback at Tsurugaoka Hachimangu Shrine, Kamakura, September 16
October
Autumn Festival of Toshogu Shrine, Nikko, October 17
Festival of Eras at Heian Shrine, Kyoto, October 22
Health Sports Day, nationwide, October 10
November
Culture Day, nationwide, November 3
Labor Thanksgiving Day, nationwide, November 23

Jordan

May
  Independence Day, nationwide, May 25
August
  King Hussein's Ascension to the Thorne Celebration, nationwide, August 11
  Jerash Festival, Jerash
October
  Exhibition of Jordanian Fine Arts, Amman

Kenya

March or April
  Safari Rally, Nairobi, always held Easter weekend, movable date
May
  Agricultural Shows, Nakuru, Mombasa, through September
June
  Madaraka Day: Anniversary of Self-Government, nationwide, June 1
October
  Kenya Agricultural Show, Nairobi
  Kenyatta Day, nationwide, October 20
November
  Sea Fishing Festival, Malindi

Korea

February
  Folk Festival, Yongsan, Kyongsangnam-do, through March
March
  Samiljol or Independence Movement Day, nationwide, March 1
April
  Arbor Day, nationwide, April 5
  King Tanjong Memorial Ceremony, Yongwol, Kangwon-do
May
  Chunhyang Festival, Namwon, North Jeolla
June
  Folk Festival, Chonju, Chollapuk-do
July
  Constitution Day, nationwide, July 17
August
  Liberation Day, nationwide, August 15
September
  Ch'usok: Korean Thanksgiving Day, nationwide, movable date
October
  Moyang Castle Festival, Gochang
November
  National Foundation Art Festival, Chinju

Luxembourg

February or March
  Prince Carnival and Carnival, nationwide, movable date
March or April
  Emaischen or Pottery Festival, Luxembourg City, always on Easter Monday, movable date
May
  International Spring Fair, Luxembourg City
May or June
  Genzefest or Broom Flower Festival, Wiltz, always on Whitmonday, movable date
  Sprangprocession or Dancing Procession, Echternach, always on Whit-Tuesday, movable date
June
  National Day, nationwide, June 23
  Remembrance Day, Ettelbruck, June 26
June/July

International Festival of Classical Music, Echternach
July
  Beer Festival, Diekrich
  Cherry Festival, Trintange
  International Open Air Theater and Music Festival, Wiltz, through August
  Theatre des Casemates: Modern Plays in Bock-Casemates of Former Fortification, Luxembourg City
August
  Antique Fair, Nospelt
  Schueberfor'er or Shepherds' Fair, Luxembourg City
  Wine and Wine-Growers Festival, Stadtbredimus
September
  Commemoration of the Liberation of the Grand-Duchy by Allied Forces in 1944, Petange, September 9
  Grape and Wine Festival, Grevenmacher
  Wine Festival, Schwebsange
October
  International Luxembourg Fall Fair, Luxembourg City
  Nuts Market, Vianden

Macao

February or March
  Chinese New Year Celebrations
  Lantern Festival
  Procession of Our Lord of Passos
April
  Anniversary of Portuguese Revolution, April 25
May
  Feast of the Bathing of Lord Buddha, movable date
  Procession of Our Lady of Fatima, May 13
June
  Feast of St. Anthony of Lisbon, June 13
  Feast of St. John the Baptist, June 24
July
  Feast of the Battle of July 13
August
  Feast of the Assumption of Our Lady, August 15
  Feast of the Hungry Ghosts, movable date
September
  Mid-Autumn Festival
October
  Republic Day, October 5

November
  Macao Grand Prix

Malaysia

January
  Thaipusam, Penang, Kuala Lumpur, Gaja Berang, through February
February
  Kula Lumpur City Day, citywide, February 1
May
  Bachok Festival of Culture, Bachok, Kelantan State
June
  Dayak Festival Day, State of Sarawak, June 1-2
August
  National Day, nationwide, August 31

Martinique (French West Indies)

February or March
  Carnival/Mardi Gras, Fort-de-France, through Ash Wednesday, movable date
March or April
  Easter Monday Picnics and Sports, islandwide, movable date
May
  Labor Day Parades, Fort-de-France, May 1
July
  Bastille Day, islandwide, July 14
  Schoelcher Day, Freedom From Slavery Observance, islandwide, July 21
August
  Assumption day, islandwide, August 15
September
  Fete Nautique de Robert or Festival of the Sea, Robert
December
  Guitar Festival, Fort-de-France

Mexico

January
  Blessing of the Animals on Feast of St. Anthony the Abbott, Mexico City, January 17

San Sebastian Festival, Guanajuato, January 20
The Three Kings, nationwide, January 6
February
Candlemas Fair, Tlacotalpan, Veracruz, February 2
February or March
Carnival, nationwide, movable date
March
Birthday of Benito Juarez, nationwide, March 21
Flower Fair, Huauchinango, Puebla
April
International Cervantes Festival, Guanajuato, through May, sometimes in Fall
San Marcos Fair, Aguascalientes, through May
May
Cinco de Mayo: Battle of Puebla, nationwide, May 5
Holy Cross Day: Construction Workers Day, nationwide, May 3
Labor Day, nationwide, May 1
San Isidro Labrador Day, Huistan, Chiapas, May 15
June
St. John the Baptist Day, nationwide, June 24
Sts. Peter and Paul Fiestas, San Pedro, Tlaquepaque, Guadalajara, June 29
July
Feast of the Virgin of Carmen, Ciudad del Carmen, Campeche, Mexico City, July 16
Monday of the Hill: Guelaguetza Dance Festival, Oaxaca, last two Mondays
August
Assumption of the Virgin Festivals, nationwide, August 15
Running of the Bulls, Huamantla, Tlaxcala, Sunday following August 15
September
Independence Day Celebration, Mexico City, nationwide, September 15-16
San Miguel Day, nationwide, September 29
October
Dia de la Raza: Day of the Race, nationwide, October 12
Fiestas de Octubre, Guadalajara, Jalisco, through November
November
All Saints Day, nationwide, November 1
All Souls Day or Day of the Dead, nationwide, November 2
Revolution Day: 1910 Revolution, Mexico City, nationwide, November 20
December
Feast of the Virgin of Guadalupe, Mexico City, nationwide, December 12
Posada Time: Processions, Pinatas and Parties, nationwide, December 16-24

Monaco

January
  International Festival of Arts, Monte Carlo, through April
February
  International Television Festival, Monte Carlo
March or April
  International Tennis Championships, Monte Carlo, always held during Easter, movable date
May
  International Flower Arrangement Competition, Monte Carlo
  Monaco Automobile Grand Prix, Monte Carlo
June
  Festival of Saint-Jean, Monte Carlo, June 23-24
July
  International Fireworks Festival, Monte Carlo, through August
November
  Monaco National Festival, nationwide, November 19
December
  International Circus Festival, Monte Carlo

Morocco

April
  Cherry Festival, Sefrou
May
  Festival of Folklore, Marrakesh
  Rose Festival, Kelaa des N'Gouna
September
  Equestrian Festival, Meknes
October
  Date Festival, Erfroud
  Fantasia/Horse Festival, Fez

Nepal

April
  The Chariot Festival of Macchendranath/Festival of the God of Rain, Patan, Kathmandu, through May
May
  Buddha Jayanti: Birth, Death and Enlightenment of Buddha, nationwide

August
    Indrajatra: End of Monsoon Season Festival, Kathmandu

Netherlands

January
    Film Festival, Rotterdam
    Indoor Six Day Cycling Event, Rotterdam
February
    Art and Antiques Fair, The Hague
    International Badminton Chapionships of Holland, Nieuwegein
March
    Art Weeks, Amsterdam
    Keukenhof, Lisse, through May
April
    Art and Antiques Fair, Breda
    Tulip Time International Music Festival, Katwijk
May
    International Lily Show, Lisse
    International Old Style Jazz Festival, Breda, through June
June
    Holland Festival, Amsterdam, Rotterdam, The Hague, June 1-23, sometimes through August
    International Albert Schweitzer Organ Festival, Deventer
    Jazz Marathon: Avant-Garde Jazz Festival, Groningen
July
    Festival of About 70 Old Crafts, Meijel
    International Folkloristic Parade, Brunssum
    International Tennis Tournament, Hilversum
    North Sea Jazz Festival, The Hague
August
    International Jazz Festival, Amsterdam
    Sneekweek: International Sailing Contests, Sneek
September
    Harvest-Fruit Pageant, Tiel
    International Gaudeamus Music Week, Hilversum, Amsterdam, Rotterdam
    Prinsjesdag: Ceremonial Procession of Queen in Golden Coach to Open New Parliamentary Season, The Hague
October
    Old Art and Antiques Fair, Delft, through early November

New Zealand

January
    Caroline Bay Carnival, Timaru
    New Zealand Grand Prix, Pukehehe
    New Zealand National Gliding Championships, Alexandra
    Rodeo, Wanganui
    Shark Fishing Tournament, Whakatane
    Summer City Festival, Wellington, through mid-February
    Yachting Regatta, Auckland
February
    Cultural Festival, Rotorua, through early March
    National Game Fishing Tournament, Napier
    New Zealand Rowing Championships, Lake Karapiro, through early March
    Summer Show, New Plymouth
March
    Auckland Festival, Auckland, held biennially, during even-numbered years only. Usually runs through April
    Christchurch Arts Festival, Christchurch, held biennially, during even-numbered years only
    Manawatu Festival of Sport and Culture, Palmerston North
April
    Floral Festival, Matamata
    Highland Games, Hastings
May
    Chrysanthemum Show, Nelson
    Society Festival of Performing Arts, Hamilton
June
    National Indoor Bowling Championships, Whangarei
    New Zealand Agricultural Field Days, Hamilton
July
    Film Festival, Wellington
August
    Festival of Arts, Hawera
    New Zealand Netball Tournament, Timaru
September
    Blossom Festival, Alexandra
October
    Festival Week, Palmerston North

Norway

January
    Monolith Ski Race, Oslo
    Ski Festival, Lillehammer

February
  International Fur Auctions, Oslo
  Opera Week, Kristiansund
March
  Holmenkollen Ski Festival, Oslo
  Jazz Festival, Voss
  Winter Festival Week, Narvik beyond the Artic Circle
March or April
  Easter Festival Week, Oslo, movable date
May
  Bergen International Festival of Music, Drama and Folklore, Bergen, through early June
  Constitution Day, nationwide, May 17
  The Ancient Marathon, Fredrikstad
June
  International Jazz Festival, Kongsberg
  North Cape Festival, Honningsvag
  North Norway Festival, Harstad
July
  International Sea Fishing Festival, Harstad
August
  Per Gynt Festival, Vinstra
  Salmon Fishing Festival, Grong
September
  Art and Antique Fair, Oslo
  Norwegian Film Festival, Skien
October
  State Autumn Exhibit, Oslo, month-long
December
  Nobel Peace Prize Presentation, Oslo, December 10

Panama

January
  Canajacua Folklore Festival, Macaracas
  Country Fair, Ocu
February
  International Film Festival, Panama City
February or March
  Carnival, Panama City, movable date
March
  International Fair of San Jose, David
April

Coffee Fair and Flower Festival, Boquete
International Underwater Fishing Tournament, Taboga and Contadora Islands
May
National Gymnastic Championship, Panama City
June
International Fishing Tournament, Panama City
July
International Boat Race, Panama City
August
Anniversary of Founding of Panama City, Panama City, August 15
Torito Grape Festival: Folkloric Festival, Anton
September
International Race, Panama City
October
Festival of the Black Christ, Portobelo, October 21

Peru

January
Feast of the Magi, Lima, January 6
International Fair of the Magi, Piura
February or March
Carnivale, nationwide, movable date
March
International Vintage Festival, Ica
Summer International Festival, Piura
May
Alasitas Fair: Popular Art Miniatures, Puno
Festivity of the Cross, Huaraz, Cuzco, May 2-3
June
Inti Raymi Fiesta or Sun Festival, San Antonio de Pichincha, Cuzco, Andahuaylas and Apurimac Valleys, June 24
July
Santa Isabel Festivity, Huaylas, July 8
August
Festidanza or Folk Festival, Arequipa
Feast of Santa Rosa de Lima, Lima, August 29-30
September
International Spring Festival, Trujillo

Philippines

January
  Ati-Atihan Festival, Kalibo, Aklan Province, Panay Island
  Constitution Day, nationwide, January 17
  Fiesta Black Nazarene, Manila, Quezon Province, Luzon Island, January 1-9
  Fiesta of the Santo Nino, Cebu Island in Visayas, third weekend
March or April
  Moriones Festival, Marinduque, southwest coast of Luzon, always Good Friday through Easter Sunday, movable date
April
  Bataan Day, nationwide, April 9
  Summer Festival, Baguio
May
  Carabao Festival, Pulilan, San Isidro, Angono, Sariaya, Quezon Province, May 14-15
June
  Independence Day, nationwide, June 12
July
  Mountain Provinces Harvest Festival, month-long
  River Festival, Bocaue, July 4-7
August
  Cultural Festival, Cagayan de Oro on coast of Mindanao
September
  Thanksgiving Day, nationwide, September 21
  Water Festival, Penafrancia, September 19
October
  Feast of Christ the King, nationwide, October 24
November
  All Saints Day, nationwide, November 1
December
  Philippine Christmas Season, nationwide, December 16-January 6

Poland

January
  Old Jazz Meeting, Warsaw
March
  Jazz on the Odra: Festival Competition of Polish Jazz Bands, Wroclaw
April
  All-Polish Student Song and Singers Festival, Cracow
May
  Chamber Music Days, Lancut Lezajsk
  Festival of Polish Contemporary Plays, Wroclaw

International Book Fair, Warsaw
June
   All-Polish Festival of Folklore and Folk Art, Plock
   Organ and Chamber Music Festival, Szczecin, Kamien Pomorski, through July
July
   Choirs Festival, Keszlin
August
   Dominican Fair, Gdansk, August 1-21
   International Chopin Festival, Duszniki Zdroj
   International Song Festival, Sopot
September
   Art Festival, Cracow
   Warsaw Autumn/International Festival of Contemporary Music, Warsaw

Portugal

February or March
   Carnival Festivities, nationwide, movable date
May
   Annual Pilgrimage to Fatima, Fatima, May 12-13
   Flower Festival, Funchal, Madeira Island
   International Fair, Lisbon
June
   Beer Festival, Silves, Algarve
   International Bach Festival, Funchal, Madeira Island
July
   Festival of the Red Waistcoat, Vila Franca de Xira
   Handicrafts Fair, Estoril, through August
August
   Celebrations of the Holy Ghost, Ponta Delgada, Sao Miguel Island, Azores
   Festival of Our Lady of Agony, Viana do Castelo
   Festival of the Green Cap and Salt Pans, Alcohete
September
   Great Wine Festival, Oporto
   International Steeplechase Championship, Penina, Algarve
   Madeira Wine Festival, Funchal
   Wine Harvest Festival, Palmela
October
   October Fair, Castro Verde-Beja
November
   National Horse Show and St. Martin's Fair, Golega, November 11

Romania

March
  Romanian Jazz Festival, Sibiu
April
  Opera and Ballet Musical Festival, Constanta
May
  Folklore Festival, Singeorz
  Folk Song and Handicraft Festival, Craiova
  Lilac Festival, Poncare Tirgu Kuu
  Youth in Spring Festival, Brasov
June
  Chamber Music Festival Brasov
  Folk Festival, Compeni Alban
July
  Ceramics Fair, Horezu
  Folk Dance and Song Festival, Felix Spa
August
  Hora de la Prislop or the Prislop Round Dance Festival, Borsa, Maramures County, second Sunday
  National Folklore Festival, Mamaia, Efore, Sinala, Constanta and Black Sea Coast
  National Light Music Festival, Mamaia
  Transylvania Men's Dance Festival, Gluj-Napoca
October
  Dionysiad, Husi, Vaslui County

Singapore

January or February
  Chinese New Year Observance, movable date
March
  Birthday of The Saint of The Poor
April
  Songkrant Festival or Water Festival: New Year Celebration at Thai Buddhist temples
May
  Birthday of the Third Prince: Third Prince of the Lotus
  Vesak Day: Birth, Death and Enlightenment of Lord Buddha, movable date
June
  Dragon Boat Festival
August

Market Festival, through early September
National Day, August 9
September
Mid-Autumn or Mooncake Festival
October
Pilgrimage to Kusu Island
Thimithi or Fire Walking Festival
December
Singapore Arts Festival

South Africa

March
Cape Show: Industrial and Agricultural Exhibition, Cape Town, through April
April
Cape Town Festival, Cape Town
Rand Show, Johannesburg, through May
May
Royal Show, Pietermaritzburg
July
Shembe/Zulu Festival, Inanda, biennially held, Sunday nearest July 25
August
Pretoria Show, Pretoria, through September

Spain

January
Festival of St. Antonio Abad, La Puebla, Mallorca, January 17
February
Festival of Moors and Christians, Bocairente, Valencia
February or March
Carnival, nationwide, movable date
March
Fallas of San Jose or St. Joseph's Bonfires, Valencia, March 12-19
Opera Festival, Las Palmas, Canary Islands
April
April Fair, Seville, Sevilla Province, follows Easter. If Easter occurs in March, the fair is held then, movable date
May
Festival of Patios, Cordoba

Festival of the Horse, Jerez de La Frontera, Cadiz
June
Feast of Corpus Christi, Toledo, movable date
International Festival of Music and Dance/Granada Festival, Granada, Granada Province, through early July
The St. John Bonfires, Alicante
July
Festival of San Fermin/Running of the Bulls, Pamplona, Navarra Province
International Festival of Music and Dance/Santander Festival, Santander, Santander Province, through August
August
Grape Harvest Festival, Requena, Valencia
The Montilla Moriles Wine Harvest, Montilla, Cordoba
September
Festival of Our Lady of Mercy, Barcelona
Jerez de Frontera Festival, Cadiz, Cadiz Province
October
Festivals del Pilar, Zaragoza
International Music Festival/Barcelona Festival, Barcelona, Barcelona Province
Saffron Rose Flower Harvest, Consuegra, Toledo
November
Start of Opera Season, Barcelona
December
Ste. Lucia's Festival, Santa Lucia, Las Palmas, December 13

Sri Lanka (Ceylon)

January
Thai Pongal Day: Hindus Festival Honoring the Sun God, nationwide
February
Independence Commemoration Day, nationwide, February 4
April
National New Year/Sinhala and Tamil New Year Observance, nationwide, movable date
May
May Day: Workers Parades, nationwide, May 1
National Heroes Day, nationwide, May 22
Vesak Festival: Birth, Enlightenment and Passing Away of Buddha, nationwide, movable date
June
Poson Full Moon Poya Day: Introduction of Buddhism to Sri Lanka in 247 B.C., nationwide, movable date

July
   Esala Perahera, Kandy, through early August, movable date

Sweden

January
   Market Fair, Hindersmassan
February
   Great Lapp Winter Fair, Jokkmokk, Lapland
March
   Ski Race, Vasa, Province of Dalarna
April
   Country Music Festival, Gothenburg
   Walpurgis Night: Bonfires and Welcome to Spring, nationwide, April 30
May
   Fladen Fishing Festival and Sea Angling Competition, Varberg
   Music Week at Uppsala Cathedral, Uppsala
   Summer Skiing, Lapland, through June
June
   Drottningholm Court Theater Season, Drottningholm near Stockholm, through August
   Midsummer Celebration, nationwide, June 22
July
   "Juliaden:" Music, Theater, Sports, Stockholm, month-long
   Swedish Open: Tennis, Bastad, Province of Skane
   The Visby Festival, Island of Gotland, through early August
August
   Jazz Days, Stockholm
September
   Cheese Fair, Skara
   St. Michael Fair, Vilhelmina, Lapland
October
   Music, Theater and Art Festival, Fershaga, Varmland, through early November
November
   Christmas Fair, Skansen, through mid-December
December
   Nobel Prize Ceremony at City Hall, Stockholm, December 10
   Santa Lucia Festival, nationwide, December 13

Switzerland

January
International Ski Races, Lauberhorn
Swiss New Year's Eve Celebration, Appenzel, Commune of Urnasch, January 13
February
International Jazz Festival, Aarau
Swiss Snow Sculpture Contest, Hoch-Ybrig
February or March
Carnival Celebrations, nationwide, movable date
March
Open Chess Tournament, Lugano
Ski-Bob Racing for Fun, Arosa
April
International Choral Festival, Montreux
Spring Festival, Zurich
May
International Festival of Lausanne, Lausanne, Vaud Canton, through early July
International June Festival, Zurich, Zurich Canton, through July
International TV Festival: Golden Rose Awards, Montreux
June
International High Alpine Ballooning Weeks, Murren, through early July
International Music Festival, Meiringen, through mid-July
July
Montreux International Music Festival/Montreux, Jazz Festival, Montreux, Vaud Canton
William Tell Festival Plays, Altdorf, Interlaken, through August
Wind-Surfing Marathon, St. Moritz
August
Festival of Music Montreux—Vevey, Montreux-Vevey, Vaud Canton, through October
Fete des Vignerons or Wine Growers' Festival, Vevey, Vaud Canton, held once every 25 years
International Festival of Music/Lucerne Festival, Lucerne, Lucerne Canton, through September
Yehudi Menuhin Festival, Gstaad
September
Wine Festival, Neuchatel
October
Chestnut Festival, Locarno

Thailand

January
   Phra Phuttabaht Temple Fair, Saraburi Province, through early February
   Red Cross Fair, Bangkok
February
   Flower Carnival, Chiang Mai
   Kite Season, Bangkok, through April
April
   Chakri Day, nationwide, April 6
   Festival of the Arts or Pattaya Festival, Pattaya
   Songkran or Water Festival: Thai New Year Observance, nationwide, April 13-15
May
   Coronation Day, nationwide, May 5
   Rocket Festival, Yasothorn Province
   Visakha Bucha: Birth, Enlightenment and Death of Buddha, nationwide, movable date
August
   Queen's Birthday Observance, nationwide, August 12
November
   Elephant Round-up, Surin, third weekend
   Loy Krathong Festival/Festival of Light, nationwide
December
   Constitution Day, nationwide, December 10
   King's Birthday and National Day, nationwide, December 5

Trinidad and Tobago

February or March
   The Trinidad & Tobago Carnival, Port-au-Spain, Monday and Tuesday before Ash Wednesday, movable date
April
   Festival of La Divina, Pastore
May
   Race Week, Tobago
June
   St. Peter's Day, all fishing villages, June 29
August
   Discovery Day by Columbus, both islands, August 1
   Independence Day, both islands, August 31
September
   Best Village Competitions, both islands, through November
   Republic Day, both islands, September 24

Tunisia

April
    Festival of the Ksars: Folklore, Tatouine
May
    Falcon Festival, El Haouaria
    Folk Art Festival, Tunis
June
    Malouf Festival: Traditional Music Festival, Testour
    Siren Festival, Kerkennah
July
    International Festival of Carthage, Carthage, North Tunis Region, through August
    International Festival of Hammamet, Hammamet, Nabeul Region, through August
    Sponge Festival, Zarzis
August
    Ulysses Festival, Djerba
    Women's Day, nationwide, August 13
September
    Memorial Day, nationwide, September 3
November
    Sahara National Festival, Douz, The South Sahara Region, through December

Turkey

January
    Camel Wrestling Festival, Selcuk
    Skiing Competitions, Bursa, Kayseri, Ankara, Erzurum, month-long
March
    Anaz Day:Anniversary of Canakkale Naval Victory (Dardanelles), Canakkale, March 18
April
    National Sovereignty and Children's Day, nationwide, April 23
    Tulip Festival, Istanbul, through early May
May
    Festival of Pergamum, Bergama/Izmir
    Selcuk Ephesus Festival of Culture and Art, Selcuk
    Youth and Sports Day, nationwide, May 19
June
    Festival of Istanbul, Istanbul, through mid-July
    Music and Art Festival, Marmaris
    Traditional Rosegrowing Competition, Konya

Wrestling Games of Kirkpinar, Edirne
July
Folklore and Music Festival, Bursa
Folklore and Water Sports Festival, Fecca north of Izmir
August
International Fair, Izmir, through mid-September
Victory Day, nationwide, August 30
September
Culture and Art Week, Bodrum
Grape Harvest and Folklore Festival, Cappadocia
Kirsehir Ahi Evran Crafts and Folklore Festival, Kirsehir
October
Film and Art Festival, Antalya
Republic Day, nationwide, October 29
December
Festival of Mevlana, Konya

Union of Soviet Socialist Republics (USSR)

May
Moscow Stars Festival, Moscow
Spring Festival, Kiev
Victory Day, nationwide, May 9
June
Music Summer Festival, Riga, through mid-August
White Nights Festival, Leningrad
August
Crimean Dawn Soviet Song Festival, Yalta
September
Arts Festival, Tashkent
October
Melodies of Soviet Transcaucasia: Arts Festival, Tbilisi, Erevan, Baku
December
Russian Winter Festival, Moscow, December 25-early January

Uruguay

January
National Festival of Folklore, Durazno
Summer Festival of the Lake of Rodo Park, Montevideo, through March
February or March

Carnival, Montevideo, movable date
March
  Semana Criolla or Creole Rodeo Week, Montevideo, through early April
July
  Constitution Day, nationwide, July 18
August
  Independence Day, nationwide, August 25
  Livestock Show, Montevideo

Venezuela

January
  Lara National Folkloric Festival, Barquisimeto
  San Sebastian International Festival, San Cristobal and throughout Tachira, January 20
February
  Dance of the Vassals Festival, La Punta
  International Carnival, Carupano
February or March
  Las Negritas Carnival/Mardi Gras, Caracas, movable date
April
  National Holiday: Declaration of Venezuelan Independence, nationwide, April 19
May
  Musical of the Cross, Caracas, through September
June
  Corpus Christi Day or Red Devils Folklore Festival, San Francisco de Yare, State of Miranda, movable date
July
  Bolivar's Birthday Observance, nationwide, July 24
  Folkloric Festival, San Carlos
  Independence Day, nationwide, July 5
August
  Feast of the Assumption, nationwide, August 14-15
  National Festival and Fair, Tariba
Movable Events
  Eastern Festival of Theater, Barcelona, Estado Anzeateguil
  International Theater Festival, Caracas, held biennially, during even-numbered years only

Yugoslavia

March
   Festival of Yugoslav Documentary Films, Belgrade, through early April
April
   International Agricultural Fair, Kranj
   International Riding Tournament, Lipica, through early May
   Spring International Grand Fair, Zagreb
May
   Festival of Pop Music, Belgrade
   Moreska Sword Dance Performances, Korcula, through September
   Yugoslav Theater Festival, Novi Sad, through early June
June
   Ljubljana Summer Festival, Ljubljana, through August
   Summer Festival, Opatija, through September
   Yugoslavia Grand Prix: Motorcycles, Opatija
July
   Dubrovnik Summer Festival, Dubrovnik, through August
   Festival of Light Music/Split Summer Festival, Split, through mid-August
   International Folklore Review, Zagreb
August
   Ceramic Pottery Exhibit, Resen, month-long
   Festival of Old Town Songs, Ohrid

Zambia

February or March
   Ku-Omboko Ceremony, Lealul Knoll, Mongu, Western Province
April
   National Fishing Competition, nationwide
May
   Africa Freedom Day, nationwide, May 25
   Copperbelt Agricultural Show, Kitwo
July
   Trade Fair, Ndola
October
   Independence Day, Lusaka, nationwide, October 24

APPENDIX: TYPES OF FESTIVALS

Agricultural

Argentina

National Festival of the Grape Harvest, Mendoza

Australia

Barossa Valley Vintage Festival, Barossa Valley, Tanunda
Royal Easter Show, Sydney

Barbados

June Crop-Over Festival, Bridgetown, islandwide

Canada

Annapolis Valley Apple Blossom Festival, Annapolis Valley Region, Nova Scotia
Eastern Nova Scotia Exhibition, Antigonish
Niagara Grape and Wine Festival, St. Catharines, Ontario
Peach Festival, Penticton, British Columbia
Potato Blossom Festival, O'Leary, Prince Edward Island

Cyprus

Limassol Wine Festival, Limassol

Malaysia

Dayak Festival Day, Sarawak

Panama

Country Fair, Ocu
International Fair of San Jose, David

Philippines

Carabao Festival, Pulilan, San Isidro, Angono, Sariaya, Quezon Province

Portugal

    October Fair, Castro Verde-Beja

South Africa

    Rand Show, Johannesburg

Tunisia

    Sahara National Harvest, Douz, The South Sahara Region

Art, Arts and Crafts

Australia

    Carnival of Flowers, Toowoomba
    Festival of Arts, Adelaide
    Festival of Perth, Perth
    Festival of Sydney, Sydney
    Moomba Festival, Melbourne

Austria

    Steirischer Herbst/Styrian Autumn, Graz, Styria

Barbados

    June Crop-Over Festival, Bridgetown, islandwide

Canada

    Acadian Festival, Caraquet, New Brunswick
    Banff Festival of Arts, Banff, Alberta
    Caribana, Toronto, Ontario
    Folklorama, Winnipeg, Manitoba
    Guelph Spring Festival, Guelph, Ontario
    Summer Festival, Quebec City, Quebec
    Summer Festival of the Arts, St. John's, Newfoundland

Denmark

    Aarhus Festival Week, Aarhus

France

    Easter Festival of Sacred Music, Lourdes
    May International Musical, Bordeaux

Great Britain

    England
    Festival of the City of London, London
    Scotland

TYPES OF FESTIVALS 249

    Edinburgh Festival, Edinburgh
    Wales
    Royal National Eisteddfod, North and South Wales

Hong Kong

    Festival of Asian Arts
    Hong Kong Arts Festival

Iceland

    Reykjavik Arts Festival, Reykjavik

Israel

    Israel Festival, Caesarea, Haifa, Jerusalem, Tel Aviv

Jamaica

    Jamaica Festival, Kingston, Montego Bay, islandwide

Jordan

    Jerash Festival, Jerash

Korea

    National Foundation Art Festival, Chinju

Mexico

    Fiestas de Octubre, Guadalajara
    International Cervantes Festival, Guanajuato

New Zealand

    Auckland Festival, Auckland
    Christchurch Arts Festival, Christchurch

Panama

    Country Fair, Ocu

Romania

    National Folklore Festival, Mamaia, Efore, Sinala, Constanta County and Black Sea Coast

Singapore

    Singapore Arts Festival

Sweden

    Great Lapp Winter Fair, Jokkmokk, Lapland

Switzerland

    International June Festival, Zurich, Zurich Canton

Tunisia

   International Festival of Hammamet, Hammamet, Nabeul Region

Turkey

   Festival of Istanbul, Istanbul
   International Fair, Izmir

Yugoslavia

   International Folklore Review, Zagreb, Croatia

Aviation

Canada

   International Air Show, Abbotsford, British Columbia

France

   Paris Air and Space Show, Paris

Ballet, Modern Dance, Folk

Australia

   Carnival of Flowers, Toowoomba
   Festival of the Arts, Adelaide
   Festival of Perth, Perth
   Festival of Sydney, Sydney

Austria

   Bregenz Festival, Bregenz, Vorarlberg
   Vienna Festival, Vienna

Bahamas

   Junkanoo Parade and Festival, Freeport, Nassau, Family Out Islands

Barbados

   June Crop-Over Festival, Bridgetown, islandwide

Bermuda

   Bermuda Festival, Hamilton

Canada

   Banff Festival of the Arts, Banff, Alberta
   Folklorama, Winnipeg, Manitoba
   Gaelic Mod, St. Ann's, Nova Scotia

Guelph Spring Festival, Guelph, Ontario
Winnipeg Folk Festival, Winnipeg, Manitoba

Colombia

Festival of Bambuco, Neiva

Czechoslovakia

Bratislava Music Festival, Bratislava
Folklore Festival of Straznice, Straznice
Prague Spring Music Festival, Prague

Denmark

Aarhus Festival Week, Aarhus

Finland

Folk Music Festival, Kaustinen
Helsinki Festival, Helsinki

France

Besancon International Music Festival, Besancon
International Festival of Lyon, Lyon
May International Musical, Bordeaux

Great Britain

England
   Aldeburgh Festival of Music and Arts, Aldeburgh, Suffolk
Wales
   International Musical Eisteddfod, Llangollen, Denbighshire

Germany, Federal Republic of

International May Festival, Wiesbaden, Hesse
Munich Opera Festival, Munich, Bavaria

Greece

Athens Festival, Athens
Festival of Demetria, Thessaloniki

Hong Kong

Festival of Asian Arts
Hong Kong Arts Festival

Iceland

Reykjavik Arts Festival, Reykjavik

Indonesia

Ramayana Dance Festival, Jogjakarta, Java-Yogyakarta District

Ireland

    The Rose of Tralee International Festival, Tralee, County Kerry

Israel

    Israel Festival, Caesarea, Haifa, Jerusalem, Tel Aviv
    Spring in Jerusalem Festival, Jerusalem

Italy

    Maggio Musicale Florence/Florentine May Musical Festival, Florence
    Spoleto Festival/Festival of Two Worlds, Spoleto

Jamaica

    Jamaica Festival, Kingston, Montego Bay, islandwide

Japan

    Osaka International Festival, Osaka

Jordan

    Jerash Festival, Jerash

Korea

    National Foundation Art Festival, Chinju

Luxembourg

    Schueberfo'er/Shepherd's Fair, Luxembourg City
    "Sprangprocession"/Dancing Procession, Echternach

Malaysia

    Bachok Festival of Culture, Bachok, Kelantan State

Mexico

    Fiestas de Octubre, Guadalajara
    International Cervantes Festival, Guanajuato

Monaco

    International Festival of Arts, Monte Carlo

Morocco

    Festival of Folklore, Marrakesh

Netherlands

    Holland Festival, The Hague/Scheveningen, Amsterdam, Rotterdam, Utrecht

New Zealand

    Auckland Festival, Auckland
    Christchurch Arts Festival, Christchurch

TYPES OF FESTIVALS 253

Norway

    Bergen International Festival of Music, Drama and Folklore, Bergen

Panama

    Canajacua Folklore Festival, Macaracas

Peru

    Festidanaza/Folk Festival, Arequipa

Poland

    Warsaw Autumn/International Festival of Contemporary Music, Warsaw

Romania

    Hora de La Prislop/The Prislop Round Dance Festival, Borsa
    National Folklore Festival, Mamaia, Efore, Sinala

Singapore

    Singapore Arts Festival

Spain

    International Festival of Music and Dance/Granada Festival, Granada
    International Festival of Music and Dance/Santander Festival, Santander

Sweden

    Drottningholm Court Theater Season, Drottningholm near Stockholm

Switzerland

    International Festival of Lausanne, Lausanne
    International June Festival, Zurich

Tunisia

    International Festival of Carthage, Carthage
    International Festival of Hammamet, Hammamet

Turkey

    Festival of Istanbul, Istanbul

Union of Soviet Socialist Republics (USSR)

    Moscow Stars Festival, Moscow
    Russian Winter Festival, Moscow
    White Nights Festival, Leningrad

Uruguay

    National Festival of Folklore, Durazno
    Summer Festival of the Lake of Rodo Park, Montevideo

Yugoslavia

    Dubrovnik Summer Festival, Dubrovnik
    International Folklore Review, Zagreb
    Ljubljana Summer Festival, Ljubljana
    Split Summer Festival, Split

Beer Festivals

Canada

    Oktoberfest, Kitchener, Waterloo, Ontario

Germany, Federal Republic of

    Oktoberfest, Munich

Carnival, Mardi Gras

Aruba

    Carnival, Oranjestad

Australia

    Carnival of Flowers, Toowoomba

Brazil

    Carnival, Rio de Janeiro

Canada

    Carnaval, Quebec City, Quebec
    Caribou Carnival and Championship Dog Derby, Yellowknife, Northwest Territories

Colombia

    Carnival, Barranquilla

Hungary

    National Floral Carnival, Debrecen

Martinique (French West Indies)

    Carnival/Mardi Gras, Fort-de-France

Panama

    Carnival, Panama City, nationwide

Trinidad & Tobago

    The Trinidad & Tobago Carnival, Port-au-Spain

Ceramics, Pottery

Luxembourg

"Emaischen" or Pottery Festival, Luxembourg City

Christmas

Austria

"Silent Night, Holy Night" Celebration, Hallein, Oberndorf, Wagrain, all of Salzburg

Ethiopia

Genna: Christmas Celebration, Addis Ababa

Philippines

Philippine Christmas Season, nationwide

Circus

Australia

Festival of Sydney, Sydney

Canada

Charlottetown Festival, Charlottetown, Prince Edward Island

Monaco

International Circus Festival, Monte Carlo

Commemorative

Bahamas

Fox Hill Day, Nassau

British Virgin Islands

Tortola Festival, Tortola

Canada

Festival of Spring, Ottawa, Ontario

Germany, Federal Republic of

Landshut Wedding 1475, Landshut, Bavaria

Great Britain

Battle of Flowers, St. Helier, Jersey, Channel Islands

Hong Kong

    Dragon Boat Festival

Italy

    Sardinian Cavalcade, Sassari, Sardinia

Japan

    Grand Festival of the Toshogu Shrine, Nikko, Toghigi Prefecture

Mexico

    Running of the Bulls, Huamantla, Tlaxcala

Philippines

    Ati-Atihan Festival, Kalibo, Aklan Province, Panay Island

Singapore

    Birthday of the Monkey God
    Mid-Autumn/Mooncake Festival

Community/Goodwill

    Antigua

        Police Week Festival, St. John's

    Denmark

        Rebild Festival of Fourth of July Celebration, Aalborg, Rebild, North Jutland

Competitions, Contests

    Antigua

        Police Week Festival, St. John's

    Bonaire

        International Regatta, Kralendijk

    Bulgaria

        Golden Orpheus, Slunchev Bryag

    Canada

        Calgary Exhibition and Stampede, Calgary, Alberta
        Gaelic Mod, St. Ann's, Nova Scotia
        Maritime Old Time Fiddling Contest, Dartmouth, Nova Scotia
        Northern Manitoba Trappers' Festival, The Pas, Manitoba

TYPES OF FESTIVALS 257

    Northern Pike Festival, Nipawin, Saskatchewan
    Snowgolf Championship, Prince George, British Columbia
    Western Festival, Saint-Tite, Quebec

Czechoslovakia

    Spartakiade, Prague

Denmark

    Sonderborg Tilting Tournament, Sonderborg

Finland

    Ounasvaara International Winter Games, Rovaniemi

France

    Besancon International Music Festival, Besancon
    Paris Marathon, Paris

Gibraltar

    International Shark Angling Competition

Great Britain

    England
        Pancake Race, Olney
    Isle of Wight
        Regatta Week, Cowes
    Wales
        International Musical Eisteddfod, Llangollen, Denbighshire
        Royal National Eisteddfod, North and South Wales

Hong Kong

    Dragon Boat Festival

Iceland

    Iceland National Horse Meet Show and Races, Skagafjordur

Ireland

    Dublin Horse Show, Dublin
    Galway Oyster Festival, Galway

Italy

    Palio of Siena, Siena, Tuscany

Japan

    Kite Battles of Hamamatsu, Hamamatsu

Kenya

    Safari Rally, Nairobi

Korea
> Chunhyang Festival, Namwon, North Jeolla
> Moyang Castle Festival, Gochang

Macao
> Macao Grand Prix

Malaysia
> Bachok Festival of Culture, Bachok, Kelantan State

Monaco
> Monaco Automobile Grand Prix, Monte Carlo

Morocco
> Fantasia/Horse Festival, Fez
> Festival of Folklore, Marrakesh

Norway
> Holmenkollen Ski Festival, Oslo

Panama
> Canajacua Folklore Festival, Macaracas

Romania
> National Folklore Festival, Mamaia, Efore, Sinala

Thailand
> Elephant Roundup, Surin
> Kite Flying Season, Bangkok

Trinidad & Tobago
> The Trinidad & Tobago Carnival, Port-au-Spain

Turkey
> Wrestling Games of Kirkpinar, Edirne

Uruguay
> National Festival of Folklore, Durazno

Crafts. See Art, Arts and Crafts

Cultural: Arts, Music, Drama, Dance
Antigua
> Police Week Festival, St. John's

TYPES OF FESTIVALS 259

Australia

    Carnival of Flowers, Toowoomba
    Festival of the Arts, Adelaide
    Festival of Perth, Perth
    Festival of Sydney, Sydney
    Moomba Festival, Melbourne

Austria

    Bregenz Festival, Bregenz
    Carinthian Summer Festival, Ossiach, Villach
    Salzburg Festival, Salzburg
    Steirischer Herbst/Styrian Autumn, Graz
    Vienna Festival, Vienna

Bahamas

    Bahamas Goombay Holiday, Freeport, Nassau
    Junkanoo Parade and Festival, Freeport, Nassau, Family Out Islands

Barbados

    June Crop-Over Festival, Bridgetown, islandwide

Belgium

    Flanders Festival, Antwerp, Bruges, Brussels, Ghent, Kortrijk, Leuven, Mechelen

Bermuda

    Bermuda Festival, Hamilton

Bulgaria

    Golden Orpheus, Slunchev Bryag
    National Humor and Satire Festival, Gabrovo

Canada

    Acadian Festival, Caraquet, New Brunswick
    Annapolis Valley Apple Blossom Festival, Annapolis Valley Region, Nova Scotia
    Banff Festival of the Arts, Banff, Alberta
    Caribana, Toronto, Ontario
    Caribou Carnival and Championship Dog Derby, Yellowknife, Northwest Territories
    Charlottetown Festival, Charlottetown, Prince Edward Island
    Festival Ottawa Opera Plus, Ottawa, Ontario
    Festival of Spring, Ottawa, Ontario
    Folklorama, Winnipeg, Manitoba
    Gaelic Mod, St. Ann's, Nova Scotia
    Guelph Spring Festival, Guelph, Ontario
    Maritime Old Time Fiddling Contest, Dartmouth, Nova Scotia
    Miramichi Folk Song Festival, Newcastle, New Brunswick
    Newfoundland Drama Festival, Provincewide

Shaw Festival, Niagara-on-the-Lake, Ontario
Stratford Festival, Stratford, Ontario
Summer Festival of the Arts, St. John's, Newfoundland
Summer Festival, Quebec City, Quebec

Colombia

Festival of Bambuco, Neiva

Cyprus

Curium Festival, Curium/Limassol

Czechoslovakia

Bratislava Music Festival, Bratislava
Folklore Festival of Straznice, Straznice
Prague Spring Music Festival, Prague

Denmark

Aarhus Festival Week, Aarhus
Hans Christian Andersen Festival, Odense
Viking Festival, Frederikssund

Finland

Folk Music Festival, Kaustinen
Helsinki Festival, Helsinki
Jyvaskyla Arts Festival, Jyvaskyla
Pori Jazz, Pori
Savonlinna Opera Festival, Savonlinna

France

Besancon International Music Festival, Besancon
Easter Festival of Sacred Music, Lourdes
International Festival of Lyon, Lyon
International Music Festival, Strasbourg
May International Musical, Bordeaux

Germany, Federal Republic of

Bayreuth Festival/Richard Wagner Festival, Bayreuth
Berlin Festival, West Berlin
Munich Opera Festival, Munich
International May Festival, Wiesbaden

Great Britain

England

Aldeburgh Festival of Music and Arts, Aldeburgh
Bath Festival, Bath
Broadstairs Dickens Festival, Broadstairs
Chichester Festival Theater Season, Chichester

TYPES OF FESTIVALS 261

>Festival of the City of London, London
>Glyndebourne Festival Opera, Glyndebourne
>King's Lynn Festival, King's Lynn
>Royal Shakespeare Company/Shakespeare Festival, Stratford-upon-Avon
>Three Choirs Festival, Gloucester, Hereford, Worcester
>York Festival and Mystery Plays, York

Scotland
>Edinburgh Festival, Edinburgh

Wales
>International Musical Eisteddfod, Llangollen, Denbighshire
>Royal National Eisteddfod, North and South Wales

Greece

Athens Festival, Athens
Epidaurus Festival, Epidaurus
Festival of Demetria, Thessaloniki
International Trade Fair, Film and Song Festival, Thessaloniki

Hong Kong

Festival of Asian Arts
Hong Kong Arts Festival

Iceland

Reykjavik Arts Festival, Reykjavik

India

Dussehra/Dasehara, Delhi, Mysore, Kulu, Calcutta

Indonesia

Ramayana Dance Festival, Jogjakarta

Ireland

The Rose of Tralee International Festival, Tralee
Wexford Festival Opera, Wexford

Israel

Israel Festival, Caesarea, Haifa, Jerusalem, Tel Aviv
Spring in Jerusalem Festival, Jerusalem

Italy

Maggio Musicale Florence/Florentine May Music Festival, Florence
Spoleto Festival/Festival of Two Worlds, Spoleto

Jamaica

Jamaica Festival, Kingston, Montego Bay, islandwide

Japan
- Osaka International Festival, Osaka

Jordan
- Jerash Festival, Jerash

Korea
- Chunhyang Festival, Namwon, North Jeolla
- National Foundation Art Festival, Chinju

Malaysia
- Bachok Festival of Culture, Bachok, Kelantan State

Mexico
- Fiestas de Octubre, Guadalajara
- International Cervantes Festival, Guanajuato

Monaco
- International Festival of Arts, Monte Carlo

Morocco
- Festival of Folklore, Marrakesh

Netherlands
- Holland Festival, The Hague/Scheveningen, Amsterdam, Rotterdam

New Zealand
- Auckland Festival, Auckland
- Christchurch Arts Festival, Christchurch

Norway
- Bergen International Festival of Music, Drama and Folklore, Bergen

Panama
- Canajacua Folklore Festival, Macaracas

Peru
- Festidanza/Folk Festival, Arequipa

Poland
- Warsaw Autumn/International Festival of Contemporary Music, Warsaw

Portugal
- International Bach Festival, Funchal, Madeira Island

Singapore

    Singapore Arts Festival

Spain

    International Festival of Music and Dance/Granada Festival, Granada
    International Festival of Music and Dance/Santander Festival, Santander
    International Music Festival/Barcelona Festival, Barcelona

Sweden

    Drottningholm Court Theater Season, Drottningholm, near Stockholm

Switzerland

    Festival of Music, Montreux-Vevey
    International Festival of Lausanne, Lausanne
    International Festival of Music/Lucerne Festival, Lucerne
    International June Festival, Zurich
    Montreux International Music Festival/Montreux Jazz Festival

Tunisia

    International Festival of Carthage, Carthage
    International Festival of Hammamet, Hammamet

Turkey

    Festival of Istanbul, Istanbul

Union of Soviet Socialist Republics (USSR)

    Moscow Stars Festival, Moscow
    Russian Winter Festival, Moscow
    White Nights Festival, Leningrad

Uruguay

    National Festival of Folklore, Durazno
    Summer Festival of the Lake of Rodo Park, Montevideo

Venezuela

    Eastern Festival of Theater, Barcelona
    International Theater Festival, Caracas

Yugoslavia

    Dubrovnik Summer Festival, Dubrovnik
    International Folklore Review, Zagreb
    Ljubljana Summer Festival, Ljubljana
    Split Summer Festival, Split

Dog/Horse Shows (Equestrian)

Colombia

Quadrilles of San Martin, San Martin

Great Britain

England
Cruft's Dog Show, London

Iceland

Iceland National Horse Meet Show and Races, Skagafjordur

Ireland

Dublin Horse Show

Italy

Palio of Siena, Siena

Morocco

Fantasia Horse Festival, Fez

Drama

Australia

Carnival of Flowers, Toowoomba
Festival of the Arts, Adelaide
Festival of Perth, Perth
Festival of Sydney, Sydney
Moomba Festival, Melbourne

Austria

Bregenz Festival, Bregenz
Salzburg Festival, Salzburg
Steirischer Herbst/Styrian Autumn, Graz
Vienna Festival, Vienna

Bahamas

Bahamas Goombay Holiday, Freeport, Nassau

Bermuda

Bermuda Festival, Hamilton

Canada

Acadian Festival, Caraquet, New Brunswick
Banff Festival of the Arts, Banff, Alberta

TYPES OF FESTIVALS 265

    Charlottetown Festival, Charlottetown, Prince Edward Island
    Guelph Spring Festival, Guelph, Ontario
    Newfound Drama Festival, provincewide
    Shaw Festival, Niagara-on-the-Lake, Ontario
    Stratford Festival, Stratford, Ontario
    Summer Festival, Quebec City, Quebec

Cyprus

    Curium Festival, Curium/Limassol

Denmark

    Aarhus Festival Week, Aarhus
    Hans Christian Andersen Festival, Odense
    Viking Festival, Frederikssund

Finland

    Helsinki Festival, Helsinki
    Jyvaskyla Arts Festival, Jyvaskyla

France

    May International Musical, Bordeaux
    Summer Festival of Paris, Paris

Germany, Federal Republic of

    International May Festival, Wiesbaden
    Oberammergau Passion Play, Oberammergau

Great Britain

    England
        Broadstairs Dickens Festival, Broadstairs
        Chichester Festival Theater Season, Chichester
        Festival of the City of London, London
        King's Lynn Festival, King's Lynn
        Royal Shakespeare Company/Shakespeare Festival, Stratford-upon-Avon
        York Festival and Mystery Plays, York
    Scotland
        Edinburgh Festival, Edinburgh

Greece

    Athens Festival, Athens
    Epidaurus Festival, Epidaurus
    Festival of Demetria, Thessaloniki

Hong Kong

    Festival of Asian Arts
    Hong Kong Arts Festival

Iceland
: Reykjavik Arts Festival, Reykjavik

India
: Dussehra/Dasehara, Delhi, Mysore, Kulu, Calcutta

Ireland
: The Rose of Tralee International Festival, Tralee

Israel
: Israel Festival, Caesarea, Haifa, Jerusalem, Tel Aviv
  Spring in Jerusalem Festival, Jerusalem

Italy
: Spoleto Festival/Festival of Two Worlds, Spoleto

Jamaica
: Jamaica Festival, Kingston, Montego Bay, islandwide

Japan
: Osaka International Festival, Osaka

Jordan
: Jerash Festival, Jerash

Korea
: National Foundation Art Festival, Chinju

Malaysia
: Bachok Festival of Culture, Bachok, Kelantan State

Mexico
: International Cervantes Festival, Guanajuato

Netherlands
: Holland Festival, The Hague/Scheveningen, Amsterdam, Rotterdam

New Zealand
: Auckland Festival, Auckland
  Christchurch Arts Festival, Christchurch

Norway
: Bergen International Festival of Music, Drama and Folklore, Bergen

Philippines
: Moriones Festival, Boac, Gasan, Marinduque Province, Marinduque Island

TYPES OF FESTIVALS 267

Singapore

  Singapore Arts Festival

Spain

  International Festival of Music and Dance/Santander Festival, Santander

Tunisia

  International Festival of Carthage, Carthage
  International Festival of Hammamet, Hammamet

Turkey

  Festival of Istanbul, Istanbul

Union of Soviet Socialist Republics (USSR)

  Russian Winter Festival, Moscow
  White Nights Festival, Leningrad

Uruguay

  Summer Festival of the Lake of Rodo Park, Montevideo

Venezuela

  Eastern Festival of Theater, Barcelona
  International Theater Festival, Caracas

Yugoslavia

  Dubrovnik Summer Festival, Dubrovnik
  Ljubljana Summer Festival, Ljubljana
  Split Summer Festival, Split

Ecology, Environmental/Conservation

Canada

  Bitowa Outdoor Festival, Tracadie, New Brunswick

Economic

Australia

  Moomba Festival, Melbourne
  Royal Easter Show, Sydney

Bahamas

  Bahamas Goombay Holiday, Freeport, Nassau

Belgium

    Begonia Festival, Lochristi
    Brussels International Fair, Brussels

Bermuda

    Bermuda College Weeks, Hamilton, St. George's
    Bermuda Festival, Hamilton

Brazil

    Carnival, Rio de Janeiro

Bulgaria

    Rose Festival, Kazanluk

Canada

    Annapolis Valley Apple Blossom Festival, Annapolis Valley region, Nova Scotia
    Bitowa Outdoor Festival, Tracadie, New Brunswick
    Buffalo Days, Regina, Saskatchewan
    Calgary Exhibition and Stampede, Calgary, Alberta
    Canadian National Exhibition, Toronto, Ontario
    Caribou Carnival and Championship Dog Derby, Yellowknife, Northwest Territories
    Eastern Nova Scotia Exhibition, Antigonish, Nova Scotia
    Folklorama, Winnipeg, Manitoba
    Gemboree, Bancroft, Ontario
    International Air Show, Abbotsford, British Columbia
    Lobster Festival, Shediack, New Brunswick
    Maritime Old Time Fiddling Contest, Dartmouth, Nova Scotia
    Niagara Grape and Wine Festival, St. Catharines, Ontario
    Northern Manitoba Trappers' Festival, The Pas, Manitoba
    Northern Pike Festival, Nipawin, Saskatchewan
    Oktoberfest, Kitchener, Waterloo, Ontario
    Peach Festival, Penticton, British Columbia
    Pioneer Days, Saskatoon, Saskatchewan
    Potato Blossom Festival, O'Leary, Prince Edward Island
    Snowgolf Championship, Prince George, British Columbia
    Western Festival, Saint-Tite, Quebec

Cayman Islands

    Pirate Week Festival, George Town, Grand Cayman

Colombia

    Quadrilles of San Martin, San Martin

France

    Paris Air and Space Show, Paris
    Summer Festival of Paris, Paris
    Three Glorious Days, Nuits-St. Georges, Beaune, Meursault

TYPES OF FESTIVALS 269

Germany, Federal Republic of
  Oktoberfest, Munich
Great Britain
  Chelsea Flower Show, London
Greece
  International Trade Fair, Film and Song Festival, Thessaloniki
  Wine Festival, Rethymon, Crete
Hungary
  National Floral Carnival, Debrecen
India
  Pushkar Fair, Pushkar
Ireland
  Galway Oyster Festival, Galway
Italy
  Milan Trade Fair, Milan
Monaco
  International Circus Festival, Monte Carlo
Netherlands
  Keukenhof, Lisse
  Old Art and Antiques Fair, Delft
Panama
  Coffee Fair and Flower Festival, Boquete
  Country Fair, Ocu
  International Fair of San Jose, David
Portugal
  October Fair, Castro Verde-Beja
Romania
  Dionysiad, Husi
South Africa
  Rand Show, Johannesburg
Spain
  April Fair, Seville
  Jerez de Frontera Festival, Cadiz

Sweden

    Great Lapp Winter Fair, Jokkmokk, Lapland

Switzerland

    International Festival of Music/Lucerne Festival, Lucerne

Thailand

    Elephant Roundup, Surin

Tunisia

    International Festival of Hammamet, Hammamet
    Sahara National Festival, Douz

Turkey

    International Fair, Izmir

Yugoslavia

    Dubrovnik Summer Festival, Dubrovnik

Ethnic

Bahamas

    Junkanoo Parade and Festival, Nassau, Freeport, Family Out Islands

Canada

    Acadian Festival, Caraquet, New Brunswick
    Canada's National Ukrainian Festival, Dauphin, Manitoba
    Caribana, Toronto, Ontario
    Festival du Voyageur, St. Boniface, Manitoba
    Folklorama, Winnipeg, Manitoba
    Gaelic Mod, St. Ann's, Nova Scotia
    Icelandic Festival, Gimli, Manitoba
    Oktoberfest, Kitchener, Waterloo, Ontario
    Vesna Festival (Ukrainian), Saskatoon, Saskatchewan

Colombia

    Quadrilles of San Martin, San Martin

Mexico

    Fiestas de Octubre, Guadalajara

Uruguay

    National Festival of Folklore, Durazno

Fairs/Markets

Australia

    Barossa Valley Vintage Festival, Barossa Valley, Tanunda
    Royal Easter Show, Sydney

Belgium

    Brussels International Fair, Brussels

Canada

    Buffalo Days, Regina, Saskatchewan
    Calgary Exhibition and Stampede, Calgary, Alberta
    Canadian National Exhibition, Toronto, Ontario
    Eastern Nova Scotia Exhibition, Antigonish, Nova Scotia

France

    Paris Air and Space Show, Paris

Germany, Federal Republic of

    Oktoberfest, Munich

Greece

    International Trade Fair, Film and Song Festival, Thessaloniki

Hungary

    National Floral Carnival, Debrecen

Iceland

    Iceland National Horse Meet Show and Races, Skagafjordur

India

    Pushkar Fair, Pushkar

Italy

    Milan Trade Fair, Milan

Korea

    National Foundation Art Festival, Chinju

Luxembourg

    Emaischen/Pottery Festival, Luxembourg-City
    Schueberfo'er/Shepherd's Fair, Luxembourg-City

Mexico

    Fiestas de Octubre, Guadalajara

Netherlands

    Old Art and Antiques Fair, Delft

Panama

    Coffee Fair and Flower Festival, Boquete
    Country Fair, Ocu
    International Fair of San Jose, David

Portugal

    October Fair, Castro Verde-Beja

South Africa

    Rand Show, Johannesburg

Spain

    April Fair, Seville

Sweden

    Great Lapp Winter Fair, Jokkmokk, Lapland

Tunisia

    Sahara National Festival, Douz

Turkey

    International Fair, Izmir

Film Festivals

Australia

    Festival of Perth, Perth
    Festival of Sydney, Sydney

Canada

    Guelph Spring Festival, Guelph, Ontario
    Summer Festival, Quebec City, Quebec

Finland

    Jyvaskyla Arts Festival, Jyvaskyla

Great Britain

    Scotland
        Edinburgh Festival, Edinburgh

Greece

    International Trade Fair, Film and Song Festival, Thessaloniki

Israel
  Israel Festival, Caesarea, Haifa, Jerusalem, Tel Aviv
Jordan
  Jerash Festival, Jerash
Mexico
  International Cervantes Festival, Guanajuato
Tunisia
  International Festival of Carthage, Carthage

Fish Festivals

Canada
  Bitowa Outdoor Festival, Tracadie, New Brunswick
  Lobster Festival, Shediac, New Brunswick
  Northern Pike Festival, Nipawin, Saskatchewan
Gibraltar
  International Shark Angling Competition
Ireland
  Galway Oyster Festival, Galway

Flowers/Floral

Australia
  Carnival of Flowers, Toowoomba
Belgium
  Begonia Festival, Lochristi
Bulgaria
  Rose Festival, Kazanluk
Canada
  Annapolis Valley Apple Blossom Festival, Annapolis Valley region, Nova Scotia
  Festival of Spring (Tulips), Ottawa, Ontario
  Potato Blossom Festival, O'Leary, Prince Edward Island
Great Britain
  England
    Chelsea Flower Show, London

Jersey, Channel Islands
    Battle of Flowers, St. Helier

Hungary

National Floral Carnival, Debrecen

Japan

Hollyhock Festival of Shimogano and Kamigano Shrines, Kyoto

Luxembourg

Genzefest or Broom Flower Festival, Wiltz

Netherlands

Keuhenhof, Lisse

Panama

Coffee Fair and Flower Festival, Boquete

Folkloric: Folk Festivals

Argentina

National Festival of the Grape Harvest, Mendoza

Barbados

June Crop-Over Festival, Bridgetown, islandwide

Belgium

Cat Festival and Parade, Ypres
Procession of The Witches, Beselare

Brazil

Carnival, Rio de Janeiro

Canada

Acadian Festival, Caraquet, New Brunswick
Caribana, Toronto, Ontario
Folklorama, Winnipeg, Manitoba
Miramichi Folk Song Festival, Newcastle, New Brunswick
Pioneer Days, Saskatoon, Saskatchewan
Toonik Tyme, Frobisher Bay, Northwest Territories
Winnipeg Folk Festival, Winnipeg, Manitoba

Colombia

Carnival, Barranquilla
Festival of Bambuco, Neiva
Quadrilles of San Martin, San Martin

Czechoslovakia

    Folklore Festival of Straznice, Straznice
    Maypole and Burning of the Witches, Postupice
    Znojmo Feast, Znojmo

Denmark

    Sonderborg Tilting Tournament, Sonderborg
    Viking Festival, Frederikssund

Ethiopia

    Maskal Festival, Addis Ababa

Finland

    Folk Music Festival, Kaustinen

France

    Three Glorious Days, Nuits-St. Georges, Beaune, Meursault

Germany, Federal Republic of

    Octoberfest, Munich
    The Master Draught Pageant, Rothenburg/Tauber

Great Britain

    Pancake Racing, Olney, England

Greece

    Wine Festival, Rethymon, Crete

Guadeloupe (French West Indies)

    Fete des Cuisineres/Cooks' Festival, Pointe-a-Pitre

Hong Kong

    Cheung Chau Festival/Festival of the Bun Hills, Island of Cheung Chau
    Dragon Boat Festival

Hungary

    National Floral Carnival, Debrecen

India

    Dussehra/Dasehara, Delhi, Mysore, Kulu, Calcutta

Indonesia

    Balinese New Year, Bali
    Ramayana Dance Festival, Jogjakarta

Ireland

    The Rose of Tralee International Festival, Tralee

Israel

   Israel Festival, Caesarea, Haifa, Jerusalem, Tel Aviv
   Spring in Jerusalem Festival, Jerusalem

Italy

   Feast of the Redeemer, Venice
   Lily Festival, Nola
   Sardinian Cavalcade, Sassari, Sardinia

Japan

   Grand Festival of the Toshogu Shrine, Nikko
   Hollyhock Festival of Shimogamo and Kamigamo Shrines, Kyoto

Korea

   Chunhyang Festival, Namwon, North Jeolla
   Moyang Castle Festival, Gochang

Luxembourg

   Emaischen/Pottery Festival, Luxembourg-City
   Genzefest/Broom Flower Festival, Wiltz
   Schueberfo'er/Shepherd's Fair, Luxembourg-City
   Sprangprocession/Dancing Procession, Echternach

Malaysia

   Dayak Festival Day, Sarawak

Martinique (French West Indies)

   Carnival/Mardi Gras, Fort-de-France

Mexico

   Fiestas de Octubre, Guadalajara

Morocco

   Fantasia/Horse Festival, Fez
   Festival of Folklore, Marrakesh

Norway

   Bergen International Festival of Music, Drama and Folklore, Bergen

Panama

   Canajacua Folklore Festival, Macaracas
   Carnival, Panama City, nationwide
   International Fair of San Jose, David

Peru

   Festidanza/Folk Festival, Arequipa

TYPES OF FESTIVALS

Philippines

    Ati-Atihan Festival, Kalibo, Aklan Province, Panay Island
    Carabao Festival, Pulilan, San Isidro, Angono, Sariaya, Quezon Province
    Fiesta Black Nazarene, Manila, Quezon Province
    Moriones Festival, Boac, Gasan, Marinduque Province
    Philippine Christmas Season, nationwide

Portugal

    Celebrations of The Holy Ghost, Ponta Delgada, Sao Miguel Island, Azores
    Festival of the Red Waistcoat, Vila Franca de Xira

Romania

    Dionysiad, Husi
    Hora de La Prislop/The Prislop Round Dance Festival, Borsa
    National Folklore Festival, Mamaia, Efore, Sinala

Singapore

    Mid-Autumn/Mooncake Festival

South Africa

    Shembe/Zulu Festival, Inanda

Spain

    April Fair, Seville
    Fallas of San Jose/St. Joseph's Bonfires, Valencia
    International Festival of Music and Dance/Santander Festival, Santander
    San Fermin Festival/Running of the Bulls, Pamplona

Sweden

    Great Lapp Winter Fair, Jokkmokk, Lapland
    Santa Lucia Festival, nationwide

Switzerland

    Fete des Vignerons/Wine Growers' Festival, Vevey
    Swiss New Year's Eve Celebration, Appenzell

Thailand

    Elephant Roundup, Surin
    Kite Flying Season, Bangkok
    Loy Krathong Festival/Festival of Light, nationwide
    Songkran/Water Festival, Paklat, Bangkok, Chiang Mai

Tunisia

    International Festival of Hammamet, Hammamet
    Sahara National Festival, Douz

Turkey

  Wrestling Games of Kirkpinar, Edirne

Uruguay

  National Festival of Folklore, Durazno

Yugoslavia

  Dubrovnik Summer Festival, Dubrovnik
  International Folklore Review, Zagreb
  Ljubljana Summer Festival, Ljubljana

Zambia

  Ku-Omboko Ceremony, Lealul Knoll, Mongu

Food Festivals

Canada

  Lobster Festival, Shediac, New Brunswick

Czechoslovakia

  Znojmo Feast, Znojmo

Guadeloupe (French West Indies)

  Fete des Cuisinieres/Cooks' Festival, Pointe-a-Pitre

Singapore

  Mid-Autumn/Mooncake Festival

Fruit Festivals

Canada

  Annapolis Valley Apple Blossom Festival, Annapolis Valley region, Nova Scotia
  Peach Festival, Penticton, British Columbia

Harvest

Argentina

  National Festival of the Grape Harvest, Mendoza

Australia

  Barossa Valley Vintage Festival, Barossa Valley, Tanunda

Barbados
> June Crop-Over Festival, Bridgetown, islandwide

Bulgaria
> Rose Festival, Kazanluk

Canada
> Niagara Grape and Wine Festival, St. Catharines, Ontario
> Peach Festival, Penticton, British Columbia

Cyprus
> Wine Festival, Limassol

India
> Onam: Harvest, Aranmula, Champ Akulam, Kottaya

Malaysia
> Dayak Festival Day, Sarawak

Panama
> Coffee Fair and Flower Festival, Boquete

Philippines
> Carabao Festival, Pulilan, San Isidro, Angono, Sariaya, Quezon Province

Spain
> Jerez de Frontera Festival, Cadiz

Tunisia
> Sahara National Festival, Douz

Heritage

Canada
> Acadian Festival, Caraquet, New Brunswick
> Gaelic Mod, St. Ann's, Nova Scotia
> Pioneer Days, Saskatoon, Saskatchewan
> Northern Games, Inuvik, Northwest Territories
> Northern Manitoba Trappers' Festival, The Pas, Manitoba

Historic

Bahamas
> Fox Hill Day, Nassau

Belgium

    Holy Blood Procession, Bruges

British Virgin Islands

    Tortola Festival, Tortola

Canada

    Festival du Voyageur, St. Boniface, Manitoba
    International Freedom Festival, Windsor, Ontario
    Klondike Days Exposition, Edmonton, Alberta
    Northern Manitoba Trappers' Festival, The Pas, Manitoba

Czechoslovakia

    Znojmo Feast, Znojmo

Denmark

    Viking Festival, Frederikssund

Germany, Federal Republic of

    Landshut Wedding 1475, Landshut
    Oberammergau Passion Play, Oberammergau
    The Master Draught Pageant, Rothenburg/Tauber

Italy

    Palio of Siena, Siena
    Sardinian Cavalcade, Sassari, Sardinia

Great Britain

    Battle of Flowers, St. Helier, Jersey, Channel Islands

Japan

    Grand Festival of the Toshogu Shrine, Nikko

Korea

    Moyang Castle Festival, Gochang

Mexico

    Independence Day Celebration, Mexico City, nationwide
    Running of the Bulls, Huamantla, Tlaxcala

Philippines

    Ati-Atihan Festival, Kalibo, Aklan Province, Panay Island

Singapore

    Mid-Autumn/Mooncake Festival

Horticultural

Australia
  Carnival of Flowers, Toowoomba
Belgium
  Begonia Festival, Lochristi
Bulgaria
  Rose Festival, Kazanluk
Canada
  Festival of Spring (Tulips), Ottawa, Ontario
Great Britain
  England
    Chelsea Flower Show, London
Hungary
  National Floral Carnival, Debrecen
Netherlands
  Keukenhof, Lisse

Humor/Satire

Bulgaria
  National Humor and Satire Festival, Gabrovo
Canada
  Toonik Tyme, Frobisher Bay, Northwest Territories

Legendary

Bahamas
  Junkanoo Parade and Festival, Freeport, Nassau, Family Out Islands
Belgium
  Cat Festival and Parade, Ypres
  Procession of the Witches, Beselare
Czechoslovakia
  Maypole and Burning of the Witches, Postupice

India

    Dussehra/Dasehara, Delhi, Mysore, Kulu, Calcutta

Japan

    Hollyhock Festival of Shimogamo and Kamigamo Shrines, Kyoto

Nepal

    The Chariot Festival of Macchendranath/Festival of the God of Rain, Patan, Kathmandu

Panama

    Festival of the Black Christ, Portobelo

Peru

    Inti Raymi Fiesta/Sun Festival, San Antonio de Pichincha, Cuzco, Andahuaylas and Apurimac Valleys

Philippines

    Moriones Festival, Boac, Gasan, Marinduque Province

Portugal

    Celebrations of the Holy Ghost, Ponta Delgada, Sao Miguel Island, Azores

Thailand

    Loy Krathong Festival/Festival of Light, nationwide

Literature/Prose, Poetry

    Australia

        Festival of the Arts, Adelaide
        Moomba Festival, Melbourne

    Austria

        Steirischer Herbst/Styrian Autumn, Graz

    Denmark

        Hans Christian Andersen Festival, Odense

    Great Britain

        England
            Broadstairs Dickens Festival, Broadstairs
            Festival of the City of London, London
        Wales
            Royal National Eisteddfod, North and South Wales

Korea

    National Foundation Art Festival, Chinju

Mexico

    International Cervantes Festival, Guanajuato

New Zealand

    Auckland Festival, Auckland
    Christchurch Arts Festival, Christchurch

Music

Australia

    Carnival of Flowers, Toowoomba
    Festival of the Arts, Adelaide
    Festival of Perth, Perth
    Festival of Sydney, Sydney
    Moomba Festival, Melbourne

Austria

    Bregenz Festival, Bregenz
    Carinthian Summer Festival, Ossiach, Villach
    Salzburg Festival, Salzburg
    "Silent Night, Holy Night" Celebrations, Hallein, Oberndorf, Wagrain, all of Salzburg
    Steirischer Herbst/Styrian Autumn, Graz

Bahamas

    Bahamas Goombay Holiday, Freeport, Nassau
    Junkanoo Parade and Festival, Freeport, Nassau, Family Out Islands

Barbados

    June Crop-Over Festival, Bridgetown, islandwide

Belgium

    Flanders Festival, Antwerp, Bruges, Brussels, Ghent, Kortrijk, Leuven, Mechelen

Bermuda

    Bermuda Festival, Hamilton

Bulgaria

    Golden Orpheus, Slunchev Bryag

Canada

    Acadian Festival, Caraquet, New Brunswick
    Banff Festival of the Arts, Banff, Alberta

Caribana, Toronto, Ontario
Charlottetown Festival, Charlottetown, Prince Edward Island
Folklorama, Winnipeg, Manitoba
Gaelic Mod, St. Ann's, Nova Scotia
Festival Ottawa Opera Plus, Ottawa, Ontario
Guelph Spring Festival, Guelph, Ontario
Maritime Old Time Fiddling Contest, Dartmouth, Nova Scotia
Miramichi Folk Song Festival, Newcastle, New Brunswick
Shaw Festival, Niagara-on-the-Lake, Ontario
Stratford Festival, Stratford, Ontario
Summer Festival, Quebec City, Quebec
Summer Festival of the Arts, St. John's, Newfoundland
Winnipeg Folk Festival, Winnipeg, Manitoba

Czechoslovakia

Bratislava Music Festival, Bratislava
Folklore Festival of Straznice, Straznice
Prague Spring Music Festival, Prague

Denmark

Aarhus Festival Week, Aarhus

Finland

Folk Music Festival, Kaustinen
Helsinki Festival, Helsinki
Jyvaskyla Arts Festival, Jyvaskyla
Pori Jazz, Pori
Savonlinna Opera Festival, Savonlinna

France

Besancon International Music Festival, Besancon
Easter Festival of Sacred Music, Lourdes
International Festival of Lyon, Lyon
International Music Festival, Strasbourg
Summer Festival of Paris, Paris

Germany, Federal Republic of

Bayreuth Festival/Richard Wagner Festival, Bayreuth
Berlin Festival, West Berlin
International May Festival, Wiesbaden
Munich Opera Festival, Munich

Greece

Athens Festival, Athens
Festival of Demetria, Thessaloniki
International Trade Fair, Film and Song Festival, Thessaloniki

TYPES OF FESTIVALS 285

  Great Britain
    England
      Aldeburgh Festival of Music and Arts, Aldeburgh
      Bath Festival, Bath
      Festival of the City of London, London
      Glyndebourne Festival Opera Season, Glyndebourne
      King's Lynn Festival, King's Lynn
      Three Choirs Festival, Gloucester, Hereford, Worcester
      York Festival and Mystery Plays, York
    Scotland
      Edinburgh Festival, Edinburgh
    Wales
      International Musical Eisteddfod, Llangollen, Denbighshire
      Royal National Eisteddfod, North and South Wales

Hong Kong

  Festival of Asian Arts
  Hong Kong Arts Festival

Iceland

  Reykjavik Arts Festival, Reykjavik

Ireland

  The Rose of Tralee International Festival, Tralee
  Wexford Festival Opera, Wexford

Israel

  Israel Festival, Caesarea, Haifa, Jerusalem, Tel Aviv
  Spring in Jerusalem Festival, Jerusalem

Italy

  Maggio Musicale Florence/Florentine May Music Festival, Florence
  Spoleto Festival/Festival of Two Worlds, Spoleto

Jamaica

  Jamaica Festival, Kingston, Montego Bay, islandwide

Japan

  Osaka International Festival, Osaka

Jordan

  Jerash Festival, Jerash

Korea

  Chunhyang Festival, Namwon, North Jeolla
  Moyang Castle Festival, Gochang
  National Foundation Art Festival, Chinju

Mexico

   Fiestas de Octubre, Guadalajara
   International Cervantes Festival, Guanajuato

Monaco

   International Festival of Arts, Monte Carlo

Morocco

   Festival of Folklore, Marrakesh

Netherlands

   Holland Festival, The Hague/Scheveningen, Amsterdam, Rotterdam

New Zealand

   Auckland Festival, Auckland
   Christchurch Arts Festival, Christchurch

Norway

   Bergen International Festival of Music, Drama and Folklore, Bergen

Panama

   Canajacua Folklore Festival, Macaracas

Peru

   Festidanza/Folk Festival, Arequipa

Poland

   Warsaw Autumn/International Festival of Contemporary Music, Warsaw

Portugal

   International Bach Festival, Funchal, Madeira Island

Romania

   National Folklore Festival, Mamaia, Efore, Sinala

Singapore

   Singapore Arts Festival

Spain

   International Festival of Music and Dance/Granada Festival, Granada
   International Festival of Music and Dance/Santander Festival, Santander
   International Music Festival/Barcelona Festival, Barcelona

Sweden

   Drottningholm Court Theater Season, Drottningholm near Stockholm

TYPES OF FESTIVALS   287

Switzerland

    Festival of Music, Montreux-Vevey
    International Festival of Lausanne, Lausanne
    International Festival of Music/Lucerne Festival, Lucerne
    International June Festival, Zurich
    Montreux International Music Festival/Montreux Jazz Festival, Montreux

Tunisia

    International Festival of Carthage, Carthage
    International Festival of Hammamet, Hammamet

Turkey

    Festival of Istanbul, Istanbul

Union of Soviet Socialist Republics (USSR)

    Moscow Stars Festival, Moscow
    Russian Winter Festival, Moscow
    White Nights Festival, Leningrad

Uruguay

    Summer Festival of the Lake of Rodo Park, Montevideo

Yugoslavia

    Dubrovnik Summer Festival, Dubrovnik
    International Folklore Review, Zagreb
    Ljubljana Summer Festival, Ljubljana
    Split Summer Festival, Split

New Year Celebrations

Bahamas

    Junkanoo Parade and Festival, Freeport, Nassau, Family Out Islands

China, Republic of (Taiwan)

    Chinese Lunar New Year, nationwide

India

    Diwali/Festival of Lights (Hindu New Year), nationwide

Indonesia

    Balinese New Year, Bali

Sri Lanka (Ceylon)

    National New Year/Sinhala and Tamil New Year Observance, nationwide

Switzerland

　　Swiss New Year's Eve Celebration, Appenzell

Thailand

　　Songkran (Water) Festival: Thai New Year, Paklat, Bangkok, Chiang Mai

Union of Soviet Socialist Republics (USSR)

　　Russian Winter Festival, Moscow

Opera/Operetta, Musicals

　Australia

　　Festival of Perth, Perth
　　Festival of Sydney, Sydney

　Austria

　　Bregenz Festival, Bregenz
　　Carinthian Summer Festival, Ossiach, Villach
　　Salzburg Festival, Salzburg
　　Vienna Festival, Vienna

　Belgium

　　Flanders Festival, Antwerp, Bruges, Brussels, Ghent, Kortrijk, Leuven, Mechelen

　Bermuda

　　Bermuda Festival, Hamilton

　Canada

　　Banff Festival of the Arts, Banff, Alberta
　　Charlottetown Festival, Charlottetown, Prince Edward Island
　　Festival Ottawa Opera Plus, Ottawa, Ontario
　　Guelph Spring Festival, Guelph, Ontario
　　Stratford Festival, Stratford, Ontario

　Czechoslovakia

　　Bratislava Music Festival, Bratislava
　　Prague Spring Music Festival, Prague

　Denmark

　　Aarhus Festival Week, Aarhus

　Finland

　　Helsinki Festival, Helsinki
　　Savonlinna Opera Festival, Savonlinna

TYPES OF FESTIVALS 289

France

    International Festival of Lyon, Lyon
    International Music Festival, Strasbourg

Germany, Federal Republic of

    Bayreuth Festival/Richard Wagner Festival, Bayreuth
    Berlin Festival, West Berlin
    International May Festival, Wiesbaden
    Munich Opera Festival, Munich

Great Britain

    England
      Aldeburgh Festival of Music and Arts, Aldeburgh
      Bath Festival, Bath
      Festival of the City of London, London
      Glyndebourne Festival Opera, Glyndebourne
    Scotland
      Edinburgh Festival, Edinburgh
    Wales
      International Musical Eisteddfod, Llangollen, Denbighshire

Greece

    Athens Festival, Athens
    Festival of Demetria, Thessaloniki

Hong Kong

    Festival of Asian Arts
    Hong Kong Arts Festival

Iceland

    Reykjavik Arts Festival, Reykjavik

Ireland

    Wexford Festival Opera, Wexford

Israel

    Israel Festival, Caesarea, Haifa, Jerusalem, Tel Aviv

Italy

    Maggio Musicale Florence/Florentine May Music Festival, Florence
    Spoleto Festival/Festival of Two Worlds, Spoleto

Japan

    Osaka International Festival, Osaka

Mexico

    Fiestas de Octubre, Guadalajara
    International Cervantes Festival, Guanajuato

Monaco

    International Festival of Arts, Monte Carlo

Netherlands

    Holland Festival, The Hague/Scheveningen, Amsterdam, Rotterdam

New Zealand

    Auckland Festival, Auckland
    Christchurch Arts Festival, Christchurch

Norway

    Bergen International Festival of Music, Drama and Folklore, Bergen

Poland

    Warsaw Autumn/International Festival of Contemporary Music, Warsaw

Singapore

    Singapore Arts Festival

Spain

    International Festival of Music and Dance/Santander Festival, Santander
    International Music Festival/Barcelona Festival, Barcelona

Sweden

    Drottningholm Court Theater Season, Drottningholm near Stockholm

Switzerland

    International Festival of Lausanne, Lausanne
    International June Festival, Zurich

Turkey

    Festival of Istanbul, Istanbul

Union of Soviet Socialist Republics (USSR)

    Moscow Stars Festival, Moscow
    White Nights Festival, Leningrad

Uruguay

    Summer Festival of the Lake of Rodo Park, Montevideo

Yugoslavia

    Dubrovnik Summer Festival, Dubrovnik
    Ljubljana Summer Festival, Ljubljana
    Split Summer Festival, Split

Pageantry

Canada

    Carnaval, Quebec City, Quebec
    Klondike Days Exposition, Edmonton, Alberta

Cayman Islands

    Pirate Week Festival, George Town, Grand Cayman

Czechoslovakia

    Znojmo Feast, Znojmo

Denmark

    Viking Festival, Frederikssund

Germany, Federal Republic of

    Landshut Wedding 1475, Landshut
    The Master Draught Pageant, Rothenburg/Tauber

Great Britain

    Battle of Flowers, St. Helier, Jersey, Channel Islands

Italy

    Palio of Siena, Siena

Luxembourg

    Sprangprocession/Dancing Procession, Echternach

Nepal

    The Chariot Festival of Macchendranath/Festival of the God of Rain, Patan, Kathmandu

Peru

    Inti Raymi Fiesta/Sun Festival, San Antonio de Pichincha, Cuzco, Andahuaylas and Apurimac Valleys

Philippines

    Carabao Festival, Pulilan, San Isidro, Angono, Sariaya, Quezon Province

Sri Lanka (Ceylon)

    Esala Perahera, Kandy

Sweden

    Santa Lucia Festival, nationwide

Switzerland

    Fete des Vignerons/Wine Growers' Festival, Vevey

Thailand

    Loy Krathong Festival/Festival of Light, nationwide

Trinidad & Tobago

    The Trinidad & Tobago Carnival, Port-au-Spain

Parades/Processions

Bahamas

    Junkanoo Parade and Festival, Freeport, Nassau, Family Out Islands

Belgium

    Cat Festival and Parade, Ypres
    Holy Blood Procession, Bruges
    Procession of the Witches, Beselare

Colombia

    Holy Week Observances and Processions, Popayan

Italy

    Sardinian Cavalcade, Sassari, Sardinia

Japan

    Grand Festival of the Toshogu Shrine, Nikko

Luxembourg

    Sprangprocession/Dancing Procession, Echternach

Macao

    Procession of Our Lord of Passos

Sri Lanka (Ceylon)

    Esala Perahera, Kandy

Patriotic

Canada

    International Freedom Festival, Windsor, Ontario

Denmark
    Rebild Festival of Fourth of July Celebration, Aalborg, Rebild, North Jutland
India
    Republic Day, New Delhi
Israel
    Spring in Jerusalem Festival, Jerusalem
Malaysia
    National Day, nationwide
Mexico
    Independence Day Celebration, Mexico City, nationwide
Singapore
    National Day
Zambia
    Independence Day, Lusaka, nationwide

Religious

Aruba
    Carnival, Oranjestad
Austria
    "Silent Night, Holy Night" Celebration, Hallein, Oberndorf, Wagrain, Salzburg
Belgium
    Holy Blood Procession, Bruges
Colombia
    Carnival, Barranquilla
    Holy Week Observances and Processions, Popayan
Ethiopia
    Genna (Christmas Celebration), Addis Ababa
    Maskal Festival, Addis Ababa
France
    Easter Festival of Sacred Music, Lourdes
Germany, Federal Republic of
    Oberammergau Passion Play, Oberammergau

Great Britain
> England
>> York Festival and Mystery Plays, York

Hong Kong
> Cheung Chau Festival/Festival of the Bun Hills, Island of Cheung Chau

India
> Diwali/Festival of Lights, nationwide

Indonesia
> Ramayana Dance Festival, Jogjakarta

Italy
> Feast of the Redeemer, Venice
> Lily Festival, Nola

Japan
> Hollyhock Festival of Shimogamo and Kamigamo Shrines, Kyoto

Luxembourg
> Sprangprocession/Dancing Procession, Echternach

Macao
> Procession of Our Lord of Passos

Malaysia
> Thaipusam, Penang, Kuala Lumpur, Gaja Berang

Martinique (French West Indies)
> Carnival/Mardi Gras, Fort-de-France

Mexico
> Running of the Bulls, Huamantla, Tlaxcala

Nepal
> The Chariot Festival of Macchendranath/Festival of the God of Rain, Patan, Kathmandu

Panama
> Carnival, Panama City, nationwide
> Festival of the Black Christ, Portobelo

Peru
> Inti Raymi Fiesta/Sun Festival, San Antonio de Pichincha, Cuzco, Andahuaylas and Apurimac Valleys

Philippines

> Ati-Atihan Festival, Kalibo, Aklan Province, Panay Island
> Fiesta Black Nazarene, Manila, Quezon Province, Luzon Island
> Moriones Festival, Boac, Gasan, Marinduque Province
> Philippine Christmas Season, nationwide

Portugal

> Celebrations of the Holy Ghost, Ponta Delgada, Sao Miguel Island, Azores

Singapore

> Birthday of the Monkey God

South Africa

> Shembe/Zulu Festival, Inanda

Spain

> Fallas of San Jose/St. Joseph's Bonfires, Valencia
> San Fermin Festival/Running of the Bulls, Pamplona

Sri Lanka (Ceylon)

> Esala Perhera, Kandy

Sweden

> Santa Lucia Festival, nationwide

Thailand

> Loy Krathong Festival/Festival of Light, nationwide

Turkey

> Festival of Mevlana, Konya

Rockhound Collecting

Canada

> Gemboree, Bancroft, Ontario

Rodeos

Canada

> Buffalo Days, Regina, Saskatchewan
> Calgary Exhibition and Stampede, Calgary, Alberta
> Western Festival, Sante-Tite, Quebec

Ships/Boats

Bonaire

International Regatta, Kralendijk

Zambia

Ku-Omboko Ceremony, Lealul Knoll, Mongu

Sports

Antigua

Police Week Festival, St. John's

Australia

Festival of Sydney, Sydney
Moomba Festival, Melbourne

Bonaire

International Regatta, Kralendijk

Canada

Bitowa Outdoor Festival, Tracadie, New Brunswick
Buffalo Days, Regina, Saskatchewan
Calgary Exhibition and Stampede, Calgary, Alberta
Carnaval, Quebec City, Quebec
Caribou Carnival and Championship Dog Derby, Yellowknife, Northwest Territories
Festival of Spring, Ottawa, Ontario
Gaelic Mod, St. Ann's, Nova Scotia
Northern Games, Inuvik, Northwest Territories
Northern Manitoba Trappers' Festival, The Pas, Manitoba
Northern Pike Festival, Nipawin, Saskatchewan
Pioneer Days, Saskatoon, Saskatchewan
Snowgolf Championship, Prince George, British Columbia
Toonik Tyme, Frobisher Bay, Northwest Territories
Top of the World Ski Meet, Inuvik, Northwest Territories
Western Festival, Saint-Tite, Quebec

Czechoslovakia

Spartakiade, Prague

Denmark

Aarhus Festival Week, Aarhus
Sonderborg Tilting Tournament, Sonderborg

Finland

Ounasvaara International Winter Games, Rovaniemi

TYPES OF FESTIVALS 297

France
> Paris Marathon, Paris

Gibraltar
> International Shark Angling Competition

Great Britain
> England
>> Cruft's Dog Show, London
> Isle of Wight
>> Regatta Week, Cowes

Hong Kong
> Dragon Boat Festival

Iceland
> Iceland National Horse Meet Show and Races, Skagafjordur

India
> Onam: Harvest, Aranmula, Champ Akulam, Kottaya

Ireland
> Dublin Horse Show, Dublin

Japan
> Kite Battles of Hamamatsu

Kenya
> Safari Rally, Nairobi

Macao
> Macao Grand Prix

Mexico
> Fiestas de Octubre, Guadalajara

Monaco
> Monaco Automobile Grand Prix, Monte Carlo

Morocco
> Fantasia/Horse Festival, Fez

Norway
> Holmenkollen Ski Festival, Oslo

Thailand

    Elephant Roundup, Surin
    Kite Flying Season, Bangkok

Turkey

    Wrestling Games of Kirkpinar, Edirne

Touristic

Bahamas

    Bahamas Goombay Holiday, Freeport, Nassau

Bermuda

    Bermuda College Weeks, Hamilton, St. George's

Canada

    Caribou Carnival and Championship Dog Derby, Yellowknife, Northwest Territories

Cayman Islands

    Pirate Week Festival, George Town, Grand Cayman

Thailand

    Elephant Roundup, Surin

Traditional Holidays

China, Republic of (Taiwain)

    Chinese Lunar New Year, nationwide
    Lantern Festival, nationwide

Great Britain

    Pancake Race, Olney, England
    Swan-Upping Season, London

Japan

    Kite Battles of Hamamatsu, Hamamatsu

Sri Lanka (Ceylon)

    National New Year/Sinhala and Tamil New Year Observance, nationwide

Thailand

    Songkran (Water Festival): Thai New Year, Paklat, Bangkok, Chiang Mai

Wine Festivals

Argentina

    National Festival of the Grape Harvest, Mendoza

Australia

    Barossa Valley Festival, Barossa Valley, Tanunda

Canada

    Niagara Grape and Wine Festival, St. Catharines, Ontario

Cyprus

    Limassol Wine Festival, Limassol

France

    Three Glorious Days, Nuits-St. Georges, Beaune, Meursault

Greece

    Wine Festival, Rethymon, Crete

Romania

    Dionysiad, Husi

Spain

    Jerez de Frontera Festival, Cadiz

Switzerland

    Fete des Vignerons/Wine Growers' Festival, Vevey

INDEX

Aarhus Festival Week, *71-72*
Academy of Chamber Music, 76
Acadian Festival, *37-38*
Agricultural festivals, 4, 6, 9, 45, 51-52, 56, 67, 247-48 (appendix). *See also* Harvest festivals
Alberta Gold Panning Championships, 30
Aldeburgh Festival of Music and the Arts, *89*
Allan, Andrew, 49
Annapolis Valley Apple Blossom Festival, *44*
Antiques fair, 140-41
Aoi Matsuri, 122-23
April Fair, *163-64*
Arts and crafts, 15, 17, 33, 35, 36, 37, 38, 41, 42-43, 54, 61, 107, 121, 125-26, 129, 133-34, 143, 146, 147, 150, 181, 183, 187, 248-50 (appendix)
Ashkenazy, Vladimir, 108-9
Association of International Festivals of France, 79, 80
Athens Festival, *101-2*
Athletic events, 35-36, 39, 40, 69, 70, 81-82, 96-97, 179-80
Ati-Atihan Festival, *152*
Aviation, 31, 81, 250 (appendix)
Auckland Festival, *143*
Australian film festival, 5
Auto racing, 126-27, 130-31, 137

Bachok Festival of Culture, *131-32*
Badran, Adnan, 125
Bahamas Goombay Holiday, *15-16*
Balinese New Year, *112*
Ballet, *See* Dance
Banff Festival of the Arts, *28-29*
Barcelona Festival, *161*
Barid, T., 154
Barossa Valley Vintage Festival, *9*
Bassinet, Andre, 80
Bassinet, George, 80
Bath Festival, *89-90*
Battle of Flowers, *98-99*
Bayreuth Festival, *83-84*
Beaverbrook, Lord, 38
Beer festivals, 48-49, 86, 133-34, 254 (appendix)
Begon, Sire, 21
Begonia Festival, *21*
Bell, A. M., 52
Bergen International Festival, *144*
Berlin Festival, *84*
Bermuda College Weeks, *22-23*
Bermuda Festival, *22*
Bernardi, Mario, 51
Besancon International Music Festival, *78-79*
Birthday of the Monkey God, *158*
Bitowa Outdoor Festival, *40*
Boats, *See* Sailing and boat races
Bosiak, Carl, 47

Bratislava Music Festival, *67*
Bregenz Festival, *11*
Briers, Jan, 18
Britten, Benjamin, 89
Broadstairs Dickens Festival, *90*
Broom Flower Festival, *130*
Brussels International Fair, *20*
Buffalo Days, *59-60*

Calgary Exhibition and Stampede, *29*
Calypsonian Competition, 5
Canada's National Ukranian Festival, *33*
Canadian Championship Dog Derby race, 43
Canadian National Exhibition, *53-54*
Canadian Tulip Festival, 50-51
Canajacua Folklore Festival, *146*
Carabao Festival, *153-54*
Caribana, *54*
Caribou Carnival and Championship Dog Derby, *43*
Carinthian Summer Festival, *13*
Carnaval, *56-57*
Carnival (Barranquilla, Colombia), *64*
Carnival (Fort-de-France, Martinique), *133*
Carnival (Oranjestad, Aruba), *4-5*
Carnival (Panama City, Panama), *147-48*
Carnival (Rio de Janeiro, Brazil), *24-25*
Carnival (Trinidad & Tobago), 54, 175-77
Carnival of Flowers, *7*
Carnivals, 4-5, 7, 24-25, 43, 56-57, 64, 108, 133, 147-48, 175-77
Cat Festival and Parade, *21-22*
Celebrations of the Holy Ghost, *156*
Ceramics, pottery, 129, 255 (appendix). *See also* Arts and crafts
Cervantes, Miguel de, 134
Chariot Festival of Macchendranath, *138-39*
Charlottetown Festival, *55*
Chelsea Flower Show, *95*
Cheung Chau Festival, *105-6*
Chichester Festival Theater Season, *91*
Chinese New Year, *62-63*
Christchurch Arts Festival, *143*

Christie, John, 92
Christmas festivals, 12, 74, 151, 255 (appendix). *See also* Religious festivals
Chunghyang Festival, *128*
Circus festivals, 5-6, 55, 136, 255 (appendix)
Clements, John, 91
Coffee Fair and Flower Festival, *145-46*
Comedow, W., 9
Commemorative festivals, 16, 25-26, 50-51, 85, 98-99, 106-7, 118-19, 123-24, 135, 152, 158, 255-56 (appendix)
Community/Goodwill festivals, 3, 70-71, 256 (appendix)
Competitions/Contests, 256-58 (appendix); arts, 16, 64, 100-101, 104, 121, 127-28, 157-58, 175-77; music, 3, 5, 10-11, 27-28, 45-47, 78-79, 100-101, 128, 138, 157-58, 175-77, 183; sports, 3, 7, 23, 29, 30, 32-33, 35-36, 39, 40, 42-43, 57, 58, 59-60, 69, 70, 73-74, 78, 81-82, 88, 94, 96-97, 98, 106-7, 109, 111, 112, 113-14, 119-20, 122, 126-27, 130-31, 137-38, 144-45, 174, 175, 179-80
Conservation, 40, 267 (appendix)
Cook, Michael, 41
Cook's Festival, *104*
Costume, 4-5, 16-17, 64, 147-48, 175-77
Country Fair, *147*
Crafts. *See* Arts and crafts
Creighton, Helen, 38
Crufts Dog Show, *94*
Culture, 258-63 (appendix). *See also* Arts and Crafts; Costume; Dance; Drama; Film; Humor; Literature; Music; National and local culture
Curium Festival, *66*

Dance, 250-54 (appendix); ballet, 11, 14, 28-29, 48, 67, 68, 71, 75, 79, 80, 85, 87, 99, 102, 103, 105, 108, 115, 117, 120, 125, 134, 136, 141, 143, 144, 162, 163, 167, 169, 178, 180, 182, 184, 185, 186, 187; folk dance, 4, 17, 24, 32, 36-38, 64, 68, 69, 77, 81, 86, 100, 101, 107, 112, 113, 114, 116,

121, 124, 125, 130, 131, 133-34, 144, 145, 146, 147, 149, 150, 157-58, 159, 163, 164, 179, 182, 183, 187, 188; modern 28-29, 102, 115, 184
Dancing Procession, *128-29*
Dasehara, *110*
Dayak Festival Day, *132*
Delamastro, Clara, 24
Delft Antique Mart, 140-41
Dickens, Charles, 90
Dionysiad, *157*
Diwali, 110
Dobrowolski, A., 154
Dog shows and races, 35-36, 39, 43, 94, 364 (appendix)
Doherty, Brian, 49
Dragon Boat Festival, *106-7*
Drama festivals, 10-11, 12, 22, 28-29, 30, 40, 41, 47-48, 49-50, 52-53, 55, 66, 71-72, 73, 75-76, 79, 86-88, 90, 91, 93-94, 97-98, 101-2, 103, 107, 108-9, 110, 113, 120, 121, 125-26, 131-32, 134, 143, 144, 159, 163, 178, 179, 180-81, 183, 184, 185-87, 264-67 (appendix)
Drottingholm Court Theater Season, *167-68*
Dublin Horse Show, *113-14*
Dubrovnik Summer Festival, *185-86*
Dubrovnik Summer Festival, *185-86*
Dussehra, *110*

Easter Festival of Sacred Music, *79-80*
Eastern Festival of Theater, *184*
Eastern Nova Scotia Exhibition, *45*
Ecology, 40, 267 (appendix)
Economic, 6, 9-10, 15-16, 20, 21, 22-23, 24-25, 27, 29, 31-33, 35-36, 37, 39, 40, 43-46, 47, 48-49, 51-52, 53-54, 56-60, 61-62, 65-66, 67, 80-82, 86, 103-4, 108, 112, 114, 117-18, 136, 40-41, 142-43, 145-57, 155, 157, 160, 161-62, 163-64, 168, 169-70, 175, 178-79, 181, 185-86, 267-70 (appendix)
Edinburgh Festival, *99-100*
Elephant Roundup, *175*
Emaischen, 129

Environment, 40, 267 (appendix)
Epidaurus Festival, *102*
Equestrian events. *See* Horse shows and races; Rodeos
Esala Perahera, *165-66*
Eskeland, Ivar, 108
Ethnic festivals, 16-17, 33-35, 37-38, 46-47, 48-49, 54, 61, 65-66, 133-34, 183, 270 (appendix). *See also* Folkloric events; Heritage festivals; National and local culture
European Association of Music Festivals, 11, 12, 14, 15, 18, 67, 68, 79, 80, 83, 84, 161, 163, 170, 180, 186
Evershed-Martin, Leslie, 91

Fairs/Markets, 6, 9, 30, 39, 45, 53-54, 59-60, 81, 86, 103-4, 108, 112, 117-18, 127, 129, 133-34, 140-41, 145-47, 155, 160, 163-64, 168, 181, 271-72 (appendix)
Falconer, John, 99
Fallas of San Jose, 164
Fantasia, *137-38*
Feast of the Redeemer, *120-21*
Festidanza, 149
Festival du Voyageur, *34-35*
Festival of Asian Arts, *107*
Festival of Bambuco, *64*
Festival of Demetria, *103*
Festival of Folklore, *138*
Festival of Istanbul, *180-81*
Festival of Light (Thailand), *173-74*
Festival of Lights (India), *110*
Festival of Mevlana, *181*
Festival of Music Montreux-Vevey, *171*
Festival of Perth, *10-11*
Festival of Spring, *50-51*
Festival of Sydney, *5-6*
Festival of the Arts, *8*
Festival of the Black Christ, *148-49*
Festival of the Bun Hills, 105-6
Festival of the City of London, *94-95*
Festival of the God of Rain, *138-39*
Festival of the Red Waistcoat, *156-57*
Festival of Two Worlds, *120*
Festival Ottawa Opera Plus, *51*
Fete des Cuisinieres, 104

Fete des Vignerons, 171-72
Fiesta Black Nazarene, *153*
Fiestas de Octubre, *133-34*
Film festivals, 5, 47-48, 58, 77-79, 100, 103-4, 115-16, 130, 178, 272-73 (appendix)
Fine Arts, 5, 28-29, 48, 99-100, 105, 108-9, 115-16, 142, 179, 248-50 (appendix)
Fish festivals, 39, 40, 59, 114, 273 (appendix)
Flanders Festival, *18-19*
Florentine Musical May, *117*
Flowers/Floral festivals, 7, 21, 27, 44, 50-51, 56, 95, 98-99, 122-23, 130, 142-43, 145-46, 273-74 (appendix). See also Horticultural shows
Folk Festival, *149*
Folklorama, *37*
Folklore Festival of Stranznice, *69-70*
Folkloric events, 274-78 (appendix); Africa, 75, 137-38, 159-60, 178-79, 188; Asia, 105-7, 110, 111, 112, 113, 122-24, 127-28, 132, 151-54, 158, 173-75; Caribbean, 17, 104, 133; Central America, 133-34, 146, 147-48; Europe, 19, 21-22, 68, 69-70, 72, 73-74, 80-81, 86, 87, 96-97, 103, 108, 118, 120-21, 128-30, 156-58, 162-64, 166-67, 168-69, 171-72, 179-80, 185-86; international, 37, 69-70, 77, 114-15, 144, 187; North America, 36-39, 54, 60; South America, 4, 24-25, 64, 65-66, 149, 183. See also Ethnic festivals
Folk Music Festival Kaustinen, *77*
Food festivals, 37, 39, 70, 104, 158, 278 (appendix)
Forum of the Nations, 20
Fourth of July Celebration (Rebild, Denmark), 70-71
Fox Hill Day, *16*
Fruit festivals, 31-32, 44, 278 (appendix)

Gaelic Mod, *46-47*
Gallego Burin, D. Antonio, 162
Galway Oyster Festival, *114*
Gawai Dayak, 132
Gemboree, *47*

Genna, *74*
Genzefest, 130
Glyndebourne Festival, *92-93*
Golden Orpheus, *27-28*
Goldschmidt, Nicholas, 48
Goodwill festivals, 3, 70-71, 255-56 (appendix)
Goombay music, 16
Granada Festival, *162*
Grand Festival of the Toshugu Shrine, *123-24*
Grand Prix Automobile de Monaco, 137
Great Lapp Winter Fair, *168*
Grieg, Edvard, 144
Gruber, Franz Xavier, 12
Guelph Spring Festival, *47-48*
Guthrie, Tyrone, 52

Hans Christian Andersen Festival, *73*
Harvest festivals, 4, 9, 17, 27, 31-32, 51-52, 67, 111, 132, 145-46, 153-54, 161-62, 178-79, 278-79 (appendix). See also Agricultural festivals
Helsinki Festival, *75-76*
Henius, Max, 70-71
Heritage festivals, 35-36, 37-38, 42-43, 46-47, 60, 279 (appendix) See also Ethnic festivals; National and local culture
Historic festivals, 19-20, 24-25, 30, 34-35, 54-55, 70, 85, 87, 98-99, 118-20, 123-24, 127-28, 135-36, 152, 158, 279-80 (appendix)
Holder, Geoffrey, 177
Holland Festival, *141-42*
Hollyhock Festival of Shimago and Kamigano Shrines, *122-23*
Holmenkollen Ski Festival, *144-45*
Holy Blood Procession, *19-20*
Holy Week Observances and Processions, 65
Hong Kong Arts Festival, *105*
Hopwood, Bing, 88
Hora de la Prislop, 157
Horse Festival, *137-38*
Horse shows and races, 58, 65-66, 73-74, 109, 113-14, 119-20, 137-38, 264 (appendix). See also Rodeos

INDEX

Horticultural festivals, 21, 27, 95, 142-43, 281 (appendix). *See also* Flowers/Floral festivals
Humor/Satire festivals, 26, 281 (appendix)
Hunter, Ian, 94
Hyde Park Festival, 5

Iceland National Horse Meet Show and Races, *109*
Icelandic Festival, *33-34*
Independence Day (Zambia), *188*
Independence Day Celebration (Mexico), *135-36*
International Air Show, *31*
International Bach Festival, *155-56*
International Cervantes Festival, *134*
International Circus Festival, *136*
International Competition for Young Conductors, 79
International Dragon Boat Races, 106-7
International events: air shows, 31, 81; circus festivals, 136; dance, 79, 99, 101-2, 105, 124-25, 130, 136-37, 143, 144, 152; drama, 8, 28-29, 79, 82, 99-100, 101-2, 105, 134, 143, 144, 185; fairs, 20, 103-4, 117-18, 146, 181; film festivals, 79, 100, 105; fine arts, 79, 99-100, 105; folklore, 37, 69-70, 77, 114-15, 144, 187; jazz, 8, 77; music, 8, 14-15, 22, 27-28, 28-29, 36-37, 38-39, 47-48, 50-51, 67, 68-69, 71-72, 75-76, 79-80, 82-83, 84, 87-88, 89-90, 92-93, 99-100, 101-2, 103-4, 105, 108-9, 117, 120, 124-25, 134, 136-37, 141-42, 143, 144, 154-56, 161, 162, 163, 169-71, 172-73, 178, 180-81; opera, 51, 67, 78, 80, 83-84, 85-86, 99-100, 101-2, 105, 115, 124-25, 136-37, 143, 144
International Fair (Izmir, Turkey), *181*
International Fair of San Jose, *146*
International Festival of Arts, *136-37*
International Festival of Carthage, *178*
International Festival of Contemporary Music, *154-55*
International Festival of Hammamet, *179*
International Festival of Lausanne, *169*

International Festival of Lyon, *80*
International Festival of Music (Lucerne, Switzerland), *169-70*
International Festival of Musical and Choreographic Film, 79
International Festival of Music and Dance (Granada, Spain), *162*
International Festival of Music and Dance (Santander, Spain), *163*
International Film Festival, 100
International Folklore Review, *187*
International Freedom Festival, *54-55*
International June Festival, *172-73*
International Musical Eisteddfod, *101*
International Music Festival (Barcelona, Spain), *161*
International Music Festival (Strasbourg, France), *83*
International Regatta, *23*
International Shark Angling Competition, 88
International Theater Festival, *185*
International Trade Fair, Film and Song Festival, *103-4*
Inti Raymi Fiesta, *149-50*
Israel Festival, *115-16*
Ives, Edward (Sandy), 38

Jamaica Festival, *121*
Jerash Festival, *125-26*
Jerez de Frontera Festival, *161-62*
Joy of Living, 7
June Crop-Over Festival, *17*
Junkanoo Parade and Festival, *16-17*
Jyvaskyla Arts Festival, *76*

Kaiser, Kurt, 11
Keukenhof, *142-43*
King's Lynn Festival, *93-94*
Kite Battles of Hamamatsu, *122*
Kite Flying Season, *174*
Klondike Days Exposition, *30*
Kotonski, W., 154
Ku-Omboko Ceremony, *188*

L'Acadie en Fete, 38
Landshut Wedding 1475, *85*
Lantern Festival, *63*

LaRue, Jan, 38-39
LeBlanc, Joseph E., 39
Legendary festivals, 16-17, 19, 21-22, 41-42, 68, 110, 122-23, 138-40, 148-50, 152-53, 156, 173-74, 281-82 (appendix)
Leissing, Eugen, 11
Les Trois Glorieuses, 80-81
Lily Festival, *118*
Limassol Wine Festival, *67*
Literature (Prose, Poetry), 8, 9-10, 12, 73, 90, 94-95, 100-101, 178, 282-283 (appendix)
Ljubljana Summer Festival, *186*
Lobster Festival, *39*
Loy Krathong Festival, *173-74*
Lucerne Festival, *169-70*
Ludwig II, King of Bavaria, 83
Lunar New Year, 62-63
Lutoslawski, W., 154

MacKinnon, Murdo, 48
Macao Grand Prix, *130-31*
Maggio Musicale Florence, *117*
Mahanuwara Esala Dalada Perehera, 165-66
Makinen, Timo, 76
Manny, Louise, 38
Mardi Gras. *See* Carnivals
Mardi Gras (Fort-de-France, Martinique), *133*
Mardi Gras (Oranjestad, Aruba), 4-5
Maritime Old Time Fiddling Contest, *45-46*
Maskal Festival, *75*
Master Draught Pageant, *87*
May International Musical, *79*
Maypole and Burning of the Witches, *68*
Menotti, Gian Carlo, 120
Menuhin, Yehudi, 89
Mid-Autumn Festival, *158*
Milan Trade Fair, *117-18*
Mildmay, Audrey, 92
Miramichi Folk Song Festival, *38-39*
Mitchell, Keith, 91
Mohr, Father Josepf, 12
Monaco Automobile Grand Prix, *137*

Montreux International Music Festival, *170-71*
Montreux Jazz Festival, *170-71*
Moomba Festival, *9-10*
Mooncake Festival, *158*
Moriones Festival, *152-53*
Morse, Barry, 50
Moscow Stars Festival, *182-83*
Moyang Castle Festival, *127-28*
Munich Opera Festival, *85-86*
Music festivals, 5, 11, 13-15, 18-19, 22, 28-29, 47-48, 57-58, 67, 68-69, 71-72, 73, 75-77, 78-80, 82, 84, 87-88, 89-90, 93-95, 99-102, 103, 115-17, 120, 124-26, 134, 136-37, 141-42, 143, 161, 162, 169-70, 171, 172-73, 178, 180-81, 182-83, 184, 185-87, 283-87 (appendix); chamber and instrumental, 8, 47-48, 67, 76, 78-79, 85, 87-88, 99-100, 101-2, 117, 163, 171, 172-73, 182-83, 184, 185-87; contemporary, 12, 82, 154-55; folk, 5, 16, 17, 24-25, 36-39, 41, 45-47, 48, 54, 57-58, 61, 69-70, 77, 101, 107, 110, 113, 115-16, 121, 128, 159, 175-77, 178, 179; jazz, 5, 8, 22, 36-37, 75-76, 77, 115-16, 125-26, 169, 170-71, 178; old time, 36-37, 38-39, 45-46; opera, 5, 11, 13, 14-15, 18-19, 22, 28-29, 51, 67, 68, 71-72, 75-76, 78, 80, 83-84, 85-86, 87-88, 89, 92-93, 94-95, 99-100, 101-2, 103, 108-9, 115-16, 117, 120, 125-26, 133-34, 143, 163, 167-68, 169, 172-73; popular, 15-16, 27-28, 41, 48-49, 57-58, 75-76; rock, 5, 125-26; vocal and choral, 12, 13, 47-48, 55, 68-69, 79-80, 87-88, 91-92, 100-101, 117, 154-55, 159, 182-83
Mystery Plays, 97-98

Nathan, Maurice, 9
National and local culture, 3, 15-16, 44, 46-47, 100-101, 107, 121, 125-26, 127. *See also* Ethnic festivals; Heritage festivals
National Day (Malaysia), *131*
National Day (Singapore), *159*
National Festival of Folklore, *183*

National Festival of the Grape Harvest, *4*
National Floral Carnival, *108*
National Folklore Festival, *157-58*
National Foundation Art Festival, *127*
National Humor and Satire Festival, *26*
National New Year, *165*
Navaratri, 110
Newfoundland Drama Festival, *40*
New Year celebrations, 16-17, 62-63, 110, 112, 165, 168-69, 174, 183, 287-88 (appendix)
Niagara Grape and Wine Festival, *51-52*
Noor, Queen of Jordan, 125
North Atlantic Festival, 108-9
Northern Games, *42-43*
Northern Manitoba Trappers' Festival, *35-36*
Northern Pike Festival, *59*
Nummi, Seppo, 76

Oberammergau Passion Play, *86-87*
October Fair (Castro Verde-Beja, Portugal), *155*
October Fair (Guadalajara, Mexico), 133-34
Oksala, Paivo, 76
Oktoberfest (Kitchener and Waterloo, Ontario, Canada), *48-49*
Oktoberfest (Munich, Germany), *86*
Old Art and Antiques Fair, *140-41*
Old Mask Parade, 5
Olivier, Sir Laurence, 91
Onam, *111*
Opera/Operetta, musicals, 5, 11, 13, 14-15, 18-19, 22, 28-29, 51, 55, 67, 68, 71-72, 75-76, 78, 80, 83-84, 85-86, 87-88, 89, 92-93, 94-95, 99-100, 101-2, 103, 108-9, 115-16, 117, 120, 125-26, 133-34, 143, 163, 167-68, 172-73, 288-91 (appendix)
Osaka International Festival, *124-25*
Ounasvaara International Winter Games, *78*

Pageantry, 30, 56-57, 61-62, 70, 72, 85, 87, 98-99, 119-20, 128-29, 138-40, 149-50, 153-54, 165-67, 171-72, 173-74, 175-77, 291-91 (appendix)

Palio of Siena, *119-20*
Pancake race (Liberal, Kansas), 97
Pancake Race (Olney, England), *96-97*
Panorama Steel Band Contest, 5
Parades, 16-17, 19-20, 21-22, 65, 118-19, 123-24, 128-29, 130, 165-66, 292 (appendix)
Paris Air and Space Show, *81*
Paris Marathon, *81-82*
"Paristory," 82
Patriotic festivals, 54-55, 70-71, 111, 116, 131, 135-36, 159, 188, 292-93 (appendix)
Patterson, Tom, 52
Peach Festival, *31-32*
Pears, Sir Peter, 89
Pearson, Lester B., 51
Perlin, John C., 41
Petterson, Bjorger, 42
Philippine Christmas season, *151*
Pioneer Days, *60*
Pirate Week Festival, *61-62*
Podolak, Mitch, 36
Poetry, 100-101, 178
Police Week Festival, *3*
Pori Jazz, *77*
Potato Blossom Festival, *56*
Pottery Festival, *129*
Prague Spring, *68-69*
Prislop Round Dance Festival, *157*
Procession of Our Lord of Passos, *130*
Procession of the Witches, *19*
Processions. *See* Parades
Pushkar Fair, *112*

Quadrilles of San Martin, *65-66*

Ramayana Dance Festival, *113*
Rand Show, *160*
Rebild Festival/Fourth of July Celebration, *70-71*
Redel, Kurt, 79
Regatta Week, *98*
Reiinhardt, Max, *13*
Religious festivals, 4-5, 12, 19-20, 64, 65, 74, 75, 79-80, 86-87, 97-98, 105-6, 110, 113, 118, 120-21, 122-24, 128-29, 130, 132, 133, 135, 138-40,

147-53, 156, 158, 159-60, 164, 165-67, 173-74, 181, 293-95 (appendix)
Republic Day, *111*
Reykjavik Arts Festival, *108-9*
Rhys ap Gruffydd, Lord, 100
Richard Wagner Festival, *83-84*
Rockhound collecting, 47, 295 (appendix)
Rodeos, 29, 58, 59-60, 175, 295 (appendix). *See also* Horse shows and races
Rose Festival, 27
Rose of Tralee International Festival, *114-15*
Royal Easter Show, *6*
Royal Horticultural Show, 95
Royal National Eisteddfod, *100-101*
Royal Shakespeare Company, *97*
Running of the Bulls (Huamantla, Mexico), *135*
Running of the Bulls (Pamplona, Spain), *162-63*
Russian Winter Festival, *183*
Russo, J. A., 88

Safari Rally, *126-27*
Sahara National Festival, *178-79*
Sailing and boat races, 23, 70, 98, 106-7, 111, 296 (appendix)
St. Joseph's Bonfires, *164*
Salzburg Festival, 13-14
Salzmann, Adolf, 11
San Fermin Festival, *162-63*
Santa Lucia Festival, *166-67*
Santander Music Festival, *163*
Sardinian Cavalcade, *118-19*
Savonlinna Opera Festival, *78*
Schueberfo'er, 129
Serocki, K., 154
Shakespeare Festival, *97*
Shaw Festival, *49-50*
Shembe, Isaiah, 159
Shembe Festival, *159-60*
Shepherd's Fair, *129*
Ships/Boats. *See* Sailing and boat races
Showalter, Harrison A., 52
"Silent Night, Holy Night" Celebration, *12*
Singapore Arts Festival, *159*

Sinhala New Year, *165*
Snowgolf Championship, *32-33*
Sonderborg Tilting Tournament, *73-74*
Songkran, 174
Southern, G. H., 51
Spartakiade, *69*
Split Summer Festival, *186-87*
Spoleto Festival, *120*
Sports festivals, 3, 5-6, 23, 29, 32-33, 35-36, 40, 41-43, 46-47, 50-51, 56-60, 69, 73-74, 78, 81-82, 88, 98, 106-7, 109, 113-14, 122, 126-27, 130-31, 133-34, 137-38, 144-45, 174, 175, 179-80, 296-98 (appendix)
Sprangprocession, 128-29
Spring in Jerusalem Festival, *116*
Steirischer Herbst, *12*
Stratford Festival, *52-53*
Strauss, Richard, 13
Styrian Autumn, *12*
Suitner, Othmar, 11
Summer Festival (Quebec City, Canada), *57-58*
Summer Festival of Paris, *82*
Summer Festival of the Arts, *41*
Summer Festival of the Lake of Rodo Park, *184*
Sun Festival, *149-50*
Swan-Upping Season, *95-96*
Swiss New Year's Eve Celebration, *168-69*

Tamil New Year, *165*
Thaipusen, *132*
Thierry of Alsace, 20
Thom, Ron, 49
Three Chors Festival, *91-92*
Three Glorious Days, *80-81*
Toonik Tyme, *41-42*
Top of the World Ski Meet, *42*
Tortola Festival, *25-26*
Touristic festivals, 15-16, 22-23, 43, 61-62, 175, 298 (appendix)
Traditional holidays, 62-63, 95-97, 122, 165, 174, 298 (appendix)
Trinidad & Tobago Carnival, 54, *175-76*
Tumba contest, 5

Vallomkali musical boat race, 111
Venables, Terry, 88
Vesna Festival, *61*
Vienna Festival, *14-15*
Viking Festival, *72*
von Hoffmanstal, Hugo, 13

Wachter, Julius, 11
Wagner, Richard, 83-84
Wagner, Wieland, 83-84
Wagner, Wolfgang, 83-84
Waldman, Yuval, 155
Warsaw Autumn, *154-55*
Waterer, Gladys, 90
Water Festival, *174*
Weadick, Guy, 29
Western Festival, *58*
Wexford Festival Opera, *115*
Whitehead, Paxton, 50
White Nights Festival, *182*
Wiesbaden May Festival, 87-88

Wine Festival (Rethymon, Crete), *103*
Wine festivals, 9, 51-52, 67, 80-81, 103, 157, 161-62, 171-72, 299 (appendix)
Wine Growers' Festival, *171-72*
Winnipeg Folk Festival, *36-37*
Winter sports, 32-33, 34-35, 57, 78, 144-45
Wobisch, Helmut, 13
Wolf, Gustave, 83
Wolf, Roger, 83
World Championship Sled Dog Race, 35
World Gold Panning Championship, 30
Wrestling Games of Kirkpinar, *179-80*

York Festival and Mystery Plays, *97-98*

Zimmerli, Jakob, 169-70
Znojmo Feast, *70*
Zulu Festival, *159-60*
Zurich May Festival, 172-73

About the Author

FRANCIS SHEMANSKI is a freelance travel writer and a contributing editor for *The Travel Agent Magazine*. She is the author of *A Guide to Fairs and Festivals in the United States* (Greenwood Press, 1984) and an active member of the Society of American Travel Writers, the New York Press Club, and The Newswomen's Club of New York. Her articles on travel and calendars of events regularly appear in *The Los Angeles Times*, *The New York Times*, *The Boston Globe*, *Chicago Tribune*, *Newsday*, *New York Daily News*, *The Star Ledger*, *The Denver Post*, *Food & Wine Magazine*, *Family Circle*, *Ladies Home Journal*, and many others.